LALITA-KOSHA

Sri Garib Das Oriental Series No.325

LALITA-KOSHA

Being a Collection of texts in Sanskrit bearing on the cult of Lalita with an Introduction and translation of the Thousand Names

Prof. S.K. Ramachandra Rao

Sri Satguru Publications

A Division of

Indian Books Centre

Delhi, India

Published by
Sri Satguru Publications,
Indological and Oriental Publishers
A Division of
Indian Books Centre
40/5, Shakti Nagar,
Delhi-110007
India

First Edition; Bangalore, 1991
Second Edition : Delhi . 2008

ISBN 81-7030-882-8

Printed at A.R. Printers, Delhi

New Preface to Second Edition

Vidyalankara Prof. S. K. Ramachandra Rao (1925-2006) was a multifaceted scholar. Born in a conservative family, he learnt Sanskrit in a pathasala even in his teens, later studied psychology at the Mysore University, and became the Head of the Department of Clinical Psychology at NIMHANS, Bangalore. He was a teacher, musician, musicologist, orator and artist. He had also been conducting classes for many decades in his residence on varied subjects like Upanishads, Brahma-sutras, Bhagavad-Gita, Indology, Agama-sastra, etc.

He had written about eighty books in Kannada, more than a hundred books in English apart from books in Sanskrit and Pali. Two of his books were given the Sahitya Academy Awards. Among his numerous publications are:

* The Encyclopedia of Indian Medicine in three volumes, published by Popular Prakashan, Mumbai;
* Tibetan Tantrik Tradition and Tibetan Meditation, published by Arnold Heinemann;
* Encyclopedia of Indian Iconography, published by Satguru Publications, Delhi;
* The Agama Encyclopedia in twelve volumes, published by Satguru Publications;
* Rg Veda Darshana in sixteen volumes, published by Kalpatharu Research Academy;
* Srividya Kosha, published by Satguru Publications.

In order to preserve his art works, reprint his books and record his lectures on CDs in order to make them available to interested people, his family members have formed a Trust, The S. K. Ramachandra Rao Memorial Trust based in Bangalore.

The Lalita kosha, which had been published more than a decade ago, has been out of print for many years. The Trust, which is desirous of reprinting all the books of Prof. S. K. Ramachandra Rao, approached Shri Sunil Gupta of Indian Books Centre, because he had already published many works of Prof. Rao. We are grateful that Shri Gupta has taken up the publication of this work.

Prof. S. K. Ramachandra Rao Memorial Trust.

Introduction

The present volume is in its nature encyclopaedic: it contains an elaborate introduction dealing with several aspects of the cult of Lalita. The thousand names have been given in English translation also, with explanations wherever necessary. Illustrations are also included. The volume comprehends almost the entire literature that is available on Lalita in Sanskrit. This may serve as a companion volume to the Tantrik practices in Sri-Vidya.

The volume also contains the text of Lalita-sahasra-nama-strotra, both in the verse-form and in the form of names as recited during worship. The portion dealing with Lalita (Lalitopakhyana) from Brahmanda-purana, and a text closely related to these two, namely Lalita-trisati are appended.

Many of the expressions like shadadhva, panchopachara, dasa-mudra, Kama-kala and so on have been explained in the author's volumes on Agama-kosha.

The illustrations included here are from sculptures in temples and from medieval manuscripts prepared in Mysore. I am grateful to the Director, Regional Design and Technical Centre (All India Handicrafts Board), Bangalore for permission to reproduce some drawings in their collection (from the artists Shri Appukuttan Achary, Shri M. S. Raman and Shri K. V. Bhandari), in additions to the drawings made by myself from old manuscripts and sculptures in temples and museums.

S. K. Ramachandra Rao.

LALITĀ – KOSHA

INTRODUCTION

There is an ancient ballad narrated in many of the purānas and in the two epics (Rāmāyaṇa and Mahābhārata) which provides a backdrop to the cult of Lalitā. The ballad is highly symbolic, and its details have inspired tāntrik speculations.

It relates to the poignant episode of Satī (the consort of Śiva) immolating herself in the sacrificial fire of her own father Dakshaprajāpati, when he heaped insults on Śiva and humiliated her. Śiva in indignnation dispatched the terrible Bhairava (or Vīrabhadra) to punish the arrogant and offending Daksha. Bhairava cut off the head of Daksha, put an end to the sacrifice and drove out all the gods and sages who had assembled there.

Śiva was still inconsolable, and grieving for his consort, withdrew himself completely from the world and retired to Himālayan solitude for austerities and contemplation. The world thus orphaned, became a prey to the outrages of the demon Tāraka. The gods decided to divert Śiva's attention to the pressing situation, and sent the god of love Kāma-rāja to disturb the contemplation in which Śiva was absorbed. Kāma-rāja succeeded in his attempt to distract Śiva and turn his attention to Pārvati, but he was reduced to ashes in the process. Śiva burnt him down with the fire of his eye.

There is an extension to the story which is not so well-known. One of the attendant spirits (gaṇas) serving Śiva, Chitrakarmā by name made a doll out of the ashes of Kāma-rāja for sport. When the gaze of Śiva fell upon this doll the doll was enlivened. The doll thereupon, chanted 'Śata-rudrīya', and the pleased Śiva granted him boons. But the doll which was made out of the ashes of Kāma-rāja's body (which was burnt by Śiva's anger) was tāmasic in character and grew to be a terrible demon, Bhaṇḍāsura by name. This asura built his fortress Śūnyaka (void) in the area called Śoṇita-pura ('the city of blood'), and began to torment gods and sages. His minister Vishaṅga and his commander Viśukra were both born out of his arms.

As the demon had obtained Śiva's boons, he was invisible and the gods and the sages had to find a way out. They engage themselves in a great sacrifice and out of the sacrificial altar flashed forth the goddess Lalitā in answer to the needs of the gods and sages. She built her own fortress in the jewel-island (maṇi-dvīpa) in the midst of the ocean of nectar (sudhā-samudra); Śyāmalā (mantriṇī) became her minister and Vārāhi (daṇḍa-nāthā) her commander.

Lalitā engaged Bhaṇḍāsura in a terrible battle and killed him; his army was destroyed. The world was liberated from all evil forces; and the gods and the sages could breathe freely once again.

This story and its significance were communicated by Hayagrīva to the sage Agasthya. *Devī-bhāgavata* has a story about the origin of the horse headed god (Hayagrīva). Vishṇu who was entrusted with the task of preserving the world, was at length tired. He supported his chin upon his great bow Śārṅga, and fell asleep. In the meantime, a horse-headed demon, Haya-grīva by name, became powerful and began tormenting the world, Vishṇu was so fast asleep that he could not be woken up. An expedient was thought of by the gods : termites were sought out to eat up the leather string that was tied to Vishṇu's bow. When this was done, the bow suddenly straightened itself out and tore away the head of Vishṇu in the process. The head which flew up could not be recovered. The gods became frantic and prayed to the goddess Tripura-sundarī. She directed them to sever the head of the horse that lay nearby and attach it to the headless body of Vishṇu. Vishṇu was thus revived; and thereafter became known as Haya-grīva.

Vishṇu as Haya-griva then attacked the demon with the same named and killed him. The gods were relieved and the world was saved. Vishṇu then approached the goddess Tripura-sundarī (Lalitā) and learnt from her the secret of Śrī-vidyā. He became the first master of Śrī-vidyā in the lineage known after him (viz. the Hayagrīva-saṁpradāya) and affiliated it to the southern recension (Dakshiṇāchāra). In the lineage, the recitation of the thousand names of Lalitā is an important detail.

The Text

One of eighteen 'great' purāṇas compiled and redacted by the celebrated sage Vyāsa, Brahmāṇḍa-purāṇa is better known for its espousal of the cause of Lalitā cult. Included in it is an elaborate account of the appearance of the Goddess as Lalitā in order to save the world from the clutches of the wicked and terrible demon, Bhaṇḍāsura. This narrative occurs almost as an appendage to the third and last division of the purāṇa (uttara and upasaṁhāra-pāda). Known as Lalitopākhyāna, it consists of forty chapters, the last five of which are regarded as especially important as they deal with actual appearance of Lalitā

(Lalitāprādurbhāva), eulogy of her greatness (Lalitā-stava-rāja), the manifestation of the god Madana-kāmeśvara, and the wedding of the goddess with the God (Vaivāhikotsava).

This portion is in the form of a dialogue between the sage Agastya and the god Hayagrīva. Better known than this narrative and more widely employed in devotional practices are two other texts which are also in the nature of dialogues between Agastya and Hayagrīva : *Lalitā-triśati* and *Lalitā-sahasra-nāma.* These are not actually portions of *Brahmāṇḍa-purāṇa,* although they are usually described to be such; they are secondary texts, evolved from the Lalitopākhyāna portion of this purāṇa. The former text eulogizes Lalitā in three hundred names (tri-śatī) and the latter in one thousand names (sahasra).

The three texts together constitute the corpus of Śrī-vidyā known after Lalitā; and they contain not only the details of 'external' worship (bahir-yāga) but suggestions for meditation and absorption (antar-yāga). In *Lalitopākhyāna,* we read that the sage Agastya asked the revered Hayagrīva to enlighten him about the great goddess known differently as Mahā-tripura-sundarī and Kāmākshī. Hayagrīva, before giving Agastya an account of the glory and exploits of the goddess reveals that she resides in the heart of all beings and that whatever occurs in the world, as thing or thought, is in reality her own sport :

यत् किंचिद्वर्तते लोके सर्वमस्या विचेष्टितम्।
किंचिच्चिन्त्यते कश्चित् स्वच्छन्दं विदधात्यसौ॥

The first of these texts, *Lalitopākhyāna* narrates the tales highlighting the greatness of the Goddess in the first of the last four chapters (41-44) of the concluding section of *Brahmāṇḍa-purāṇa;* the second among these chapters brings out the significance of the sixteen-lettered mantra of the goddess (shoḍaśāksharī-vidyā), and the benefits and powers that are acquired by the practitioner who perfects this mantra; the third of these chapters gives an account of gestures and postures (mudrās) that must be assumed by the practitioner; the next chapter deals with initiations (dīkshā), meditations (dhyāna) and other associated details like guru and so on; and the concluding chapter deals with the mystical placement (nyāsa) of the deities involved in the sacred Śrī-chakra.

The other text is known as *Lalitā-triśati,* because of the three hundred names of the goddess that figure prominently. These names are arranged in the order of letters that constitute the celebrated fifteen-lettered mantra (pañchadaśī-vidyā). The text has a prologue (pūrva-pīṭ hikā) and an epilogue (uttara-piṭhikā). There is a well-known commentary on this work ascribed to the great vedāntin, Śaṁkara. However, the authorship is not certain.

The text, celebrated as *Lalitā-sahasra-nāma,* consists of 320 verses in three chapters. The first chapter (in 51 verses) relates that the thousand secret names of Lalitā were first recited by Vaśinī and other Vāgdevatās as commanded by the Goddess herself, and includes a 'nyāsa' giving the following details : the Vāgdevatās headed by Vaśinī are the seers who saw these sacred names which are strung together as a garland of mantras; the metre in which the verses contain these names is anushṭup; the great goddess is Lalitā, the deity invoked by these names; the vāgbhavakūṭa (the first of the three kūṭas constituting by Śrī-vidyā) is the 'seed', the Kāma-rāja-kūṭa (the second of the three kūṭas) the 'power', and the Śakti-kūṭa (the third) the 'spike'; the purpose of the recitation of the names is to accomplish the grace of the goddess Lalitā, and thereby to procure the benefits that one longs for :

अस्य श्रीललितासहस्रनामस्तोत्रमालामन्त्रस्य वशिन्यादि वाग्देवता ऋषयः।

अनुष्टुप् छन्दः। श्री ललिता परमेश्वरी देवता। श्री मद्वाग्भव कूटेति बीजम्। मध्यकूटेति शक्तिः। शक्तिकूटेति कीलकम्। श्री ललिता महात्रिपुरसुन्दरी प्रसाद सिद्धिद्वारा चिन्तितफलावप्त्यर्थे जपे विनियोगः।।

The second chapter contains the thousand mystic names of the goddess in 182-1/2 verses. The third chapter (86-1/2 verses) enumerates the benefits that are got by reciting these thousand names.

The commentaries

The text, which is exceedingly popular among the devotees given to Śākta form of worship, even as Vishṇu-sahasra-nāma (extracted from Mahābhārata) is among the Vaishṇava devotees, is among the best known and widely used hymnal collections in the country. It occupies a unique position, because it has mystical overtones which are both profound and suggestive. Although affiliated to the *Brahmāṇḍa-purāṇa* corpus, it enjoys an independent and august status and has merited numerous glosses and commentaries, among which the following are important:

1. *Saubhāgya-bhāskara* (an elaborate commentary by the celebrated tāntrik authority Bhāskara-rāya-makhin, whose initiatory name was Bhāsurānanda-nātha);

2. *Vidyāraṇya-bhāshya* (in nine chapters, 1500 ślokas in extent, by Vidyāraṇya-muni, who is described as a disciple of Ānandāraṇya-pūjya-pāda);

3. Commentary by Vimarśānanda-nātha (a work of 2000 slokas in nine sections, disciple of Vimalānanda-nātha);

4. *Saubhāgya-ratnākara* (in 36 taraṅgas by Śrīnivāsa-sundara, whose initiatory name was Vidyānanda-nātha, disciple of Śacchidānanda-nātha);

5. Commentary (a work of 2500 ślokas) by Bhaṭṭ anārāyaṇa, (who describes himself as the disciple of Śivānandanātha, and describes his work as inspired by the goddess Lalitā herself).

All these are works of Tāntrik initiates, and contain esoteric doctrines preserved in several traditions, or mārgas (lines or pathways meant for tāntrik practitioners). They have different ways of classifying the thousand names. For instance, the commentary of Vimarśānanda-nātha, which has nine chapter, has this classification :

1. Prathama-bhūmikā (names 1 to 64)
2. Viśvādhika-pariccheda (65 to 84)
3. Śakti-chandra-kalā-pariccheda (85-111)
4. Śakti-trayottīrṇa-pariccheda (112-256)
5. Sākshi-pariccheda (257-274)
6. Pañchama-pariccheda (275-300)
7. Purushārtha-pariccheda (301-354)
8. Paśu-pāśa-pariccheda (356-408)
9. Śrītattva-pariccheda (493-503 and 997-1000)

Some commantaries are encyclopaedic in character. *Saubhāgya-ratnākara,* for example, treats of all topics concerning Tāntrik worship (daily as well as occasional), varieties of and preparations for initiations, fire-ablutions, rituals of benign and malignant significance, recitation of sacred hymns as a ritual, the division of the Śri-vidyā cult, and good conduct :

श्रीविद्यायाः सभेदाय नित्य नैमित्तिकार्चनं कामार्चन।। दीक्षांगभूतं प्रत्यगंसाधनं

दीक्षाभेदं पुरश्चर्यान् तत्तत्कर्मनियमादिकान् काम्यहोमविधिश्चैव सौम्यक्रूरविभेदत:

समस्तव्यस्तविद्याया: जपात् काम्यफलोदय: सदाचारादिकं चैव लिख्यते रत्नवारिधौ।।

But the information provided in most cases is fragmentary and pedantic, and offers little clue to the practical character of these cultic traditions. Probably, this was deliberately meant to be so, for the esoteric aspects of the tradition cannot be expected to be made explicit for those who are devoid of necessary equipment and who are not properly initiated.

The best among the commentaries and most frequently consulted, is Bhāskara-rāya's *Saubhāgya-bhāskara*. The author who lived between 1690 and 1785 A.D. was a versatile scholar and prolific writer on general subjects. Among his tāntrik works, the commentary on *Nityā-shoḍaśikārṇava* (Vāmakeśvara-tantra) entitled, *Setu-bandha*, the exposition on the Pañcha-daśī-vidyā known as *Varivasyā-rahasya*, the commentary on *Lalitā-sahasranāma* known as *Saubhāgya-bhāskara* and a work on worship based on *Paraśu-rāma-kalpa-sūtra* entitled *Nityotsava* are popular and famous. He was an ardent devotee of the Mother-goddess, and was recipient of all higher initiations in the Śākta-tantra. His name as a dikshita was Bhāsurānanda-nātha, and his teacher was Śiva-datta-śukla. He pays homage in his works to his father (Gaṁbhīra-rāya), his teachers Nṛsiṁha-adhvarī or Nṛsiṁhānandanātha (vidyā-guru) and Śiva-datta-śukla (dīkshā-guru). His writings number more than 40, and include works on Veda, Vedānta, Nyāya, Mīmāṁsā, Chhandas, Smṛti and mantra-śāstra. He wrote commentaries on some Upanishads (like Kaulopanishad and Tripuropanishad), on Śrī-sūkta, and on Durgā-sapta-śati section of Mārkaṇḍeya-purāña, entitled

Gupta-vatī. His vast erudition and profound acquaintance with tāntrik practitioners make his works a mine of valuable information concerning Tantra and Mantra. He performed several Vedic sacrifices also, and thereby came to be known as a 'mankhin'.

His commentary on *Lalitā-sahasra-nāma* was based on some notes on technical and terminological matters (Paribhāshā) prepared by his tāntrik-preceptor, whom he does not name :

गुरुचरणसनाथो भासुरानन्दनाथो
विवृतिमातिरहस्यां वीररवृन्दैर्नमस्याम्।
रचयति ललिताया नामसाहस्रिकाया
गुरुकृत परिभाषाः सविवृण्वन्नशेषाः॥

He also draws extensively from all available sources, both of the Vedic tradition and the Tāntrik tradition. The commentary is divided into twelve sections (called kalās). The first chapter called upodghāta-prakaraṇa deals with the first fifty-one verses of *Lalitā*-sahasra-nāma, and the last chapter known as 'kshamā' with the enumeration of benefits (phala-śruti); the other ten chapters deal with a hundred each of the thousand names. The ten chapters dealing with the thousand names are named Tāpanī, Dhūmrikā, Marīchī, Jvālinī, Ruchi, Sushumṇā, Bhogadā, Viśvā, Bodhinī, and Dhāriṇī. The colophon at the end of the first chapter describes the author as a devotee of the sacred feet of his teacher Nṛsiṁhayajvā, who is claimed to the "Śrīmat-pada-vākya-pramāṇapārāvāra-pāriṇa-dhurīṇa-sarva-tantra-svatantra', the customary description of a great and venerable teacher who is proficient in Vyākaraṇa, Mīmāṃsā and Nyāya and who is an independent authority in matters of all religious and philosophical disciplines. The author's father's name is given as

Gaṃbhīra-rāya-dīkshita who bore the surname 'Bhārati'.

Hayagrīva and Agastya

The text, like *Lalitopākhyāna* and *Lalitā-triśatī*, is, as said earlier, in the form of a dialogue between the sage Agastya and the god Hayagrīva. Hayagrīva is represented as the teacher ('deśikendra') who communicates the mysterious thousand names to Agastya who is here a disciple. Hayagrīva is the horseheaded incarnation of Vishṇu, the occasion for the assumption of this form being variously given. The most popular story is that he assumed this form to kill the demon Hayagrīva (who was horseheaded). But the more ancient narrative (cf. *Pañcha-viṃśa-brahmāṇa*, 7, 5, 6 and *Taittirīya-āraṇyaka*, 5, 1) mentions that Vishṇu as the personification of sacrifice (yajña) was deprived of his head in a skirmish with the other gods, and that later a horse's head was fixed on the trunk of yajña, which was resuscitated. *Skandapurāṇa*, however, has it that Vishṇu having lost his head, performed austerities in Dharmāraṇya and obtained a horse's head as a boon bestowed by Śiva. Bhāskara-rāya refers to Devībhāgavata (first skanda) for the story.

Agastya was a sage of great renown, and he has been immortalized by a celestial position (the star canopus, agastyodaya being the arising of the star on the seventh day of the second half of the month Bhādra, when water-offerings, tarpaṇa, is offered to the sage Agastya) being accorded to him. The legends ascribe his origin to the semen of the twin-gods Mitrā-Varuṇa which were dropped into a jar (hence known as Kuṁbha-sambhava, "potborn", and also as Maitrā-vāruṇi, "off-spring of Mitrā-Varuṇa") and to the conjoint action of fire and wind.

The celebrated sage Vasishṭha was his half-brother, according to Yāska's *Nirukta*. Among the many exploits of Agastya were the drinking of the entire ocean, the destruction of the demon Vātāpi and the humbling of the mountain Vindhyā (hence his name Agastya, which means one who fixed the mountain, "na gacchhatīty agah, parvatah; tam vindhyanāmānam styāyati; styānam stambhanam). He is also the patron-saint of South India, and a system of indigenous medicine practised in Tamil Nādu till this day (viz. the Siddha) is said to be his legacy.

The verse that is commonly recited while making offerings to him on the occasion of Agastyodaya runs as follows :

काशपुष्पप्रतीकाश अग्निमारुतसंभवं।
मित्रावरुणयोः पुत्र कुम्भयोने नमोऽस्तु ते॥

His wife Lopāmudrā was the princess of Vidarbha, and was reputed for her devotion to the sage Agastya (cf. for her birth, *Mahābhārata,* Vana-parva, 96 ff). She is eligible for the pious offerings on the occasion of Agastyodaya, and the verse recited on the occasion is given in *Mala-māsa-tattva* as follows :

लोपामुद्रे महाभागे राजपुत्रि पतिव्रते।
गृहाणार्घ्यं मया दत्तं मैत्रावरुणिवल्लभे॥

They were married in Mahā-sindhu-tīrtha (*Mahābhārata*, Śānti-parva, 88, 343 and Vana-parva 130, 5) and lived in Gaṇgādvāra. Both Agastya and Lopamudra were great devotees of the Mother-goddess, and they are eulogized by the Goddess herself in *Lalitā-tri-śati.* Lopāmudrā is regarded by Tāntriks as one of the architects of a Śri-vidyā division, and her name is identified with a mantra of the goddess. Bhāskara-rāya describes Agastya as 'Śrī-vidyopāsakāgresara' ("the front-ranking devotee of Śrī-vidyā").

Agastya's meeting with Hayagrīva has been described at the beginning of *Lalitopākhyāna* (3, 5 in the *Brahmāṇḍa-purāṇa,* after the fourth chapter in the Uttara-bhāga):

अगस्त्यो नाम देवर्षिः वेदवेदांगपारगः।
सर्वसिद्धान्तसारज्ञो ब्रह्मानन्दरसात्मकः॥

चचाराद्भुतहेतूनि तीर्थान्यायतनानि च।
शैलारण्यापगामुख्यान् सर्वा जानपदानपि॥

तेषु तेष्वखिलाञ्जन्तूनज्ञानतिमिरावृतान्।
शिश्नोदरपरान् दृष्ट्वा चिन्तयामास तान्प्रति॥

तस्य चिन्तयमानस्य चरतो वसुधामिमां।
प्राप्तमासीन्महापुण्यं कांचीनगरमुत्तमम्॥

तत्र वारणशैलेन्द्रमेकाम्रनिलयं शिवम्।
कामाक्षीं कलिदोषघ्नीमपूजयदथात्मवान्॥

लोकहेतोर्दयार्द्रस्य धीमतश्चिन्तनो मुहुः।
चिरकालेन तपसा तोषितोऽभूज्जनार्दनः॥

हयग्रीवां तनुं कृत्वा साक्षाच्चिन्मात्रविग्रहाम्।
शंखचक्राक्षवलयपुस्तकोज्वलबाहुकाम्॥

पूरयित्रीं जगत्कृत्स्नं प्रभया देहजातया।
प्रादुर्बभूव पुरतो मुनेरमिततेजसा॥

The great sage Agastya was once visiting several places of pilgrimage and when he saw people steeped in ignorance and concerned only with their creature-comforts and sensual pleasures, he was greatly agitated and pondered over their lot and fate. He came in due course to Kāñchi. He worshipped Ekāmranātha and Kāmākshī and performed austerities for a long time there. Pleased with his devotion, Vishṇu appeared before him in the horse-headed form and asked him what he desired. The sage prostrated before the god, and inquired how the poor worldly folk could be released from the fetters of ignorance. Vishṇu thereupon told Agastya that the same inquiry had been made first by Śiva, then by Brahmā, and later by Durvāsa. He explained that He is in fact a primaeval spirit, the primordial principle, source of everything and cause of creation, preservation and dissolution. He involves in himself the three forms (Brahmā, Vishṇu and Śiva) and the three guṇas (sattva, rajas and tamas); and yet beyond both forms and guṇas. Sporting out of free will, He, who is Pradhāna (primordial matter) and Purusha (the conscious spirit) at once, divides himself into two distinct aspects: the Pradhāna aspect transformed itself into the universe; the other aspect remained beyond the guṇas, transcendental and supreme. One who understands this dual nature of Godhead gets released from worldly fetters. It is possible to achieve this freedom, by the performance of austerities of great lengths of time, observances and self-discipline, renunciation and elimination of evil propensities. However, it is difficult to give up worldly pleasures and renounce completely. But the worship of the supreme goddess that abides in oneself will *achieve the purpose* of liberation easily; and this is true for all people, whether they come within the fold of three varnas or not, and even for the sinful folk. Mere contemplation on the Goddess will transform malevolent inclinations to beneficent ones. The worship of the Goddess may or may not be conducted according to prescribed regimen; but its reward will surely be release from all bondages. Śiva, Brahmā and all the gods have worshipped the goddess Tripurā and obtained their powers. By no other means can worldly prosperity and ultimate liberation together be accomplished.

Vishṇu concluded by saying that this was revealed out of compassion for the mankind, and suggested that Agastya spread this message among gods, adepts and human beings for their weal and welfare. When the sage desired further knowledge about the form of the Goddess which was absolute and undifferentiated, Vishṇu directed him to approach his incarnatory form, Hayagrīva in his hermitage, and disappeared from Agastya's view. Agastya met the divine sage Hayagrīva, with devotion and reverence, and sought enlightenment concerning the great Goddess, who, as told by Hayagrīva, is without beginning or end, who is the foundation for the entire universe, who could be apprehended only in meditative absorption, and also abides in the heart of all beings.

Thus, the cult of Lalitā was communicated by Hayagrīva to Agastya. It is said that Hayagrīva it was that discovered the sixteen-lettered mantra of the Goddess (śhoḍaśī-vidyā, with the addition of the syllable Śrīṁ to the usual pañchadaśī). In the cult of Śrī-vidyā, there is a traditional lineage beginning with Hayagrīva (Hayagrīva-saṁpradāya), which is one of the three lineages current in the Tāntrik circles (the other two being Ānanda-bhairavasaṁpradāya and Dakshiṇā-mūrti-saṁpradāya). The linage of Hayagrīva aligns itself to Dakshiṇāchāra (for details see the author's *Tāntrik Practices in Śrī-vidya),* and the worship of the goddess is carried on with 'the thousand names' of Lalitā, or alternately with 'the three hundred names' (tri-śatī), or with 'one hundred and eight names' (ashṭottara-śata-nāma). This tradition is distinguished by the omission of the three concentric circles (tri-vṛtta) inside the outer square (bhūpura) of Śrī-chakra design in worship. It may be mentioned that the Ānandabhairava tradition retains the three circles but does not include it in worship, while the Dakśhiṇāmūrti tradition not only retains them but also offers worship to them.

Lopamudra

The customary lineage of the division of Śrī-vidyā known as Kādi (viz. where the mantra of Śrī-vidya begins with the syllable 'Ka'), begins with Śrī-parama-śiva and continues with Durvāsa, Hayagrīva and Agastya. Hayagrīva is the teacher and Agastya his disciple. Curiously enough, the lineage of the other division of Śrī-vidyā known as Hādi (viz. where the mantra begins with the syllable 'Ha') involves the wife of Agastya, Lopāmudrā, prominently. This division, which is said to be later (kādeh paśchād eva hader uddhārah), counts twelve pioneers of Śrī-vidyā : Manu, Chandra, Kubera, Lopāmudrā, Manmatha (Kāma-rāja), Agastya, Nandiśa, Sūrya, Vishṇu, Skanda, Śiva and Durvāsa (cf. also *Śrī-vidyārṇavatantra,* 7, 1). Lopāmūdra is credited with having initiated her husband Agastya into Śrī-vidyā. Manmatha (Kāma-rāja) is said to have inaugurated the Kādi lineage, while Lopāmudrā and Agastya were responsible for the other lineage. The main difference between the two lineages is that the number of effective (viz. not repeated) letters in the Hādi lineage is five, while in the Kādi lineage the number of such letters is seven.

The mantra of Kādi lineage takes this form

क ए ई ल ह्रीं। ह स क ह ल ह्रीं। स क ल ह्रीं।।

while that of the Hādi lineage is

ह स क ल ह्रीं। ह स क स ल ह्रीं। स क ल ह्रीं।।

The Kādi-vidyā is said to have been derived from *Devyatharva-śirsha* belonging to Atharva-veda:

कामो योनिः कमला वज्रपाणि-

(क) (ए) (ई) (ल)

गुहा ह सा मातरिश्वाभ्रमिन्द्रः।

(ह्रीं) (क) (ह) (ल)

पुनर्गुहा स क ला मायया च

(ह्रीं) (ह्रीं)

पुरूच्च्रैषा विश्वमातादिविद्या।।

It has (according to *Chatuś-śatī*) three sections (Khaṇḍa or Kūṭa), constituting fifteen letters (akshara), twenty-seven ingredients and thirty-six units (representing the 36 tattvas of Śākta philosophy :

Section I : 5 letters; 9 ingredients (4 consonants, 3 vowels, 1 nāda, 1 bindu)

Section II : 5 letters; 10 ingredients (7 consonants, 1 vowel, 1 nāda, 1 bindu)

Section III : 4 letters; 8 ingredients (5 consonants, 1 vowel, 1 nāda, 1 bindu)

Total 15 Total 27

[Each Section has three tattvas separately; thus the mantra has altogether nine tattvas, which when added to the 27 ingredients will constitute a total of 36 tattvas. In Śākta philosophy the following tattvas are enumerated : Śiva, Śakti, Sadāśiva, Iśvara, Śuddha vidhyā, Māyā, Kalā, Vidyā, Rāga, Niyati, Purusha, Prakṛti, Ahaṁkāra, Buddhi, Manas, 10 indriyas (5 for cognition and 5 for action), 5 tanmātras and 5 mahābhūtas].

व्याप्ता पंचदशगुणैर्या विद्या भूतगुणात्मिका।

पंचाभिश्च तथा षड्भिश्चतुर्भिरपि चाक्षरैः।।

स्वरव्यंजनभेदेन सप्तविंशप्रभेदिनी।

सप्तविशंप्रभेदेन षट्त्रिंशत्तत्त्वरूपिणी।

तत्त्वातीतस्वभावा च विद्यैषा भासते सदा।

Lalitā-triśatī is supposed to be the main text of the Kādi-tradition, and the three hundred names are arranged in the order mentioned above for the Kādi version of pañchadaśī-vidyā.

Śrī-vidyārṇava-tantra (1, 17) distinguishes between Kāmarāja-krama (viz. Kādi) and Lopāmudrā-krama (viz. Hādi) within ūrdhvāmnāya. The same text later (7th Śvāsa, as told by Īśvara) refers to Lopāmudrā-vidyā as a variant of Kāmarāja-vidyā:

कामराजविद्यायाः शक्तिं तुर्यं च सुन्दरि।

हित्वा मुखे शिवेन्द्राढ्या लोपामुद्रा प्रकाशिता॥

In the first kūṭa of Kādi-vidyā, we have ए and ई which are omitted in the version ascribed to Lopāmudrā, and this version begins with ह and has स also in the first kūṭa (vāgbhava). Other wise the two vidyās are similar. There is another version of Kāmarāja-vidyā, followed by Agastya as well as by Lopāmudrā :

क ए ई ल ह्रीं। ह स क ह ल ह्रीं। ह स स क ल ह्रीं।

इत्यगस्त्योपासिता श्रीविद्या।

तथा 'लोपामुद्राप्रभावेण साक्षाद् ब्रह्मस्वरूपिणी' इतीयं विद्या लोपामुद्रयाप्युपासितेत्यर्थः।

एतेनेयं द्वितीया लोपामुद्रोपासिता श्रीविद्येति।

(*Śrī-vidyārṇava-tantra,* 7, 8)

There is also a third version which is associated with Lopāmudrā (Śakti-lopāmudrā, Śakti represented by the syllable स which is added to Kāmarāja-vidyā).

शक्तिर्महेशः कामश्चन्द्रबीजं ततः परम्।
महामाया ततः पश्चात्तव स्नेहान्प्रकीर्तितम्।

The addition of स at the beginning of the fifteen-lettered Kāmarāja-vidyā would make it the Lopāmudrā version of sixteen lettered vidyā:

लोपामुद्रा वाग्भवं तु पृथिव्यन्ते शिवयोजनात्।
सकारं कामराजादौ लोपा तु षोडशाक्षरी।।

The eighteen-lettered vidyā which is again ascribed to Lopāmudrā takes this form :

ऐ ह स क ल ह्रीं। क्लीं ह स क ह ल ह्रीं। सौः स क ल ह्रीं।।

This has been described as incomparable and most meritorious, providing prosperity as well as liberation, and accomplishing directly all human objectives :

एषाप्यष्टादशी प्रोक्ता सर्वसिद्धिप्रदायिका।
भोगमोक्षप्रदा साक्षात् पुरुषार्थप्रदायिका।।
अनया सदृशी विद्या न विद्यार्णवगोचरे।
नास्ति नास्ति पुनर्नास्ति सत्यं सत्यं वदाम्हम्।।

Lopāmudrā, although born as a princess, lived austerely in a hermitage after she married Agastya; she had a son by Agastya, Dṛdhasyū (or Idhma-vāha) by name.

Śrī-chakra and worship of Lalitā

All the three texts pertaining to the goddess Lalitā (*Lalitopakhyāna, Lalitā-sahasra-nāma* and *Lalitā-triśatī*) involve the ideology of Śrī-chakra and are employed while worship is conducted to Śrī-chakra (for details of Śrī-chakra, see the author's *Śrī-chakra,* Śrī Satguru Publications, Delhi, 1989 and the *Tāntrik Practices in Śrī-vidya,* Kalpatharu Research Academy, Bangalore, 1990). The cult of Lalitā is distinguished by its devotion to the fifteen-lettered mantra of the Goddess (pañchadaśī-vidyā), which is itself regarded as the embodiment of the Goddess. The thousand names or the three hundred names are recited while worshipping Śrī-chakra, and the ideology is that the names are in reality the elaboration of the implications of pañchadaśī-vidyā while the Śrī-chakra design (whether as a linear diagram, rekhā-yantra or as an icon, meru) itself is the visual representation of the same vidyā. The construction of Śrī-chakra follows the symbolism of the three kūṭas and the significances of the fifteen letters of the Śrī-vidyā. The arrangement of the names of Lalita follows the scheme, especially in the *Lalitā-triśatī.* The correspondance between the Śrī-chakra as a yantra and pañchadaśi-vidyā as a mantra is achieved by the mindful recitation of the names of Lalitā :

Kūṭa I	-	the central dot (bindu)
	-	the triangle (trikoṇa)
	-	the eight angled figure (vasu-koṇa)
	-	inner ten-sided figure (antar-daśāra)
Kūṭa II	-	the fourteen sided figure (chatur-daśāra)
	-	the circle that is outside the above (prathama-valaya)
	-	the eight-petalled lotus (ashṭa-dala)
	-	the second (middle) circle (dvitīya-valaya)
	-	the sixteen-sided figure (shoḍaśāra)
	-	the third (outer) circle (tṛtīya-valaya)
Kūṭa III	-	the inner line forming the square enclosure (bhūpura)

- the middle lines
- the outer lines
- the presiding pair of deities, Śiva-kāmeśvarī,

Among the letters that go to compose the Śrī-vidyā, the three 'ka's and the two 'ha's are regarded as the Śiva aspect, the other effective letters represent the Śakti aspect; the conjunct letter 'hrīṁ' that occurs after each kūṭa is composite of Śiva and Śakti.

कत्रयं हद्वयं चैव शैवो भागः प्रकीर्तितः।

शक्त्यक्षराणि शेषाणि ह्रींकार उभयात्मकः॥

Pañchadaśī thus involves a conjoint presence of Śiva and Śakti; and the Śrī-chakra also conveys the same message. According the Bhāskara-rāya the central point (bindu) represents the letter 'ī' as well as the three 'ka's of the Pañchadaśī. The triangle which encloses the bindu is the first 'hrīm'; and the eight-angled figure represents the other two 'hrīm's. The two ten-sided figures (inner and outer) and the figure with fourteen-angles stand for the two 'ha's and 'e'. The eight petalled lotus and the sixteen-petalled lotus symbolize the two 'sa's. The outer enclosure, square in shape and with a portal on each of the sides, represent the three 'la's of the Pañchadaśī:

क त्रितयादीकाराद् बिन्दुर्जातः तदग्रमे चक्रे।

हृल्लेखाभिस्तत्परचक्रत्रितयं हकाराभ्यां।

एकारेण च तत्परचक्रे जाते सकाराभ्यां।

चतुरस्त्राणि लकारैव विद्याक्षरेण चक्रजनिः॥

(वरिवस्यारहस्ये)

Bhāskara-rāya's identification of the details of Śrī-chakra with the letters of the mantra is in terms of the construction of the design from the letters.

Lalitā-sahasra-nāma speaks of Pañchadaśī as the monarch of the mystic formulae (mantras) and Śrī-chakra as the monarch of mystic design (yantras); and the two will be enriched by the recitation of the mystic names of the Goddess whose body is Śrī-chakra and whose spirit is Pañchadaśī :

मन्त्रराजजपश्चैव चक्रराजार्चनं तथा।

रहस्यनामपाठश्च नाल्पस्य तपसः फलम्॥

Yoginī-hṛdaya rightly speaks of the three-fold symbolism and the hidden import (saṅketa) that must be fully comprehended by the practitioner : (1) the symbolism of the fifteen-lettered mantra (mantra-sanketa); (2) the symbolism of Śrī-chakra (chakra-saṅketa); and (3) the symbolism of worship involving meditation and the recitation of the mystic names (pūjā-sanketa). The last detail, also called yāga or saparyā, is external (bahir-yāga) or internal (antar-yāga). The external worship consists of several sequences, and involves various materials and equipment; it is the worship that is normally seen. The internal worship, on the other hand, is entirely a matter of mental attitudes and meditations; it is the worship meant for the advanced devotees. And the internal worship is further of two varieties : (1) with support (sādhāra) like the Śrī-chakra or visualized form of the Goddess which is worshipped mentally with great devotion; and (2) without support (nirādhāra), viz. worship conducted purely in consciousness and involving total absorption in the object of worship. The latter, of course, is the most superior :

पूजा याभ्यन्तरा सापि द्विविधा परिकीर्तिता।

साधारा च निराधारा निराधारा महत्तरा॥

साधारा या तु साधारे निराधारा तु संविदि।

आधारे वर्णसंकृप्तविग्रहे परमेश्वरीम्।

आराधयेदतिप्रीत्या गुरुणोक्तेन वर्त्मणा।

या पूजा संविदि प्रोक्ता सा तु तस्यां मनोलयः॥

संविदेव परा शक्तिः नेतरा परमार्थतः।

अतः संविदि तां नित्यां पूजयेन्मतिमत्तमः॥

(सूतसंहितायां, १, ५)

The goddess that is worshipped in Śrī-chakra and by the repetition of Pañchadaśī-vidyā is called Lalitā or Lalitā-tripurā-sun-darī. The expression Lalitā literally signifies 'desiring' (lallyate), 'adorning' (śṛngāre) or 'charming' (sundarī). The commentators, however, take the word in the sense of playing or sporting. Bhāskara-rāya relying on a statement in *Padma-purāṇa* interprets the word to mean one who sports, having transcended the world (lokānatītya lalate lalitā tena chochyate). The Goddess known as Lalitā is also known by other names, such as Tripurā, Kāmeśvarī, Sundarī or Rāja-rājeśvari. She is called Tripurā ('one who was three cities') because the Pañchadaśī-vidya has three 'kūṭa's (Vāgbhava, Kāma-rāja and Śaktī), and the mantra is three-lettered (ka, la, īm):

ककारे सर्वमुत्पन्नं कामकैवल्यदायकम्।

लकारे सकलैश्वर्यं ईकारे सर्वसौख्यदम्।

एवं बीजत्रयं देवि विद्यानां सारसंग्रहम्॥

(श्रीक्रमे)

The goddess is represented by the triangle (trikoṇa), standing for the three pīthas : Kāmagiri, Jālandhara and Pūrṇā-giri) in Śrī-chakra, and her form as Kuṇḍalinī is also three-fold (iḍā, pingalā and sushumnā). She is also called the supreme and sovereign mistress (parā-bhaṭṭ ārikā).

The goddess Lalitā is invoked in Śrī-chakra, contemplated upon by the japa of Pañchadaśī-vidyā (in the Kādi-krama) which is most sacred for the goddess, and worshipped by the recitation of the thousand names, after the japa is completed.

तन्त्रेषु ललितादेव्यास्तेषु मुख्यमिदं मुने।
श्रीविद्यैव तु मन्त्राणां तत्र कादिर्यथा परा॥

चक्राधिराजमभ्यर्च्य जप्त्वा पंचदशाक्षरीम्।
जपान्ते कीर्तयेन्नित्यमिदं नामसहस्त्रकम्॥

जपपूजाद्यशक्तश्चेत्पठेन्नामसहस्त्रकम्॥

(ललिता सहस्त्रनामस्तोत्रे, १, २३)

If one is unable to perform the sequences of worship or japa, he should at least recite the thousand names. While reciting the names, he should first articulate each name clearly, and holding the flower (or kuṁkuma) in the cupped hand he should utter the formula 'Hrīm Śrīm Śrī-matryai namah" and then place the flower (or kumkuma) on top of the bindu in Śrī-chakra. As regards the suitable flowers, the text suggests lotus, tulasī, and bilva-leaves (1, 21); and the list is expanded to include kalhāra, kadaṁba, champaka, jāti, mallikā, karavīra, utpala, and so on. *Phetkāriṇī-tantra* prescribes that the flower must always be held upward in the hand in the posture of offering (añjali), and never facing the ground :

अधोमुखार्पणं नेष्टं पुष्पांजलिविधिं विना।

It may be pointed out that contrary to the injunction of *Lalitāsahasra-nāma, Rudra-Yāmala* prohibits the employment of tulasī, bilva-leaves and dhātri-leaves in the worship of Śrī-chakra.

तुलसीबिल्वपत्राणि धात्रीपत्राणि पार्वति।
अर्चने चक्रराजस्य नोचितान्येव सर्वथा॥

The recitation of the names of Lalitā upon Śrī-chakra must be done every day (japen nityam) after the customary bath and ablutions, and after the sandhyā is done in both the Vedic and Tāntrik manners. The devotee must approach the Śrī-chakra with reverence and worship it in the prescribed way. Then he must repeat the pañchadaśī-vidyā a thousand times, three hundred times or at least a hundred times.It is only after this is completed, on must recite the thousand names of Lalitā :

प्रातःस्नात्वा विधानेन संध्याक्रमं समाप्य च।
पूजागृहं ततो गत्वा चक्रराजं समर्चयेत्॥

विद्यां जपेत् सहस्त्रं वा, त्रिशतं शतमेव वा।
रहस्यनामसाहस्त्रमिदं पश्चात्पठेन्नरः॥

(तत्रैव, २३९-१४०)

But the recitation of the thousand names of Lalitā is itself most meritorious and it alone may be done everyday. If, however, one finds it difficult to recite it everyday, he may do it on Fridays or on the ninth or fourteenth day of the bright-half of the lunar month; recitation on a full-moon night is specially recommended. If even this is impossible, then it may be done on special and auspicious days like Sankrānti or Vishu. Recitation on the day on which falls one's own birthday, one's wife's birthday or one's child's. Should this also prove difficult, one may recite the thousand names once at least in a life-time (janma-madhye sakṛcchāpi), or at least one of the thousand names (rahasya-nāma-sāhasre namaikam api). All the sins committed by the devotee will completely be got rid of.

When the full-moon night is chosen for the recitation (and night is the best time of this), the Goddess must be visualized in the lunar orb, and must be mentally worshipped with five-fold ministrations (pañchopachāra, viz. gandha, pushpa, dhūpa, dīpa and naivedya). The devotee must identify himself with the Goddess with the lunar orb and then recite the thousand names :

प्रतिमांस पौर्णमास्यामेभिर्नामसहस्त्रकैः।

रात्रौ यश्चक्रराजस्थामर्चयेत्परदेवताम्॥

स एक ललितारूपस्तद्रूपा ललिता स्वयम्।

न तयोर्विद्यते भेदो भेदकृत्पापकृद् भवेत्॥

(तत्रैव, २७९-२९०)

पौर्णमस्यां चन्द्रबिम्बे ध्यात्वा श्रीललिताम्बिकाम्।

पंचोपचारैः सम्पूज्य पठेन्नामसहस्त्रकम्॥

(तत्रैव, २५५)

Bhāskara-rāya explains that 'worship' here means the devotee identifying himself with the lubar orb, and then identifying the lunar orb with the Goddess :

तद्योहं सोऽसौ योसौ सोहं तत्त्वमेव त्वमेव तदित्यादि परस्पर प्रतियोगित्वरूपसम्यक्त्वेनप स्वात्मदेवतयोरैक्यं विभाव्यम्॥

Numerous benefits consequent upon the recitation are recounted in the final portion of text (*Lalitā-sahasranāma,* Phala-śruti). The recitation of names is regarded as what can be accomplished with little effort (svalpāyāsa-sādhya), but productive of great and various benefits (bahu-phala-prada). Especialy so in the present age, when evil prevails and virtuous conduct is conspicuous by its absence. In an age like this, people can hardly do anything better than merely recite the names. It is impossible to perform the rituals and other religious activities prescribed in the Vedas and Tantras :

कलौ पापैकबहुले धर्मानुष्ठानवर्जिते।
नामानुकीर्तनं मुक्त्वा नृणां नान्यत्परायणम्॥

(तत्रैव, ३०१)

Therefore, the recitation of names which easily secures the grace of the Goddess has been prescribed as the most suitable conduct for all classes of people in the present degenerate time. And its rewards are many and significant. Among the benefits are mentioned the cure of all types of diseases, the obtainment of all wealth, the avoidance of premature death and prolongation of life, expiation of sins, elimination of obstacles to prosperity and emancipation. And the text wonders how any one god or man, with limited equipment as he is, can even understand the benefits that attend the worship of Lalitā in a Śrī-chakra and with the thousand names; the Goddess herself truly knows; and no one else.

सा वेत्ति ललिता देवी स्वचक्रार्चनजं फलम्।
अन्ये कथं विजानीयुर्ब्रह्माद्याः स्वल्पमेधसः॥

(तत्रैव, ३०१)

Benefits will accrue even when the thousand names are written in a book and the book worshipped (282).

THE THOUSAND NAMES

It is an old custom to use as a devotional device a string of names or epithets concerning a deity; it will also be an aid for concentration. The name (nāman) in Sanskrit is derived from the root 'mnā' meaning that which serves the purpose of repeated employment (abhyāse); mnāyate abhyasyate yat tat nāmah. It is commonly used as a designation (abhidhāna), a denotation (ākhyā), an adoration (sambhāvanā), and invitation (āhvā), a description (lakshaṇa), or a symbol (saṁjñā). There is a secondary meaning which signifies mind's inclination towards an object (namayati, namyate anena vā); the mind bends towards what the name points to. As a devotional device, it is what reveals the deity, the aspects of the deity and the relevance of the deity to the devotee.

When the names of the deity are recited continuously and with devotion, the mind acquires a facility for concentration. The notion of 'sankīrtana' ('singing the glory of godhead') involves the narration of the acts of the deity as well as the numerous qualities that are unique to Godhead (guṇādi-kathanam). The devotional sects look upon Godhead not only in its universal and absolute aspect, but also as a personalized Deity (ishta-devatā), bearing an intimate relationship with the devotee.

The same deity is called by different names and described by several attributes; and this forms the content of multiple names (1000, 300 or 108). The nāma-samkīrtana (or nāma-smaraṇa, recollecting the glory of God through a standardized list of names) is different from japa. While the latter is repitition of a single formula (mantra) over and over again, the former is recitation of a large number of different names, which may or may not constitute a unity. Pañchadaśī-vidyā, for instance, is a mantra (mystic formula) and is meant for japa, where as *Lalitā-sahasra-nāma* is really a stotra (prayer), which has to be articulated (pāṭha). The ingredient letters in a mantra are all closely inter-related, and all of them together have one spiritual import and impact. The constitutent names of a sahasra-nāma, triśatī or ashṭottara-śaṭa are all independent of each other and the expression of unity is formal and collective. One many indeed select out of the standard list only the names that appeal to him and recite those names. The text itself suggests that the recitation of a single name among the thousand would suffice.

The recitation of names is indicated in formal and 'external' worship (bahir-yāga) as well as in 'internal' and mental worship (antaryāga), and this is its distinction. It may be employed as a sequence in the elaborate ritual of Lalitā worship, or it may be all that the worship involves. The names of Lalitā are meant more for contemplation than for mere articulation. Therefore they are all packed with ideas characteristic of the cult. We have it on good authority that when the names are recited as part of the ritual, the symbolism of each name must be fully comprehended for rendering the recitation effective.

Bhāskara-rāya compares pronouncing the words without a knowledge of their meaning to the performance of the ritual of oblations to the fire, not in fire but in ash; the ghee poured on the ash will not help to produce the blaze of fire. And he likens the person who has made a study of various texts without under standing the import of those texts to the donkey carrying a load of sandalwood (not knowing the value of the load on its back) (cf. *Varivasyā-rahasya,* Amśa, 2, 54-55).

अर्थज्ञानरहितशब्दोच्चारणस्य निन्दया पापानुमानाच्चार्थज्ञानमावश्यकमाह–

नार्थज्ञानविहीनं शब्दोच्चारणं फलति।

भस्मनि बह्निविहीने न प्रक्षिप्तं ज्वलति॥

अर्थमजानानां नानाविधशब्दमात्रपाठवताम्।

उपेयश्चक्रीवान्मलयजभारस्य वोढैव॥ (वरिवस्यारहस्ये २, ५४–५५)

The importance of understanding the import of each name and its relevance to the deity can hardly be exaggerated. The names included in the list are described as having 'secret' or 'hidden' meaning (rahasya-nāmāni), which can be communicated only to a deserving disciple from a competent master. it is interesting to read in the *Lalitā-sahasra-nāma* that even the sage Agastya, to whom all details about nyāsa etc., antar-yāga and bahir-yāga and worship rituals were imparted, was not considered worthy enough by Hayagrīva to receive the 'Thousand names'. It is only when he felt that all that he had learnt till then from Hayagrīva did not set his mind at rest, and that he had to receive specially the "Lalitā-devyāh nāma-sahasrakam' to crown all other initiations, Hayagrīva offered to instruct him. And the teacher specified that the 'thousand names of Lalitā' must be given only to one who is devoted to the Mother-goddess, who is well-versed in the cult of Śrī-vidyā, and who is a practitioner, filled with purity :

श्रीमातृभक्तियुक्ताय श्रीविद्याराजवेदिने।
उपासकाय शुद्धाय देयं नामसहस्रकम्॥

(ललिता, १, १६)

Bhāskara-rāya enumerates different kinds of meaning for traditional Tāntrik expression, illustrated by the 'Thousand names'. The thousand names of Lalitā are distinguished by the absence of words which are by themselves meaningless (like 'cha', 'tu'), which are inserted only to satisfy the requirements of prosody. And further, they are free from the flaw of repitition of ideas. Although apparently words like 'Aṁbā', "Jananī and 'Mātā' mean only mother, and words like 'Deveśī' and 'Sura-nāyikā mean only the rule of the hosts of gods, each of the words in the Thousand Names has a distinct connotation (pṛthaktva-niveśitasvābhāvyah). What this special nuance is can only be known from masters of the tradition. Bhāskāra-rāya provides a list of fifteen shades of meaning :

1. The comprehensive import, taking into consideration also the words that are not articulated, like the pūrṇa-gāyatrī, the fourth quarter of which is usually not uttered :
2. The general import (bhāvārtha), overlooking the customary and literary expressions and concentrating on the spirit of the text.
3. The traditional meaning (sampradāyārtha), which can be learnt only at the feet of an accredited master.
4. The mystic (hidden) meaning (nigarbhārtha), which becomes evident when the act of initiation has begun to mature.
5. The cultic meaning (kaulikārtha), which is imparted at the time of initiation.
6. The secret import (rahasyārtha), which becomes apparent in contemplative sessions.
7. The great metaphysical meaning (mahātattvārtha) which emerges when thought about it deeply.
8. The explicit nominal meaning (nāmārtha), which can be apprehended by those who are brilliant even though not initiated.
9. The literal meaning (śabda-rūpartha), which can be got by
10. The partial but relevant meaning (nāmaikadeśaga).

11. The Śākta meaning (Śāktārtha), which can be conveyed in terms of the theory and practice of the Śāktas.
12. The integrative meaning (sāmarasyārtha), which is produced by comparative study.
13. The cumulative meaning (samastārtha), which covers all aspects but not in depth.
14. The secondary meaning (guṇārtha), which focusses attention on particular aspects or purposes.
15. The final and overriding significance (mahā-vākhyārtha).

It must be conceded that most of these meanings are not available to us to-day, and that many of them have become obsolete and irrelevant to the uninitiate layman. The commentaries of Bhāskara-rāya and others have preserved fragments of some of these meanings in so far as they relate to Śrī-vidyā and Śrī-chakra for the text itself holds that the three are intimately related (1, 25, 'chakra-rājārchanam devya japo nāmnām cha kīrtanam').

The composition of the Thousand Names of Lalitā as eulogy is ascribed to the eight Vāgdevatās (1, 27-32). Stationed in the eight-sided figure (ashṭāra) known as "Sarva-roga-hara chakra' of Śrī-chakra the eight goddesses (Vaśinī, Kāmeśī, Modinī, Vimalā, Aruṇā, Jayinī, Sarveśī and Kaulinī) are very close to the Mother goddess, Tripurā or Lalitā, who assumes the form of the central triangle known as Vāgbhava; they constitute the inner circle of attendant-divinities, and the Mother-goddess reveals the entirety of Her mysteries only to them ('macchakrasya rahasyajña); and they are fully acquainted with the Śrī-chakra structure and symbolism. And they are said to have crystallized their wisdom concerning the Goddess in these

Thousand Names, which they themselves recite without a break ('mama nāma-parāyanāh'). Tradition holds that out of an infinitely large number of names, they selected a Thousand, to help the devotees quickly realize the benefits.

देव्या अनन्तेषु नामसु शीघ्रं साधकोपकारकत्वेन नामानि वाग्देवताभिरिहं संगृहीतानि।

(सौभाग्यभास्करे, २, १)

When the *Lalitā-sahasra-nāma* is regarded as a mālā-mantra, these speech-goddesses are considered the seers thereof.

श्रीललितासहस्रनामस्तोत्रमालामन्त्रस्य वशिन्यादयो वाग्देवताभ्य ऋषिभ्यो नमः।

These are described as 'deities of speech' (Vāgīśī, Vāngamayī, Sarasvatī, Vāk-pradhāraṇā). They are engaged always in japa ('etā devyo japa-parāh, *Lalitopākhyāna*, 37, 7), and are brilliantly charming with their poetic compositions in adoration of the Goddess; and they entertain the Goddess with their sweet and musical voice.

एता देव्यो जपरता मुक्ताभरणमण्डिताः।
सदा स्फुरद्गद्यपद्यलहरीललिता मताः॥

काव्यैश्च नाटकैश्चैव मधुरैः कर्णहारिभिः।
विनोदयन्त्यः श्रीदेवीं वर्तते कुंभसंभव॥

(ललितोपाख्याने, ३७, ७-५)

There are several ways of classifying the Thousand Names of Lalitā. Most of them have characteristic feminine endings (like Śrī-mātā, Varadā, Pūrṇā, Hrīṁkārī, and Veda-jananī; but some have masculine endings (like Guṇa-nidhī) and some neuter (Paramjyoti). Bhāskara-rāya cites an authority which says that the divinity may be visualized as having a male form or a female form, or contemplated as having no form whatever but as mere existence, pure consciousness and bliss :

पुंरूपं वा स्मरेद्देवीं स्त्रीरूपं वा विचिन्तयेत्।
अथवा निष्कलं ध्यायेत्सच्चिदानन्दलक्षणम्॥

(सौभाग्यभास्करे उद्धृतः, १, १७)

Classification is sometimes made on the basis on the length of the name, and depending on a Tāntrik classification of mantras. If the mantra (any mystic formula, in the case any of the Thousand Names of Lalitā) has only one letter, it is called a piṇḍa, if there are two letters, it is kartarī; if from three to nine letters, it is known as bīja; if the letters are ten or more but less than twenty, it is mantra;and if more than twenty it is called a mālā-mantra :

एकाक्षरा पिण्डाः कर्तर्यो द्व्यक्षरा मताः।
वर्णत्रयं समारभ्य नवार्णा विधिबीजकाः॥

ततो दशार्णमारभ्य यावद्विंशति मन्त्रकाः।
तत ऊर्ध्वं गता मालास्तासु भेदो न विद्यते॥

It is usual to take the entire collection of the thousand names as a 'mālā-mantra'. But there is also a method of classifying the names in the method mentioned above. There is a single example of the 'piṇḍa' variety ("Ī", 712), leaving out of consideration the case-endings of the word and the usual expression for submission'-namah').Illustrations for the 'kartarī'variety are Rasyā (311), Ramā (313), Dhṛti (446), and Śānti (447). The next variety 'bīja' is illustrated by a large number of names, like Śrī-mātā (1), Ramaṇī (310), Śātodarī (130, Sarvāruṇā

(49), Anavadyāṅgī (50), Bhagamālinī (276), Sampradāyeśvarī (710), Ksharāksharātmikā (757), Kadaṁba-vana-vāsinī (60), and Shaḍadhvātita-rūpiṇī (991). Quite a few names belong to the "mantra" variety. Tarā-kānti-tiraskārināsābharaṇa-bhāsurā (20), Janma-mṛtyu-jarā-tapta-jana-viśrāntidāyinī (851), Samsāra-paṅka-nirmagna-samuddharaṇa-paṇḍitā (880), and so on.

There is another classification which groups the thousand names under ten heads according to a formula 'gaṃ-ga-sya-la-ka-vala-ra-sa-bha'; the names beginning with each of these letters constitute a group (cf. Bhāskara-rāya, on 1, 16).

The *Paribhāshā-śesha* has a scheme whereby the thousand names are classified into ten groups with a hundred names in each group. The name marking the beginning of a centum (śataka) is given to the group. The ten groups are :

1. Śrī-mātā
2. Maṇi-pūrāntar-uditā
3. Sadgati-pradā
4. Hrīṁ-kārī
5. Vividhākārā
6. Guḍānna-prītī-mānasā
7. Dur-āndolita-dīrghākshā
8. Deśa-kāla-paricchhinnā
9. Pushṭā
10. Nāda-rūpiṇī

Lalitopākhyāna also refers to this classification, but the last names given in this text are Sāvitrī, Rasa-śevadhi and Vijñānakalikā.

The beginning letters of the names have also been

considered while classifying the names. Unlike *Lalitā-triśati*, which has names begining with the fifteen letters of Pañchadaśī (Kādi) vidya in a regular order, the *Sahasra-nāma* does not follow any order in selecting the first letters of the names. But out of the 51 letters of the Sanskrit alphabet only 32 have been selected and the rest left out. Among the vowels, the first and 'e', 'o' and 'aṁ' have only been chosen; and among the consonants, 'gha', 'ṅ'; 'jha', 'ṅ'; 'ṭa', 'ṭha' 'dha', 'ṇa,' 'tha', 'pha'; and 'la' have been omitted (altold nineteen). The names commencing from 'a' are 40; 'a', 10; 'ī' 3; 'i' 2; 'u' 5; 'e' 1, 'o' 2; 'aṁ' 4; 'ka' 51; 'kha' 1; 'ga' 24; 'cha' 29; 'chha' 1; 'ja' 19; 'da' 2; 'ta' 46; 'da' 37; 'ḍha' 14; 'na' 75; 'pa' 81; 'ba' 24; 'bha' 37; 'ma' 112; 'ya' 13; 'ra' 38, 'la' 14; 'va' 79; 'śa' 59; 'sha' 5; 'sa' 122; 'ha' 11 and 'ksha' 9. The letters that have been selected are said to represent the 'mātrkas' (letter-divinites) that help the devotee approach the Goddess. Contrarily the letters which are omitted are regarded as harmful (cf. Nṛsimha's *Paribhāshā*).

But the letter of the Sanskrit alphabet selected and the number of names beginning with those letters in the *Sahasra-ṇāma* seem to bear no relation with each other. And the letters omitted are obviously the letters with which no word can possibly begin (like ṅ, ñ, na and la) or with which few words begin (like gha, jha, ṭha, tha, dha and pha). Names of the Goddess beginning with these letters are indeed exceedingly hard to make up.

Further, all the letter of the alphabet are alike mātṛkās, and in the tantrik lore no distinction is made among them. Even the vāgdevatās, to whom the composition of *Lalitā-sahasra-nāma* is ascribed are grouped among all the letters of the alphabet (see figure). And in the *Sahasra-nāma*, the goddess is described as the very form of all the letter ('mātṛkā-varṇa-rūpiṇī, 577, 'varṇa-rupiṇi, 850).

Each name has three distinct parts. The first part which is common to all the names is the 'praṇava' or 'Oṁ'. The second part is the actual name in the fourth case-ending (chaturthī-vibhaktyanta). And the third part, which again is common to all the names is the expression of obesience and submission, 'namaḥ'. The name in effect is a statement of the devotee taking refuge in the Goddess, an aspect or attribute of whom is brought to focus in the particular name. For instance, the first name would take the form :

"Oṁ / Śrī-matre / namah"

However, the actual text of *Lalitā-sahasra-nāma* is in the form of couplets in the anushtup metre retaining only the names in the nominative absolute case-ending, omitting the first and the third parts (Oṁ and namah). Each line will contain one name (when the name is long) or more usually two or more names, and thus the thousand names are in a string or an unbroken chain of 183 couplets constituting the second chapter of the text, which is more properly named *Lalitā-sahasra-nāma-stotram.* The last line says : "Thus the thousand names of the Goddess Lalitā were uttered (by the vāgdevatās)".

एवं श्रीललितादेव्याः नाम्नां साहस्रकं जगुः॥

When the text is recited as a chant (pāṭha), the verses are read or sung as they actually are; but when the names are used for worship, the names are taken out individually an pronounced along with the first and the third parts (Oṁ and namah), which are added to each of the names. For instance the chant of the first verse would be :

Śrī-mātā Śrī-mahārājñi śrīmat-śiṁhāsaneśvarī,
chidagni-kuṇḍa-saṁbhūtā deva-kārya-samudyatā

As rendered during worship, it would be as follows.

Oṁ Śrī-mātre namah

Oṁ Śrīmat-siṁhāśaneśvaryai namah

Oṁ Chidagni-kuṇḍa-saṁbhūtayai namah

Oṁ Deva-kāya-samudyatāyai namah

The significance of the first part (viz. Oṁ) is too well- known to need elaboration. The expression 'Oṁ' is regarded as the very first sound that emerged when Brahman manifested himself in the phenomenal context, and the expression denotes the absolute Brahman (Oṁ tat sat) as well as all the manifestations thereof. It is customary to utter Om before commencing any serious religious activity like study of scriptures (veda-pāṭha), oblations in fire (homa), sacred recitation (japa), ritual of food offerings (bali), oblations to the manes (tarpaṇa), meditation (dhyāna), expiations (prāyaśchitta), daily devotions (sandhyā) and so on. Especially while perfecting a mantra, Om is added at the beginning of the mantra as well as at the close of it. When the mantra is thus enclosed by two 'Oṁ's, it is called 'saṁpuṭita'. It is said that the mantra does not get fixed unless Oṁ is uttered before it, and that the power of the mantra will run away unless Om is uttered after it (cf. *Kālikā-purāṇa,* cited in *Saubhāgya-bhāskara* :)

स्त्रवत्यनोंकृतपूर्व परस्ताञ्च विशीर्यते।

According to the tāntrik lexicon *Mātṛkā-kosha,* 'Oṁ' is what contributes stability to the mantra and makes it effective.

ओंकारो वर्तुलस्तारो मन्त्राद्यः प्रणवो ध्रुवः।

The expression 'Oṁ' is not only a mystic ejaculation, the mere utterance of which will heighten the power and enrich the meaning of the mantra, but it is composite of three vocables (trimātrā), 'a', 'u' and 'ma' which represent several triads like the three gods (Brahmā, Śiva and Vishṇu), the three divine functions (creation, preservation and dissolution), the three Vedas (Ṛg, Yajus and Sāma), the three worlds (bhū, bhuva and svah; the earth, the mid-region and the heavens), the three divinities which control the three regions (Agni, Soma and Sūrya), the three states of existence (wakefulness, dream and deep-sleep), the three conditions of consciousness (antah-prajña, bahih-prajña and ghana-prajña, corresponding to the three states of existence), the three phases of time (past, present and future) and the three genders (liṅgas; puṁ, strī and niskhala). All things in the universe are thus pervaded by Oṁ; and without Oṁ, no sound can be uttered and nothing can be communicated (cf. *Bṛhat-parāśara-smṛti*).

It has been, however, debated whether the names in a stotra like *Lalitā-sahasra-nāma,* can properly be regarded as a mantra. If the name is not a mantra, then the employment of 'Om' is not indicated. But Bhāskararāya cites numerous authorities to show that not only each of the names in *Lalitā-sahasra-nāma* is a mantra, but the entire collection is a mala-mantra. *Lalitopākhyāna* for instance, refer to Hayagrīva's admonition to Agastya (pūrvapiṭhikā) :

केवलं नामबुद्धिस्ते न कार्या तेषु कुंभज।
मन्त्रात्मकत्वमेतेषां नाम्नां नामात्मतापि च॥

(ललितोपाख्याने)

The names are not doubt epithets which are descriptive of the beauty, might and glory of the Goddess, but the names are also so many mantras denoting the one Goddess, whose various manifestations are recounted in the names. The undercurrent in all the names, and contributing unity and continuity to the Thousand names, is the notion of one and secondless supreme principle, pervading the universe and transcending it. This principle (tattva) is devoid of form, gender, attribute or character; it is nirguna and nishkala. It is, in other words, the supreme Brahman. This aspect of the names, which is common to all of them, is suggested by the addition of 'Oṁ' (which is an ancient expression for parabrahman) to each of the names :

तस्य च समस्तस्य ब्रह्मैवार्थः।

'Oṁ' is added to the names in the sahasra-nāma only at the beginning of each name. And while reciting the names continuously, care must be taken to introduce a slight pause after each 'varnah' (coming at the end of the name), so that the next name starts disinctly with an 'Oṁ', the expression 'namah' (meaning prayer, bowing, adoration) is the proper termination of each name as a mantra, even as 'Oṁ' is the proper comencement. The name articulated without an Oṁ as its beginning would fail to be a mantra, and would thus be ineffective.

THE GODDESS

Before the ceremonial recital of a mantra, it is usual (if not mandatory) to remind ourselves of the nature of the deity (devatā), the 'seer' (ṛshi) of the mantra (discoverer or one who was responsible for its composition or revelation), the metre in which the mantra occurs (chhandas), and the purpose for which the recitation is undertaken (viniyoga). Then follows the descriptive verse for contemplation and the visualization of the deity (dhyāna-śloka).

As regards, the 'seers' of this mantra (or rather malamantra), the eight vāgdevatās headed by Vaśinī are mentioned. *Lalitāsahasra-nāma* mentions that when the Goddess commanded, Vaśinī and other Vāgdevātās got up in their respective seats, folded their hands in an attitude of supplication and praised the Goddess by the thousand names which they themselves had composed (1, 38-39).

तेषु दृष्टोपविष्टेषु स्वे स्वे स्थाने यथाक्रमम्।
तत्र श्रीललितादेवीकटाक्षाक्षेपनोदिताः॥
उत्थाय वशिनीमुख्या बद्धाञ्जलिपुटास्तदा।
अस्तुवन्नामसाहस्रैः स्वकृतैर्ललिताम्बिकाम्॥

(ललितासहस्रनामस्तोत्रे, १, ३५-३९)

And the metre in which the composition appears is given as anushṭup. There is a custom of formally and symbolically placing the three details (devatā, ṛshi and chhandas) on one's own body parts. This procedure is known as 'aṅga-nyāsa'. The 'goddess' is located in the heart, the 'seers' on the head, and the 'metre' on the tongue. This is because the 'seer' is the preceptor and so must be held on top of the devotee's head. The goddess is to be meditated upon, and so must be placed in the heart. The metre has to be articulated and so must be located on the tongue :

ऋषिर्गुरुत्वाच्छिरसि ध्येयत्वाद्देवता हृदि।
छन्दोक्षरत्वाज्जिह्वायां न्यस्तव्यं मन्त्रवित्तमैः॥

The devotee makes an explicit acknowledgement of this three-fold placement thus :

अस्य श्रीललितासहस्रनामस्तोत्रमालामन्त्रस्य वशिन्यादिभ्यो वाग्देवताभ्य ऋषिभ्यो नमः शिरसि। अनुष्टुप्छन्दसे नमः मुखे। श्रीमहात्रिपुरसुन्दर्यै देवतायै हृदि।

The purpose of the recitation of the thousand names of Lalita is the obtainment of all the four values of life, viz. virtue (dharma), wealth (artha), pleasures (kāma) and liberation (moksha):

चतुर्विधपुरुषार्थसिद्ध्यर्थे जपे विनियोगः।

For *Lalitā-sahasra-nāma,* the deity is, of course, Lalitā (Lalitāmbā, Lalitā-parā-bhaṭṭārikā, Lalitā-tripura-sundarī). The section known as Lalitopākhyāna in *Brahmāṇḍa-purāṇa* begins with this verse which describes the deity :

चतुर्भुजे चन्द्रकलावतंसे

कुचोन्नते कुंकुमरागशोणे।

पुंड्रेक्षुपाशांकुशपुष्पबाण-

हस्ते नमस्ते जगदेकमातः॥

She, the mother of all the worlds, is four-armed, carrying in her hands the sugar-cane stalk as bow, the flowers as arrows, noose and goad; her head is adorned with the crescent moon.

According to Bhāskara-rāya, *Lalitā-sahasra-nāma* has this dyāna-śloka :

सिन्दूरारुणविग्रहां त्रिनयनां माणिक्यमौलिस्फुर

त्तारानायकशेखरां स्मितमुखीमापीनवक्षोरुहाम्।

पाणिभ्यामलिपूर्णरत्नचषकं रक्तोत्पलं बिभ्रतीम्

सौम्यां रत्नघटस्थरक्तचरणां ध्यायेत्परामम्बिाम्॥

The goddess is visualized as ruddy in complexion like red lead or sindūra, having three eyes, smiling countenance, and large breasts, her bejewelled crown is adorned by the brilliant moon. She holds in one of her hands the jewel-studded bowl filled with nectar, and red lily in the other. Beneath her foot, daubed with red lac, is a bejewelled pot.

Another version of the same text has a different dhyānaśloka :

श्रीविद्यां जगतां धात्रीम्

सर्गस्थितिलयेश्वरीम्।

नमामि ललितां नित्याम्

महात्रिपुरसुन्दरीम्॥

Here she is identified with the fifteen-lettered mantra (pañchadaśī) which is familiarly known as Śrī-vidyā. She is also the nourisher of the worlds : she is responsible for creation, preservation and dissolution. She is an enduring spirit (nityā), and the great Tripura-sundarī.

Lalitā-triśatī has this dhyāna-śloka included in the prologue (pūrva-pīṭhikā) :

सकुंकुमविलेपनामलकचुम्बिकस्तूरिकाम्।

समन्थहसितेक्षणां सशरचापपाशांकुशाम्।

अशेषजनमोहिनीमरुणमालाविभूषाम्बराम्।

जपाकुसुमभासुरां जपविधौ स्मरेदम्बिकाम्॥

Here the goddess is visualized as red in complexion, and wearing reddish garments and ornaments. Red is the colour of the Goddess because, according to *Bhāvano-panishat* (29), red signifies the aspect of vimarśā (which is represented by Śakti, as the Prakāśa aspect is Śiva).

लौहित्यमेतस्य सर्वस्य विमर्शः।

There is a name in the *Sahasra-nāma* which identifies the goddess with vimarsā (vimarśā-rūpiṇī 548). She is charming in appearance and has four arms, carrying bow, arrow, noose and goad in her hands.

The *Lalitā-sahasra-nāma* itself has names descriptive of the goddess suitable for visualization :

chidagni-kuṇḍa-saṁbhūtā (4) : she emerges out of the firealtar of consciousness.

deva-kārya-samudyatā (5) : she is engaged in accomplishing the task for the good of the gods.

udyad-bhānu-sahasrābhā (6) : she is resplendent like the rising sun

chaturbāhu-samanvitā (7) : she has four arms

rāga-svarūpa-pāśādhyā (8) : she holds in one of her hands noose, which symbolizes love and worldliness

krodhākārānkuśojjvalā (9) : she holds in another hand goad, which symbolizes divine displeasure

mano-rūpekshu-kodaṇḍā (10) : she holds in the third hand sugar-cane-stalk as bow, symbolizing mind

pañcha-tanmātra-sāyakā (11) : she holds in the fourth hand arrows, representing the five basic elements of the phenomenal world (earth, water, fire, air and ākāśā).

The symbolism of the weapons is explained in *Bhāvanopanishat*

शब्दादितन्मात्राः पंच पुष्पबाणाः।

मनः इक्षुकोदण्डः।

रागः पाशम्।

द्वेषोऽङ्कुशः।

Further, this text identifies the supreme goddess Lalitā with the devote's own self, ever filled with bliss :

सदानन्दपूर्णः स्वात्मैव परदेवता ललिता।

Bhāskara-rāya commenting on this sentence quotes a verse from *Tantra-rāja-tantra,* in support of this idea :

स्वात्मैव देवता प्रोक्ता ललिता विश्वविग्रहा।

लौहित्यं तद्विमर्शः स्यादुपास्तितिरिति भावना॥

(तन्त्रराजतन्त्रे)

The *Sahasra-nāma* has several names (65 to 87) recounting the occasion for the appearance of the Goddess (viz. to kill Bhandāsura), as given in *Lalitopākhyāna*. And her identification with *Śri-vidyā* is the import of several other names (85-89)

vāgbhava-kūṭaika-svarūpa-mukha-pañkajā;

kaṇthādhah-kaṭi-paryanta-madhya-kūṭa-svarūpiṇī;

śakti-kūṭaikatāpanna-katyadhobhāga-dhāriṇī;

mūla-mantrātmikā;

mūla-kūta-traya-kalevarā.

The figure of the goddess is composed of the first unit of the pañchadaśī-vidyā (known as vāgbhava-kūṭa, क ए इ ल ह्रीं।) as her face, the middle unit (kāmarāja-kūṭa ह स क ह ल ह्रीं।) as her torso, and the third unit (śakti-kūṭa, स क ल ह्रीं।) as the limbs below the waist. Her form is that of the pañchadaśī-vidyā itself (referred to here as mūla-mantra). She is elsewhere also described as having three units ('tri-kūṭa', 588), as being the six-lettered vidyā viz. panchadasī with the addition of Śrīṁ as turīya-kūṭa (587), as 'śrī-vidyā' (584), as worshipped by Kāma ('kāma-sevitā, 585), i.e. the Kādi-vidyā, as well as by Lopāmudrā (647), i.e. the Hādi-vidyā.

She is also described as residing in Śri-chakra ('śri-chakra-rāja-nilayā' 955, 'chakra-rāja-niketanā, 245), and is of the form of the primary triangle in it ('tripurā, 626, 'kāma-kalā-rūpā, 321, 'sumeru-śṛṅga-madhyasthā', 55). There are names which describe elaborately the form of Śrī-chakra as 'the abode of wishfulfilment' (chintāmaṇi-gṛha, 57), 'the glorious city' (śrīmannagara', 56), 'the peak of the golden moutain' (sumer-śṛṅga, 55; meru, 775), 'the great garden of lotus-flowers' (mahā-padmāṭavī,

59), 'the forest of kadaṁba trees' (kadamba-vana,60) and 'the ocean of nectar' (sudhā-sāgara, 61). The source of this imagery is *Lalitopākhyāna* (chapters 35 to 37). Inside this splendid palace she is seated on a cot composed of the five inert gods representing the five tattvas (pañcha-brahmāsanā, 58; pañcha pretamañchādhi-śāyinī, 947; pañcha-pretāsanāsīnā, 249); and she sits on the lap of her consort Kameśvara (śiva-kāmeśvarānkasthā, 52) who is identified with the central point inside the primary triangle (bindu) (hence 'baindavāsangā, 905). And the goddess represents the unity of Śiva and Śakti (Śiva-śaktyaikya-rūpiṇī, 999).

Following the idea of the correspondence of Śrī-chakra with the six chakras of Kuṇḍalinī-yoga,

त्रिकोणं चाधारं त्रिपुर तनु तेऽष्टारमनघे
तव स्वाधिष्ठानं भगवति दशारं मणिपुरम्।
दशारं ते संवित् कमलमथ मन्वस्त्रकमुमे
विशुद्धं स्यादाज्ञा शिव इति ततो बैन्दवगृहम्॥
(सुभगोदये)

Lalitā is said to reside in each of the six chakras, and also in the space transcending them (shaṭ-chakropari-saṁsthitā, 108; daharākāśa-rūpiṇī 608); she also breaks through the three 'knots' of the constitution, during the upward passage of Kuṇḍalinī. Among the names in *Sahasra-nāma,* we find the following :

mūlādhāraika-nilayā (109)
Brahma-granthi-vibhedinī (100)
maṇipūrāntar-uditā (101)
Vishṇu-granthi-vibhedinī (102)
ājhā-chakrāntarāla-sthā (103)
Rudra-granthi-vibhedinī (104)

sahasrārāmbujārūḍhā (105)
sudhā-sārābhi-varshiṇī (106)
taḍil-latā-sama-ruchi (107)
mahā-śakti (109)
kuṇḍalinī (110)

In another context later on, we have a complete list of the six chakras :

mūlādhārāṁbujārūḍhā (514)
svādhishṭhānāṁbuja-gata (504)
maṇipūrābja-nilayā (495)
anāhatābja-nilayā (485)
viśuddhi-chakra-nilayā (476)
ājñā-chakrābja-nilayā (521)
sahasra-dala-padma-saṁsthā (528)

The goddess is, likewise, identified with each of the three states of experience (waking, dream and sleep), while she is actually beyond them :

1) viśva-rūpā (256)
   jāgariṇī (257)
2) taijasātmikā (259)
   svapantī (258)
3) prājñatmikā (261)
   suptā (260)
   turyā (262)
   sarvāvasthā-varjitā (263).

She is also recognized as the inner awareness (pratyak-chitirūpā, 367) in all beings, and the goddess transcending all the beings (parā-devatā, 369). She is also the stages of the manifestation of the fundamental urge to articulate : 'parā' (366), 'paśyantī' (368), 'madhyamā' (370) and 'vaikharī' (371).

PARIBHĀSHĀ

Mention has already been made of a cryptic but clear gloss (paribhāshā) on the Sahasra-nāma, by Nṛsiṁhānanda-nātha, based on which his disciple Bhāskara-rāya-makhin prepared his commentary (bhāshya, entitled *Saubhāghya-bhāskara*) This gloss consisting of forty verses (maṇḍala) is intended to show the correct tradition (sat-saṁpradāya-gamakam) with regard to the recitation and interpretation of the thousand names. He claims to follow the chhalākshara-scheme in his work which not only fixes the total number of verses in the *Sahasra-nāma-stotra* but classifies the thousand names in different ways, based essentially on the letters of the names, which are regarded as significant.

The analysis of the text, according to this gloss, is also made in accordance with the speakers of the verses. The total number of verses which constitutes the whole text is given as 320. The introductory section (pūrva-pīṭ hikā) has fifty verses; after this there is a dhyāna-śloka;

followed by the thousand names in verse-form with 182 verses and half-verse; and the text ends with a eulogy of three thousand names in 86 verses.

Of them the sage Agastya is credited with ten verses at the very beginning which mark the commencement of the text. This is followed by one verse by Sūta-purāṇika, the author of *Brahmāṇḍapurāṇa,* explaining which the sage Agastya made a request to the god Hayagrīva to communicate the thousand names ot Lalitā. Hayagrīva then proceeds to answer Agastya in 16 verses and a half-verses. During Hayagrīva's response there are three additional verses and a half-verse by the mother (Aṁbā), nine more verses by Hayagrīva, six more verses by the mother, and finally three verses and a half-verse by Hayagrīva.

The text is essentially a dialogue between the sage Agastya who assumes the role of a devotee and the god Hayagrīva who is the teacher. The entirety of the main portion (the stotra section) consisting of 182 verses and a half-verse is the speech of Hayagrīva. The thousand names of the goddess are given in 182 verses and the last half-verses concludes that these thousand names were uttered by the Vāgdevatās.

The final portion of the text (uttara-pīṭhikā) is also mainly Hayagrīva's speech explaining the benefits to be derived by the recitation of the thousand names (85 verses and a half-verses); and the last verse is by Sūta-paurāṇika, the author of the purāṇa, narrating that after communicating the thousand names to the sage, Hayagrīva was happy contemplating on the goddess Lalitā.

After this analysis the gloss proceeds to enumerate the number of 'names' that begin with the several letters of the alphabet. Among vowels, five of them after the fifth are omitted (akshu sarat sarva-varṇān) viz. u, ṛi, ṛii, lṛi, and lṛii. Among the grouped consonants the final two letters of the two groups beginning with 'ka' and 'cha' are also omitted ('tatas samānāntimau ka-cha-yoh) viz. gha, ri, jha and r. In the group of letters beginning with 'ṭa' only the third is retained (viz. ḍa) and all other letters are left out (ṭa, ṭha, ḍha and ṇa). In the next two groups beginning with 'ta' and 'pa' the second letters are left out, viz. 'tha' and 'pha'. And among the ungrouped consonants, the ninth (viz. ḷa) is also left out (antye tyajen navamam).

SCHEMATA IN SAHASRA-NĀMA

The names included here are varied in significance and context. While the purpose of the Sahasra-nāma is to eulogize her as the supreme goddess, as the Brahman of the Upanishads, the names take into account both the aspected (sakala) and the unaspected (nishkala) view of the Divine Being. The names bring out the truth that they are only views, and that they do not diversify reality. The one principle of consciousness (chit, chaitanya, chin-mātra) manifests itself in a myriad of forms, filling the universe as well as the constitution of all living beings. It occurs as the will (icchhā), the wisdom (jñāna) and the action (kriyā), wherever they are found. The goddess of the thousand names is the enlivening, energizing and directive force behind everything.

The names can convey complete meaning only for those who are well acquainted with the Upanishadic ideology, with the Vedāntic system, with the mythological lore as found in the purāṇas, with the tāntrik outlook and practice, and with the kuṇḍalinī-yoga. She is identified with Śrī-chakra, and correspondances are indicated between the structure of Śri-chakra and the psychic constitution of the human being. Thus the names cover a wide range of details. Some of the names are purely descriptive of the beauty and glory, might and mercy of the goddess; poetic imagery is frequently employed in such descriptions. Some names refer to the stories of her fight with demons, and her victory over the evil forces. Some names are obviously philosophical in import and symbolic in significance. Some refer unmistakably to occult practices, and some are sublime and subtle. There is an especial association with the tāntrik cult known as Kaula-mārga; but some names suggest a preference for the samaya-mārga, another cult.

1. The names that describe the physical beauty of the goddess, her ornaments and decorations are illustrated in the numbers 6 to 64.

2. The purpose and methods of her mainfestation are recounted in names numbered 4, 5 and 865 to 867.

3. The fight between the goddess and the demon called Bhaṇḍāsura forms an important detail in *Brahmāṇḍapurāṇa.* The gods begged the goddess to vanquish this demon; and the victory of the goddess over the demon is hailed as the supreme achievement. This episode is in the background of the names numbered 65 to 83.

4. The glory of the goddess as Durgā is the theme of the names 189 to 198, as Lakshmī of names 684 to 698, as Sarasvatī of the names 704 to 707, 798-799 and 833, as Mahākālī of the names 750 to 754, and as Bhū-devī of the names 718 to 724.

5. Her aspect as Bālā is adored in the names numbered 965 to 975.

6. Her all-pervasive, all-comprehending and all-enlivening nature is referred to in the names 282-284, 341-

343, 400-401, 413, 673, 679, 750-754, 779-781, 808, 862 872-875, 895, 907 and 942.

7. Her role in the creation, maintenance and dissolution of the universe is mentioned in the names 264-272, 249, 281, 325, 438, 440, 539, 550, 562, 622, 637-638, 648, 658-665, 718-719, 723, 757, 778, 788, 792, 796, 798, 826, 831-832, 837, 843, 881, 935 and 947-949.

8. The fifteen-lettered mantra (pañcha-daśī) is referred to in the names 85 to 89 and 301-302; the sixteen-letered mantra (shoḍaśī) in the names 236-237, 455, 578-590, 794 and 799; the mantra in general in the names 204, 227, 539-540, 624, 798, 812, 844 and 846.

9. Śrī-vidyā in general is the subject matter of the names 239-245, 330, 333, 382, 391, 536, 575-576, 585, 592, 610-615, 717, 792, 853-858, 879, 910, 918, 929 and 973; the same called Mahā-vidyā is referred to in the names 289-290, 327-328, 338, 355, 385-386, 584, 705, 707, 762 and 827.

10. The identification of the goddess with Kuṇḍalinī-śākti and its several centres (chakras) is the theme of the names 99-111, 352, 422, 440, 458, 460, 466, 470-474, 513-514, 520, 591-625, 775, 905, 974 and 976-993 (Kuṇḍalinī-śakti); 99, 100, 352, 514-520, 588, 597-598 and 986 (mūlādhāra); 504-513 (svādhisṭhāna); 101-102, 495-503 (maṇipūra); 336, 485-494, 595-596 and 647 (anāhata)(; 475-484 (viśuddha); 103-104, 521-527, 594, 609, 610 and 905 (ājñā); and 55-61, 105, 108, 245, 303, 386, 428, 528-537, 578, 591-592, 905 and 996 (sahasrāra).

11. Antaryāga (internal worship) is mentioned in the names 230, 381, 535 and 597; ātma-vidyā (self-knowledge) in the names 238, 335, 472, 539-540, 549, 583, 645, 709-711, 844-846, 852, 859, 887-888 and 918-919; the samaya-mārga in the names 97-111, 291, 363,

475-544, 548-549, 570, 591-625, 608, 641, 643-644, 651-657, 666-668, 672, 626, 680, 725, 742, 771, 773, 851, 870-871, 881-883, 908, 909, 918-919, 926, 946, 950, and 976-981; and the mudrās in the names 378-383, 706-709, 711, 977-979, 982-983.

12. The role of devotion (bhakti) is referred to in the names 112-121, 353, 372, 404, 567 and 747.

13. The four states of individual existence (avasthas) (jāgrat, svapna, sushupti and turīya) form the subject matter of the names 256-263, 290, 625 and 926.

14. The four-fold aspects of sound (parā, paśyantī, madhyamā and vaikharī) and the significance of the primaeval sound 'OM' are dealt with in the names 236, 237, 299, 328, 350, 266-371, 455, 457, 597, 630, 633-657, 678, 706-707, 709, 711, 715, 733-735, 738, 741-749, 797, 833, 846, 850, 853-855, 857, 901, and 909.

15. The liberated souls (the jīvanmuktas) are referred to in the names 571, 473-576, 613, 666, 726-732 and 816.

The conception of 'Chhālakshara' is significant in the tāntrik context, because while all the letter of the Sanskrit alphabet are'matrices' (mātṛkās), The letters omitted here do not serve as seeds for the names to grow out of them. This bears relevance to the four-fold division of sound into parā, paśyantī, madhyamā and vaikharī. The names in the Sahasra-nāma illustrate the vaikharī (or explicitly articulate) variety; they are the gross forms the sound assumes. The matrices that they arise from represent the intermediate stage of the subtle transforming itself into the gross (madhyamā); these are the letters with which the names begin and which are dealt with in the *Paribhāshā*. The praṇava (om) which is common to all the names, and which precedes the names and also follow them is the barely cognizable 'paśyantī'. In the Śākta ideology, madhyamā is the principle of Sadāśiva and pasyanti is principle of Śakti. The bindu, which is beyond the level of pasyanti, is parā, the altogether inexpressible and hence called transcendental; it is the unmanifest Brahman. It is the 'mahā-kāraṇa' : the great cause of the other three divisions which comprehend the entire universe of objects, words and meanings.

Alternately, the matrices of the *Sahasra-nāma* constitute the 'vimarśā' aspect of the mind (deliberation), while the pranava is the 'prakāśa' aspect (illumination). Prakāśa is likened to the fire, while vimarśā is like butter that melts in the fire. When the prakāśa (which is white or śveta, in colour) and the vimarśā (which is red or lohita) are in a state of unison, we have the mantra, which is black in colour (śyāma). Śiva (or Brāhman) represents prakāśa, and Śakti (or māyā) represents vimarśā; their union is the spiritual energy known as kuṇḍalinī; which significes the sādhaka as well as the sādhya; the person as well as the goal. The three aspects, prakāśa, vimarśā and their union (mithuna) are in fact what the expression 'tri-pura' (the three cities or realms) suggests.

PRESUPPOSITIONS

The preliminary section (pūrva-pīṭhikā) of *Lalitā-sahasra-nāma* mentions that Hayagrīva had already communicated in great detail (vistareṇa) to Agastya several details of the Lalitā cult : the appearance of Lalitā (prādurbhāva), and the slaying of the demon Bhaṇḍāsura (vadha). There is also the suggestion of a book, six chapters from which have been mentioned by name : Nyāsa-khaṇḍa Pūjā-Khaṇḍa, Puraścharaṇa-khaṇḍa, Homa-khaṇḍa, Rahasya khaṇḍa and Stotra-khaṇḍa. The chapters are said to have dealt with the ritual placements (like shoḍhā-nyāsa), procedures of internal and external worship (antar-yāga and bahir-yāga krama), the nature and method of japa, the fire-rituals and the articles needed for them, the secret teachings about the identity ('tādātmyam') of the Śrī-chakra, Śrī-vidyā, the goddess, the guru and the practitioner ('chakra-rājasya vidyāyāh śrī-devayā deśikātmanoh'), and many kinds of eulogies ('bahu-vidhāh stutayah') respectively.

However, it is not certain what this book was. It is likely that *Lalitopākhyāna* (of the *Brahmāṇḍa-purāṇa*) was meant, as it deals with most of the topics mentioned above, although not in the same order. And it is significant that this book prescribes the worship of Lalitā in Śrī-chakra installed in front of the icon of the goddess with the sixteen-lattered mantra (shoḍaśī) and the sandal paste :

श्रीदेव्याः पुरतो चक्रं हेमशैप्यादिनिर्मितम्।
निधाय गन्धैरभ्यर्च्य षोडशाक्षरविद्यया॥

The sixteen-lettered mantra has been described as mantra-rāja, which is an improvement over the fifteen-lettered Kāma-rājamantra :

एतस्याः मन्त्रराजस्तु श्रीविद्यैव तपोधन।
कामराजाख्यमन्त्रान्ते श्रीबीजेन समन्वितः।
षोडशाक्षरविद्येयं श्रीविद्येति प्रकीर्तिता॥

The text prescribes only the japa of this mantra (prajapan), worship of the Śrī-chakra (archayet) and thinking of the goddess (bhāvayan eva). It is said here that the japa of the mantra one lakh of times will undo even the great sins done during the life-time, two lakhs of japa will help get rid of the sins done during seven lives, three lakhs of japa will cleanse the devotee of sins acquired during a thousand lives and so on; finally sixteen lakhs of japa will bring the devotee to the goddess herself ('devī-sānnidhyam āpnuyāt'). The japa involves worship three times every day (pūjā traikālikī nityam), recitation and repetition (japa), offerings of food (tarpaṇa) fire oblations (homa) and feeding of pious brahmins (brāhmaṇabhukti). And the text insists that worship must be carried out according to the prescribed method ('kuryāc cha vidhi-vat-pūjām', 40, 70)

No mention of *Sahasra-nāma* or its recitation is to be found here. From the introductory section of *Sahasra-nāma* (pūrvapīṭhikā), we learn from Agastya's request to Hayagrīva that there were eulogies of 'thousand names' for Mantriṇī (Śyāmalā) and Daṇḍinī (Vārāhi), who were attendants of Lalitā, but Agastya had not heard of the thousand names of Lalitā.

मन्त्रिणी दण्डिनी देव्योः प्रोक्ते नामसहस्त्रके।

न तु श्री ललितादेव्याः प्रोक्तं नामसहस्त्रकम्॥

The pūrva-pīṭhikā not only prescribes that the *Sahasra-nāma* should be recited after the japa without fail ('japānte kīrtayen nityam idam nāma-sahasrakam'), but also provides that even if one is unable to worship and do the japa, the thousand names have to be recited ('japa-pūjādyaśaktaś chet paṭhen nāma-sahasrakam'). And the recitation of the *Sahasra-nāma* is said to be all that is necessary and sufficient for a devotee. The goddess herself is made to say : "you may or may not worship me; you may or may not do the japa of the sixteen-lettered mantra; but do recite the thousand names without fail, and it will please me. You will obtain without doubt the fulfilment of all your desires"

मामर्चयतु वा मा वा विद्यां जपतु वा न वा।

कीर्तयेन्नामसहस्त्रमिदं मत्प्रीतये सदा।

मत्प्रीत्या सकलान् कामान् लभते नात्र संशयः।

तस्मान्नामसहस्त्रं मे कीर्तयध्वं सदादरात्॥ (२, ४५-४६)

Thus the *Sahasra-nāma* is held out not only as a substitute for pūjā and japa, but as more effective than them. But the section after the *Sahasra-nāma* (uttara-pīṭ hikā) does not share this view. It prescribes that the devotee must worship the Śrīchakra and do the japa of the Śrī-vidyā (the sixteen lettered manra) one thousand times, three hundred times or at least a hundred times before reciting the thousand names :

पूजागृहं ततो गत्वा चक्रराजं समर्चयेत्।

विद्यां जपेत् सहस्त्रं वा त्रिशतं शतमेव वा।

रहस्यनाम सहस्त्रमिदं पश्चात्पठेन्नरः॥

Of course, the section extols (in great detail) the merits of reciting the thousand names. It provides the recitation of even one name out of the thousand, and that once only, would be productive of great benefit, if one is unable for any reason to recite all the thousand names (3, 13).

Further, this section commends that worship of the goddess must be done, using these thousand names ('archayen nāmasahasraiah', 3, 58). And on special occasions, one must, according to the section, perform the worship in five sequences before he recites the thousand names ('panchopachārais sampūjya pathen nāma-sahasrakam', 3, 22).

If the Sahasra-nāma is in the nature of an after-thought to *Lalitopākhyāna,* and a device to dispense with the elaborate pūjā and japa which *Lalitopākhyāna* prescribes, *Lalita-triśatī* is a sequel to the *Sahasra-nāma* claiming better results with only three hundred names. At the beginning of this work, the sage Agastya confesses that he is dissatified with the thousand names which Hayagrīva was pleased to communicate to him ('tathāpi mama chittasya paryāptir naiva jāyate'). But Hayagrīva does not know anything better, and is at a loss to oblige the sage. However, (after the lapse of three years during which period Agastya held the feet of Hayagrīva firmly and without getting up, much to the discomfort and concern of Hayagrīva) Lalitā manifests herself before him, along with her consort Kāmeśvara, and gives him the 'three hundred names' (tri-śatī). If the 'Thousand names' are the composition of the eight immediate attendants (vāgdevatās), the 'three hundred names' are the composition of Lalitā herself, assisted by Kāmeśvara('mayā kāmeśvareṇā pi kṛitvā sā gopitā bhṛśam'), hence the superior merit of this work.

Hayagrīva tells Agastya that the 'three hundred names', which he had now received are holier than the 'thousand names' which he had communicated earlier and that therefore this is very necessary for the devotees of Lalitā.

रहस्यनामसाहस्त्रात् अतिगुह्यतमं मुने।
आवश्यकं ततो ह्येतत् ललितां समुपासताम्।।

But the preliminary section to the *Triśatī* makes a specific mention of the fifteen-lettered mantra, the constituent letters of which have provided the three hundred names ('śrīmatpañchadaśāksharyāh kādivarṇa-kramāt'); from each of the letters of the mantra twenty names of Lalitā have been formed ('pṛthak viṁśati-nāmāni'), thus making the total number of names three hundred ('āhatya nāmnām tri-śatī').

शिववर्णानि नामानि श्रीदेवीकथितानि वै।
शक्त्यक्षराणि नामानि कामेशकथितानि च।
उभयाक्षरनामानि ह्युभाभ्यां कथितानि वै।।

(३, २-३)

Of these three hundred names, the initial letters follow the order of letters the pañchadaśāksharī-mantra, which has 'masculine letters' (śiva-varṇāni, the three 'ra'-s and the two 'ha-'s), 'feminine letters' (śaktyaksharāṇi, all the other letters excepting hrim) and letters which are both (ubhyātmaka, 'hrīm'). The 'masculine' names were given by Devī (Lalitā) and the 'feminine' names by Kāmeśvara; the names which are both 'masculine' and 'feminine' were composed by both of them together.

रहस्यनाभसाहस्रपाठे यत्फलमीरितम्।
तत्फलं कोटिगुणितं एकनामजपाद्भवेत्।।

(३, २९)

The text also insists that this division must be well understood by the devotees; otherwise their japa or recitation of the names would be utterly useless (3, 10-11). The three hundred names are arranged to highlight this wisdom, while the 'thousand names' do not involve this knowledge. It is therefore that the recitation of even one name among the 'three hundred' is claimed to be crore of times more meritorious than the repetition of the 'thousand names"

वाग्देवीरचिते नामसाहस्त्रे यद्यदीरितम्।
तत्तत् फलमवाप्नोति नाम्नोप्येकस्य कीर्तनात्।।

(४२)

and the recitation once of the 'three hundred names' is immensely more effective than the repetition a crore of times of the 'thousand names'for the simple reason that the former is the composition of Lalitā and Kāmeśvari,while the latter is the work of the vāgdevatās, albeit at the command of Lalitā.

रहस्यनामसाहस्त्रकोट्यावृत्त्यास्तु यत्फलम्।
तद्भवेत् कोटिगुणितं भवेत् नामशतत्रयात्॥

(४४)

The *Triśatī* also is said be a part of the *Brahmaṇḍa-purāṇa (uttara-khaṇḍa),* even as the *Sahasra-nāma* is; and both texts are said to be the teaching of Hayagrīva to Agastya. The composition of the former text is obviously later than that of the latter, for we get numerous references to the *Sahasra-nāma* in the *Triśatī* while the *Sahasranāma* makes no mention whatever of the *Triśatī*. The claims of the *Triśatī* apart, the arrangement of the 'three hundred names' is certainly more methodical and is more intimately associated with the fifteen-lettered mantra of Śrī-vidyā than the scheme followed in the 'thousand names'. But the canvas of the *Sahasranāma* is much wider, and involves all the details of the Śrī-Vidyā ideology. And the *Sahasra-nāma* has the advantage of an elaborate commentary by the person who popularized the Śrī-vidyā cult in the country (viz., Bhāskara-rāya). The gloss on *Triśatī*, ascribed to some Śaṁkara (not the great Bhāshya-kāra) does not compare favourably with *Saubhāgya-bhāskara* (commentary on *Sahasra-nāma* by Bhāskara-rāya). It does not abound in tāntrik explanations, or in helpful insights into the cult of Lalitā. It is therefore that the *Triśatī* is not so well-known as the *Sahasra-nāma,* nor so widely employed.

(from Minakshi temple Museum Madurai)

॥ श्रीः ॥

श्रीललितासहस्त्रनामस्तोत्रम्।

पूर्वभागः

श्रीललितमहात्रिपुरसुन्दर्यै नमः

प्रथमोऽध्यायः

अगस्त्य उवाच–

अश्वानन महाबुद्धे सर्वशास्त्रविशारद।
कथितं ललितादेव्याश्चरितं परमाद्भुतम्।।१।।

पूर्वं प्रादुर्भवो मातुस्ततः पट्टाभिषेचनम्।
भण्डासुरवधश्चैव विस्तरेण त्वयोदितः।।२।।

वर्णितं श्रीपुरं चापि महाविभवविस्तरम्।
श्रीमत्पञ्चदशाक्षर्या महिमा वर्णितस्तथा।।३।।

षोढान्यासादयो न्यासा न्यासखण्डे समीरिताः।
अन्तर्यागक्रमश्चैव बहिर्यागक्रमस्तथा।।४।।

महायागमश्चैव पूजाखण्डे प्रकीर्तिताः।
पुरश्चरणखण्डे तु जपलक्षणमीरितम्।।५।।

होमखण्डे त्वया प्रोक्तो होमद्रव्यविधिक्रमः।
चक्रराजस्य विद्यायाः श्रीदेव्या देशिकात्मनोः।।६।।

रहस्यखण्डे तादात्म्यं परस्परमुदीरितम्।
स्तोत्रखण्डे बहुविधाः स्तुतयः परिकीर्तिताः।।७।।

मन्त्रिणीदण्डिनीदेव्योः प्रोक्ते नामसहस्रके।
न तु श्रीललितादेव्याः प्रोक्तं नामसहस्रकम्।।८।।

तत्र मे संशयो जातो हयग्रीव दयानिधे।
किं वा त्वया विस्मृतं तज्ज्ञात्वा वा समुपेक्षितम्।।९।।

मम वा योग्यता नास्ति श्रोतुं नामसहस्रकम्।
किमर्थं भवता नोक्तं तत्र मे कारणं वद।।१०।।

सूत उवाच–

इति पृष्टो हयग्रीवो मुनिना कुम्भजन्मना।
प्रहृष्टो वचनं प्राह तापसं कुम्भसंभवम्।।११।।

श्रीहयग्रीव उवाच–

लोपामुद्रापतेऽगस्त्य सावधानमनाः श्रुणु।
नाम्नां सहस्रं यन्नोक्तं कारणं तद् वदामि ते।।१२।।

रहस्यमिति मत्वाहं नोक्तवांस्ते न चान्यथा।
पुनश्च पृच्छते भक्त्या तस्मात् तत् ते वदाम्यहम्।।१३।।

ब्रूयाच्छिष्याय भक्ताय रहस्यमपि देशिकः।
भवता न प्रदेयं स्यादभक्ताय कदाचन।।१४।।

न शठाय न दुष्टाय नाविश्वासाय कर्हिचित्।
श्रीमातृभक्तियुक्ताय श्रीविद्याराजवेदिने।।१५।।

उपासकाय शुद्धाय देयं नामसहस्रकम्।
यानि नामसहस्राणि सद्यः सिद्धिप्रदानि वै।।१६।।

तन्त्रेषु ललितादेव्यास्तेषु मुख्यमिदं मुने।
श्रीविद्यैव तु मन्त्राणां तत्र कादिर्यथा परा॥१७॥

पुराणं श्रीपुरमिव शक्तीनां ललिता यथा।
श्रीविद्योपासकानां च यथा देवो वरः शिवः॥१८॥

तथा नामसहस्रेषु वरमेतत् प्रकीर्तितम्।
यथास्य पठनाद् देवी प्रीयते ललिताम्बिका॥१९॥

अन्यनामसहस्रस्य पाठान्न प्रीयते तथा।
श्रीमातुः प्रीतये तस्मादनिशं कीर्तयेदिदम्॥२०॥

बिल्वपत्रैश्चक्रराजे योऽर्चयेल्ललिताम्बिकाम्।
पद्मैर्वा तुलसीपुष्पैरेभिर्नामसहस्रकैः॥२१॥

सद्यः प्रसादं कुरुते तत्र सिंहासनेश्वरी।
चक्रधिराजमभ्यर्च्य जप्त्वा पञ्चदशाक्षरीम्॥२२॥

जपान्ते कीर्तयेन्नित्यमिदं नामसहस्रकम्।
जपपूजाद्यशक्तश्चेत् पठेन्नामसहस्रकम्॥२३॥

साङ्गार्चने साङ्गजपे यत् फलं तदवाप्नुयात्।
उपासने स्तुतीरन्याः पठेदभ्युदयो हि सः॥२४॥

इदं नामसहस्रं तु कीर्तयेन्नित्यकर्मवत्।
चक्रराजार्चनं देव्या जपो नाम्नां च कीर्तिनम्॥२५॥

भक्तस्य कृत्यमेतावदन्यदभ्युदयं विदुः।
भक्तस्यावश्यकमिदं नामसाहस्रकीर्तनम्॥२६॥

तत्र हेतुं प्रवक्ष्यामि श्रुणु त्वं कुम्भसंभव।
पुरा श्रीललितादेवी भक्तानां हितकाम्यया।।२७।।

वाग्देवीर्वशिनीमुख्याः समाहूयेदमब्रवीत्।

देव्युवाच–

वाग्देवता वशिन्याद्याः श्रुणुध्वं वचनं मम।।२८।।

भवत्यो मत्प्रसादेन प्रोल्लसद्वाग्विभूतयः
मद्भक्तानां वाग्विभूतिप्रदाने विनियोजिताः।।२९।।

मच्चक्रमस्य रहस्यज्ञा मम नामपरायणाः।
मम स्तोत्रविधानाय तस्मादाज्ञापयामि वः।।३०।।

कुरुध्वमङ्कितं स्तोत्रं मम नामसहस्त्रकैः।
येन भक्तैः स्तुताया मे सद्यः प्रीतिः परा भवेत्।।३१।।

हयग्रीव उवाच–

इत्याज्ञप्ता वचोदेव्यो देव्या श्रीललिताम्बया।
रहस्यैर्नामाभिर्दिव्यैश्चक्रुः स्तोत्रमनुत्तमम्।।३२।।

रहस्यनामसाहस्त्रमिति तद् विश्रुतं परम्।
ततः कदाचित् सदसि स्थित्वा सिंहासनेऽम्बिका।।३३।।

स्वसेवावसरं प्रादात् सर्वेषां कुम्भसंभव।
सेवार्थमागतास्तत्र ब्रह्माणीब्रह्मकोटयः।।३४।।

लक्ष्मीनारायणानां च कोटयः समुपागता।
गौरीकोटिसमेतानां रुद्राणामपि कोटयः।।३५।।

मन्त्रिणीदण्डिनीमुख्याः सेवार्थं याः समागताः।
शक्तयो विविधाकारास्तासां संख्या न विद्यते।।३६।।

दिव्यौघा मानवौघाश्च सिद्धौघाश्च समागता:।
तत्र श्रीललितादेवी सर्वेषां दर्शनं ददौ।।३७।।

तेषु दृष्टोपविष्टेषु स्वे स्वे स्थाने यथाक्रमम्।
तत: श्रीललितादेवीकटाक्षाक्षेपचोदिता:।।३८।।

उत्थाय वशिनीमुख्या बद्धाञ्जलिपुटास्तदा।
अस्तुवन्नामसाहस्रै: स्वकृतैर्ललिताम्बिकाम्।।३९।।

श्रुत्वा स्तवं प्रसन्नाभूल्ललिता परमेश्वरी।
सर्वे ते विस्मयं जग्मुर्ये तत्र सदासि स्थिता:।।४०।।

तत: प्रोवाच ललिता सदस्यान् देवातागणान्।

देव्युवाच–

ममाज्ञयैव वाग्देव्यश्चक्रु: स्तोत्रमनुत्तमम्।।४१।।

अङ्कितं नामाभिर्दिव्यैर्मम प्रीतिविधायकै:।
तत् पठध्वं सदा यूयं स्तोत्रं मत्प्रीतिवृद्धये।।४२।।

प्रवर्तयध्वं भक्तेषु मम नामसहस्रकम्।
इदं नामसहस्रं मे यो भक्त: पठते सकृत्।।४३।।

स मे प्रियतमो ज्ञेयस्तस्मै कामान् ददाम्यहम्।
श्रीचक्रं मां समभ्यर्च्य जप्त्वा पञ्चदशाक्षरीम्।।४४।।

पश्चान्नामसहस्रं मे कीर्तयेन्मम तुष्टये।
मामर्चयतु वा मा वा विद्यां जपतु वा न वा।।४५।।

कीर्तयेन्नामसाहस्रमिदं मत्प्रीतये सदा।
मत्प्रीत्या सकलान् कामाँल्लभते नात्र संशय:।।४६।।

तस्मान्नामसाहस्रं मे कीर्तयध्वं सदादरात्।

हयग्रीव उवाच–

इति श्रीललितेशानी शास्ति देवान् सहानुगान्।।४७।।

तदाज्ञया तदारभ्य ब्रह्मविष्णुमहेश्वराः।
शक्तयो मन्त्रिणीमुख्या इदं नामसहस्रकम्।।४८।।

पठन्ति भक्त्या सततं ललितापरितुष्टये।
तस्मादवश्यं भक्तेन कीर्तनीयमिदं मुने।।४९।।

आवश्यकत्वे हेतुस्ते मया प्रोक्तो मुनीश्वर।
इदानीं नामसाहस्त्रं वक्ष्यामि श्रद्धया श्रुणु।।५०।।

न्यास :

अस्य श्रीललितासहस्रनामस्तोत्रमालामन्त्रस्य वशिन्यादिवाग्देवता ऋषयः, अनुष्टुप् छन्दः, श्रीललितापरमेश्वरी देवता, श्रीमद्वाग्भवकूटेति बीजम्, मध्यकूटेति शक्तिः, शक्तिकूटेति कीलकम्, श्रीललितामहात्रिपुरसुन्दरीप्रसाद सिद्धिद्वारा चिन्तितफलावाप्त्यर्थे जपे विनियोगः।

ध्यानम्–

सिन्दूरारुणविग्रहां त्रिनयनां माणिक्यमौलिस्फुर-
त्तारानायकशेखरां स्मितमुखीमापीनवक्षोरुहाम्।
पाणिभ्यामलिपूर्णरत्नचषकं रक्तोत्पलं बिभ्रतीं
सौम्यां रत्नघटस्थरक्तचरणां ध्यायेत परामम्बिकाम्।।५१।।

इति श्रीब्राह्माण्डपुराणे उत्तरखण्डेश्रीहयग्रीवागस्त्यसंवादे
श्रीललितानामसहस्रपूर्वभागो नाम
प्रथमोऽध्यायः।

द्वितीयोऽध्यायः

श्रीमाता श्रीमहाराज्ञी श्रीमत्सिंहासनेश्वरी।
चिदग्निकुण्डसंभूता देवकार्यसमुद्यता॥१॥

उद्यद्भानुसहस्राभा चतुर्बाहुसमन्विता।
रागस्वरूपपाशाढ्या क्रोधाकाराङ्कुशोज्ज्वला॥२॥

मनोरूपेक्षुकोदण्डा (१०) पञ्चतन्मात्रसायका।
निजारुणप्रभापूरमज्जद्ब्रह्माण्डमण्डला॥३॥

चम्पकाशोकपुंनागसौगन्धिकलसत्कचा।
कुरुविन्दमणिश्रेणीकनत्कोटीरमण्डिता॥४॥

अष्टमीचन्द्रविभ्राजदलिकस्थलशोभिता।
मुखचन्द्रकलङ्काभमृगनाभिविशेषका॥५॥

वदनस्मरमाङ्गल्यगृहतोरणचिल्लिका।
वक्त्रलक्ष्मीपरीवाहचलन्मीनाभलोचना॥६॥

नवचम्पकपुष्पाभनासादण्डविराजिता।
ताराकान्तितिरस्कारिनासाभरणभासुरा (२०)॥७॥

कदम्बमञ्जरीक्लृप्तकर्णपूरमनोहरा।
ताटङ्कयुगलीभूततपनोडुपमण्डला॥८॥

पद्मरागशिलादर्शपरिभाविकपोलभूः।
नवविद्रुमबिम्बश्रीन्यक्कारिरदनच्छदा॥९॥

शुद्धविद्याङ्कुराकारद्विजपङ्क्तिद्वयोज्ज्वला।
कर्पूरवीटिकामोदसमाकर्षद्दिगन्तरा॥१०॥

निजसंलापमाधुर्यविनिर्भर्त्सितकच्छपी।

मन्दस्मितप्रभापूरमज्जत्कामेशमानसा॥११॥

अनाकलितसादृश्यचिबुकश्रीविराजिता।

कामेशबद्धमाङ्गल्यसूत्रशोभितकंधरा(३०)॥१२॥

कनकाङ्गदकेयूरकमनीयभुजान्विता।

रत्नग्रैवेयचिन्ताकलोलमुक्ताफलान्विता॥१३॥

कामेश्वरप्रेमरत्नमणिप्रतिपणस्तनी।

नाभ्यालवालरोमालिलताफलकुचद्वयी॥१४॥

लक्ष्यरोमलताधारतासमुन्नेयमध्यमा।

स्तनभारदलन्मध्यपट्टबन्धवलित्रया॥१५॥

अरुणारुणकौसुम्भवस्त्रभास्वत्कटीतटी।

रत्नकिङ्किणिकारम्यरशनादामभूषिता॥१६॥

कामेशज्ञातसौभाग्यमार्दवोरुद्वयान्विता।

माणिक्यमकुटाकारजानुद्वयविराजिता (४०)॥१७॥

इन्द्रगोपपरिक्षिप्तस्मरतूणाभजङ्घिका।

गूढगुल्फा कूर्मपृष्ठजयिष्णुप्रपदान्विता॥१८॥

नखदीधितिसंछन्ननमज्जनतमोगुणा।

पदद्वयप्रभाजालपराकृतसरोरुहा॥१९॥

शिञ्जानमणिमञ्जीरमण्डितश्रीपदाम्बुजा।

मरालीमन्दगमना महालावण्यशेवधिः॥२०॥

सर्वारुणाऽनवद्याङ्गी (५०) सर्वाभरणभूषिता।
शिवकामेश्वराङ्कस्था शिवा स्वाधीनवल्लभा।।२१।

सुमेरुमध्यशृङ्गस्था श्रीमन्नगरनायिका।
चिन्तामणिगृहान्तःस्था पञ्चब्रह्मासनस्थिता।।२२।।

महापद्माटवीसंस्था कदम्बवनवासिनी (६०)।
सुधासागरमध्यस्था कामाक्षी कामदायिनी।।२३।।

देवर्षिगणसंघातस्तूयमानात्मवैभवा।
भण्डासुरवधोद्युक्तशक्तिसेनासमन्विता।।२४।।

संपत्करीसमारूढसिंधुरव्रजसेविता।
अश्वारूढाधिष्ठिताश्वकोटिकोटिभिरावृता।।२५।।

चक्रराजरथारूढसर्वायुधपरिष्कृता।
गेयचक्ररथारूढमन्त्रिणीपरिसेविता।।२६।।

किरिचक्ररथारूढदण्डनाथपुरस्कृता (७०)
ज्वालामालिनिकाक्षिप्तवाह्निप्राकारमध्यगा।।२७।।

भण्डसैन्यवधोद्युक्तशक्तिविक्रमहर्षिता।
नित्या पराक्रमाटोपनिरीक्षणसमुत्सुका।।२८।।

भण्डपुत्रवधोद्युक्तबालाविक्रमनन्दिता।
मन्त्रिण्यम्बाविरचितविषङ्गंवधतोषिता।।२९।।

विशुक्रप्राणहरणवाराहीवीर्यनन्दिता।
कामेशवरमुखालोककल्पितश्रीगणेश्वरा।।३०।।

महागणेशनिर्भिन्नविघ्नयन्त्रप्रहर्षिता।
भण्डारसुरेन्द्रनिर्मुक्तशस्त्रप्रत्यस्त्रवर्षिणी॥३१॥

कराङ्गुलिनखोत्पन्ननारायणदशाकृतिः (८०)।
महापाशुपतास्त्राग्निनिर्दग्धासुरसैनिका॥३२॥

कामेश्वरास्त्रनिर्दग्धसभण्डासुरसैनिका (शुन्यका)।
ब्रह्मोपेन्द्रमहेन्द्रादिदेवसंस्तुतवैभवा॥३३॥

हरनेत्राग्निसंदग्धकामसंजीवनौषधिः।
श्रीमद्वाग्भवकूटैकस्वरूपमुखपङ्कजा॥३४॥

कण्ठाधः कटिपर्यन्तमध्यकूटस्वरूपिणी।
शक्तिकूटैकतापन्नकट्यधोभागधारिणी॥३५॥

मूलमन्त्रात्मिका मूलकूटत्रयकलेबरा।
कुलामृतैकरसिका (९०) कुलसंकेतपालिनी॥३६॥

कुलाङ्गना कुलान्तःस्था कौलिनी कुलयोगिनी।
अकुला समयान्तःस्था समयाचारतत्परा॥३७॥

मूलाधारैकनिलया ब्रह्मग्रन्थिविभेदिनी (१००)।
मणिपूरान्तरुदिता विष्णुग्रन्थिविभेदिनी॥३८॥

आज्ञाचक्रान्तरालस्था रुद्रग्रन्थिविभेदिनी।
सहस्त्राराम्बुजारूढा सुधासाराभिवर्षिणी॥३९॥

तटिल्लतासमरुचिः षट्चक्रोपरि संस्थिता।
महासक्तिः कुण्डलिनी (११०)बिसतन्तुतनीयसी॥४०॥

भवानी भावनागम्या भवारण्यकुठारिका।
भद्रप्रिया भद्रमूर्तिर्भक्तसौभाग्यदायिनी।।४१।।

भक्तिप्रिया भक्तिगम्या भक्तिवश (१२०) भयापहा।
शांभवी शारदाराध्या शर्वाणी शर्मदायिनी।।४२।।

शांकरी श्रीकरी साध्वी शरच्चन्द्रनिभानना।
शातोदरी (१३०) शान्तिमती निराधारा निरञ्जना।।४३।।

निर्लेपा निर्मला नित्या निराकारा निराकुला।
निर्गुणा निष्कला (१४०) शान्ता निष्कामा निरुपप्लवा।।४४।।

नित्यशुद्धा नित्यबुद्धा निरवद्या निरन्तरा:।
निष्कारणा निष्कलङ्का निरुपाधिर्निरीश्वरा।।४५।।

नित्यमुक्ता निर्विकारा निष्प्रपञ्चा निराश्रया।
नीरागा रागमथनी निर्मदा मदनाशिनी।।४६।।

निश्चिन्ता (१६०) निरहंकारा निर्मोहा मोहनाशिनी।
निर्ममा ममताहन्त्री निष्पापा पापनाशिनी।।४७।।

निष्क्रोधा क्रोधशमनी निर्लोभा (१७०) लोभनाशिनी।
नि:संशया संशयघ्नी निर्भवा भवनाशिनी।।४८।।

निर्विकल्पा निराबाधा निर्भेदा भेदनाशिनी।
निर्नाशा (१८०) मृत्युमथनी निष्क्रिया निष्परिग्रहा।।४९।।

निस्तुला नीलचिकुरा निरपाया निरत्यया।
दुर्लभा दुर्गमा दुर्गा (१९०) दुःखहन्त्री सुखप्रदा।।५०।।

दुष्टदूरा दुराचारशमनी दोषवर्जिता।
सर्वज्ञा सान्द्रकरुणा समानाधिकवर्जिता।।५१।।

सर्वशक्तिमयी सर्वमङगला (२००) सद्गतिप्रदा।
सर्वेश्वरी सर्वमयी सर्वमन्त्रस्वरूपिणी।।५२।।

सर्वयन्त्रात्मिका सर्वतन्त्ररूपा मनोन्मनी।
माहेश्वरी महादेवी महालक्ष्मी-(२१०) मृडप्रिया।।५३।।

महारूपा महापूज्या महापातकनाशिनी।
महामाया महासत्त्वा महाशक्तिर्महारतिः।।५४।।

महाभोगा महैश्वर्या (२००) महावीर्या महाबला।
महाबुद्धिर्महासिद्धिर्महायोगेश्वरेश्वरी।।५५।।

महातन्त्रा महामन्त्रा महायन्त्रा महासना।
महायागक्रमाराध्या (२३०) महाभैरवपूजित।।५६।।

महेश्वरमहाकल्पमहाताण्डवसाक्षिणी।
महाकामेशमहिषी महात्रिपुरसुन्दरी।।५७।।

चतुःषष्ट्युपचाराढ्या चतुः षष्टिकलामयी।
महाचतुः षष्टिकोटियोगिनीगणसेविता।।५८।।

मनुविद्या चन्द्रविद्या चन्द्रमण्डलमध्यगा(२४०)।
चारुरूपा चारुहासा चारुचन्द्रकलाधरा।।५९।।

चराचरजगन्नाथा चक्रराजनिकेतना।
पार्वती पद्मनयना पद्मरागसमप्रभा।।६०।।

पञ्चप्रेतासनासीना पञ्चब्रह्मस्वरूपिणी।(२५०)
चिन्मयी परमानन्दा विज्ञानघनरूपिणी॥६१॥

ध्यानध्यातृध्येयरूपा धर्माधर्मविवर्जिता।
विश्वरूपा जागरिणी स्वपन्ती तैजसात्मिका॥६२॥

सुप्ता (२६०) प्राज्ञात्मिका तुर्या सर्वावस्थाविवर्जिता।
सृष्टिकर्त्री ब्रह्मरूपा गोप्त्री गोविन्दरूपिणी॥६३॥

संहारिणी रुद्ररूपा तिरोधानकरी (२७०) (ई)श्वरी।
सदाशिवाऽनुग्रहदा पञ्चकृत्यपरायणा॥६४॥

भानुमण्डलमध्यस्था भैरवी भगमालिनी।
पद्मासना भगवती पद्मनाभसहोदरी (२८०)॥६५॥

उन्मेषनिमिषोत्पन्नविपन्नभुवनावलिः।
सहस्रशीर्षवदना सहस्राक्षी सहस्रपात्॥६६॥

आब्रह्मकीटजननी वर्णाश्रमविधायिनी।
निजाज्ञारूपनिगमा पुण्यापुण्यफलप्रदा॥६७॥

श्रुतिसीमन्तसिन्दूरीकृतपादाब्जधूलिका।
सकलागमसंदोहशुक्तिसंपुटमौक्तिका(२९०)॥६८॥

पुरुषार्थप्रदा पूर्णा भोगिनी भुवनेश्वरी।
अम्बिकाऽनादिनिधना हरिब्रह्मेन्द्रसेविता॥६९॥

नारायणी नादरूपा नामरूपविवर्जिता(३००)।
ह्रींकारी ह्रीमती हृद्या हेयोपादेयवर्जिता॥७०॥

राजराजार्चिता राज्ञी रम्या राजीवलोचना।
रञ्जनी रमणी (३१०) रस्या रणत्किङ्किणिमेखला।।७१।।

रमा राकेन्दुवदना रति रूपा रतिप्रिया।
रक्षाकरी राक्षसघ्नी रामा रमणलम्पटा (३२०)।।७२।।

काम्या कामकलारूपा कदम्बकुसुमप्रिया।
कल्याणी जगतीकन्दा करुणारससागरा।।७३।।

कलावती कलालापा कान्ता कादम्बरीप्रिया(३३०)।
वरदा वामनयना वारुणीमदविह्वला।।७४।।

विश्वाधिका वेदवेद्या विन्ध्याचलनिवासिनी।
विधात्री वेदजननी विष्णुमाया विलासिनी(३४०)।।७५।।

क्षेत्रस्वरूपा क्षेत्रेशी क्षेत्रक्षेत्रज्ञपालिनी।
क्षयवृद्धिविनिर्मुक्ता क्षेत्रपालसमर्चिता।।७६।।

विजया विमला वन्द्या वन्दारुजनवत्सला।
वाग्वादिनी (३५०) वामकेशी वह्निमण्डलवासिनी।।७७।।

भक्तिमत्कल्पलतिका पशुपाशविमोचिनी।
संहृताशेषपाषण्डा सदाचारप्रवर्तिका।।७८।।

तापत्रयाग्निसंतप्तसमाह्लादनचन्द्रिका।
तरुणी तापसाराध्या तनुमध्या (३६०) तमोऽपहा।।७९।।

चितिस्तत्पदलक्ष्यार्था चिदेकरसरूपिणी।
स्वात्मानन्दलवीभूतब्रह्माद्यानन्दसंततिः।।८०।।

परा प्रत्यक्चितीरूपा पश्यन्ती परदेवता।
मध्यमा (३७०) वैखरीरूपा भक्तमानसहंसिका॥८१॥

कामेश्वरप्राणनाडी कृतज्ञा कामपूजिता।
श्रृङ्गाररससंपूर्णा जया जालन्धरस्थिता॥८२॥

ओड्याणपीठनिलया बिन्दुमण्डलवासिनी(३८०)।
रहोयागक्रमाराध्या रहस्तर्पणतर्पिता॥८३॥

सद्यः प्रसादिनी विश्वसाक्षिणी साक्षिवर्जिता।
षडङ्गदेवतायुक्ता षाड्गुण्यपरिपूरिता॥८४॥

नित्यक्लिन्ना निरुपमा निर्वाणसुखदायिनी(३९०)।
नित्याषोडशिकारूपा श्रीकण्ठार्धशरीरिणी॥८५॥

प्रभावती प्रभारूपा प्रसिद्धा परमेश्वरी।
मूलप्रकृतिरव्यक्ता व्यक्ताव्यक्तस्वरूपिणी॥८६॥

व्यापिनी (४००) विविधाकारा विद्याविद्यास्वरूपिणी।
महाकामेशनयनकुमुदाह्लादकौमुदी॥८७॥

भक्तहार्दतमोभेदभानुमद्भानुसंततिः।
शिवदूती शिवाराध्या शिवमूर्तिः शिवकरी॥८८॥

शिवप्रिया शिवपरा (४१०) शिष्टेष्टा शिष्टपूजिता।
अप्रमेया स्वप्रकाशा मनोवाचामगोचरा॥८९॥

चिच्छक्तिश्चेतनारूपा जडशक्तिर्जडात्मिका।
गायत्री (४१०) व्याहृतिः संध्या द्विजबृन्दनिषेविता॥९०॥

तत्त्वासना तत्वमयी (तत् त्वम् अयी) पञ्चकोशान्तरस्थिता।
निःसीममहिमा नित्ययौवना (४३०) मदशालिनी॥९१॥

मदघूर्णितरक्ताक्षी मदपाटलगण्डभूः।
चन्दनद्रवदिग्धाङ्गी चाम्पेयकुसुमप्रिया॥९२॥

कुशला कोमलाकारा कुरुकुल्ला कुलेश्वरी।
कुलकुण्डालया (४४०) कौलमार्गतत्परसेविता॥९३॥

कुमारगणनाथाम्बा तुष्टिः पुष्टिर्मतिर्धृतिः।
शान्तिः स्वस्तिमती कान्तिर्नन्दिनी (४५०) विघ्ननाशिनी॥९४॥

तेजोवती त्रिनयना लोलाक्षी कामरूपिणी।
मालिनी हंसिनी माता मलयाचलवासिनी॥९५॥

सुमुखी नलिनी (४६०) सुभ्रूः शोभना सुरनायिका।
कालकण्ठी कान्तिमती क्षोभिणी सूक्ष्मरूपिणी॥९६॥

वज्रेश्वरी वामदेवी वयोऽवस्थाविवर्जिता(४७०)।
सिद्धेश्वरी सिद्धविद्या सिद्धमाता यशास्विनी॥९७॥

विशुद्धचक्रनिलयाऽऽरक्तवर्णा त्रिलोचना।
खट्वाङ्गादिप्रहरणा वदनैकसमन्विता॥९८॥

पायसान्नप्रिया (४८०) त्वक्स्था पशुलोकभयंकरी।
अमृतादिमहाशक्तिसंवृता डाकिनीश्वरी॥९९॥

अनाहताब्जनिलया श्यामाभवदनद्वया।
दंष्ट्रोज्ज्वलाऽक्षमालादिधरा रुधिरसंस्थिता(४९०)॥१००॥

कालरात्र्यादिशक्त्यौघवृता स्निग्धौदनप्रिया।
महावीरेन्द्रवरदा राकिण्यम्बास्वरूपिणी॥१०१॥

मणिपूराब्जनिलया वदनत्रयसंयुता।
वज्रादिकायुधोपेता डामर्यादिभिरावृता॥१०२॥

रक्तवर्णा मांसनिष्ठा (५००) गुडान्नप्रीतमानसा।
समस्तभक्तसुखदा लाकिन्यम्बास्वरूपिणी॥१०३॥

स्वाधिष्ठानाम्बुजगता चतुर्वक्त्रमनोहरा।
शूलाद्यायुधसंपन्ना पीतवर्णाऽतिगर्विता॥१०४॥

मेदोनिष्ठा मधुप्रीता (५१०) बन्दिन्यादिसमन्विता।
दध्यन्नासक्तहृदया काकिनीरूपधारिणी॥१०५॥

मूलाधाराम्बुजारूढा पञ्चवक्त्राऽस्थिसंस्थिता।
अङ्कुशादिप्रहरणा वरदादिनिषेविता॥१०६॥

मुद्गौदनासक्तचित्ता साकिन्यम्बास्वरूपिणी।(५२०)
आज्ञाचक्राब्जनिलया शुक्लवर्णा षडानना॥१०७॥

मज्जासंस्था हंसवती मुख्यशक्तिसमन्विता।
हरिद्रान्नैकरसिका हाकिनीरूपधारिणी॥१०८॥

सहस्रदलपद्मस्था सर्ववर्णोपशोभिता।
सर्वायुधधरा (५३०) शुक्लसंस्थिता सर्वतोमुखी॥१०९॥

सर्वौदनप्रीतचित्ता याकिन्यम्बास्वरूपिणी।
स्वाहा स्वधामतिर्मेधा श्रुतिः स्मृति- (५४०) रनुत्तमा॥११०॥

पुण्यकीर्तिः पुण्यलभ्या पुण्यश्रवणकीर्तना।
पुलोमजार्चिता बन्धमोचनी बर्ब (बन्धु) रालका॥१११॥

विमर्शरूपिणी विद्या वियदादिजगत्प्रसूः(५५०)।
सर्वव्याधिप्रशमनी सर्वमृत्युनिवारिणी॥११२॥

अग्रगण्याचिन्त्यरूपा कलिकल्मषनाशिनी।
कात्यायनी कालहन्त्री कमलाक्षनिषेविता॥११३॥

ताम्बूलपूरितमुखी दाडिमीकुसुमप्रभा।(५६०)
मृगाक्षी मोहिनी मुख्या मृडानी मित्ररूपिणी॥११४॥

नित्यतृप्ता भक्तनिधिर्नियन्त्री निखिलेश्वरी।
मैत्र्यादिवासनालभ्या (५७०) महाप्रलयसाक्षिणी॥११५॥

परा शक्तिः परा निष्ठा प्रज्ञानघनरूपिणी।
माध्वीपानालसा मत्ता मातृकावर्णरूपिणी॥११६॥

महाकैलासनिलया मृणालमृदुदोर्लता।
महनीया (५८०) दयामूर्तिर्महासाम्राज्यशालिनी॥११७॥

आत्मविद्या महाविद्या श्रीविद्या कामसेविता।
श्रीषोडशाक्षरीविद्या त्रिकूटा कामकोटिका॥११८॥

कटाक्षकिङ्करीभूतकमलाकोटिसेविता(५९०)।
शिरःस्थिता चन्द्रनिभा फालस्थेन्द्रधनुःप्रभा॥११९॥

हृदयस्था रविप्रख्या त्रिकोणान्तरदीपिका।
दाक्षायणी दैत्यहन्त्री दक्षयज्ञविनाशिनी(६००)॥१२०॥

दरान्दोलितदीर्घाक्षी दरहासोज्ज्वलन्मुखी।
गुरुमूर्तिर्गुणनिधिर्गोमाता गुहजन्मभूः॥१२१॥

देवेशी दण्डनीतिस्था दहराकाशरूपिणी।
प्रतिपन्मुख्यराकान्ततिथिमण्डलपूजिता(६१०)॥१२२॥

कलात्मिका कलानाथा काव्यालापविनोदिनी।
सचामररमावाणीसव्यदक्षिणसेविता॥१२३॥

आदिशक्तिरमेयात्मा परमा पावनाकृतिः।
अनेककोटिब्रह्माण्डजननी (६२०) दिव्यविग्रहा॥१२४॥

क्लींकारी केवला गुह्या कैवल्यपददायिनी।
त्रिपुरा त्रिजगद्वन्द्या त्रिमूर्तिस्त्रिदशेश्वरी॥१२५॥

त्र्यक्षरी (६३०) दिव्यगन्धाढ्या सिन्दूरतिलकाञ्चिता।
उमा शैलेन्द्रतनया गौरी गन्धर्वसेविता॥१२६॥

विश्वगर्भा स्वर्णगर्भावरदा वागधीश्वरी(६४०)।
ध्यानगम्यापरिच्छेद्या ज्ञानदा ज्ञानविग्रहा॥१२७॥

सर्ववेदान्तसंवेद्या सत्यानन्दस्वरूपिणी।
लोपामुद्रार्चिता लीलाक्लृप्तब्रह्माण्डमण्डला॥१२८॥

अदृश्या दृश्यरहिता (६५०) विज्ञात्री वेद्यवर्जिता।
योगिनी योगदा योग्या योगानन्दा युगंधरा॥१२९॥

इच्छाशक्तिज्ञानशक्तिक्रियाशक्तिस्वरूपिणी।
सर्वाधारा सुप्रतिष्ठा (६६०) सदसद्रूपधारिणी॥१३०॥

अष्टमूर्तिरजाजैत्री लोकयात्रविधायिनी।
एकाकिनी भूमरूपा निर्द्वैता द्वैतवर्जिता॥१३१॥

अन्नदा वसुदा (६७०) वृद्धा ब्रह्मात्मैक्यस्वरूपिणी।
बृहती ब्राह्मणी ब्राह्मी ब्रह्मानन्दा बलिप्रिया॥१३२॥

भाषारूपा बृहत्सेना भावाभावविवर्जिता (६८०)।
सुखाराध्या शुभकरी शोभनासुलभा गतिः॥१३३॥

राजराजेश्वरी राज्यदायिनी राज्यवल्लभा।
राजत्कृपा राजपीठनिवेशितनिजाश्रिता॥१३४॥

राज्यलक्ष्मीः कोशनाथा (६९०) चतुरङ्गबलेश्वरी।
साम्राज्यदायिनी सत्यसंधा सागरमेखला॥१३५॥

दीक्षिता दैत्यशमनी सर्वलोकवंशकरी।
सर्वार्थदात्री सावित्री सच्चिदानन्दरूपिणी(७००)॥१३६॥

देशकालापरिच्छिन्ना सर्वगा सर्वमोहिनी।
सरस्वती शास्त्रमयी गुहाम्बा गुह्यरूपिणी॥१३७॥

सर्वोपाधिविनिर्मुक्ता सदाशिवपतिव्रता।
संप्रदायेश्वरी (७१०) साध्वी (साधु-ई) गुरुमण्डलरूपिणी॥
कुलोत्तीर्णा भगाराध्या माया मधुमती मही।
गणाम्बा गुह्यकाराध्या (७२०) कोमलाङ्गी गुरुप्रिया॥१३९॥

स्वतन्त्रा सर्वतन्त्रेशी दक्षिणामूर्तिरपिणी।
सनकादिसमाराध्या शिवज्ञानप्रदायिनी॥१४०॥

चित्कलानन्दकलिका प्रेमरूपा (७३०) प्रियंकरी।
नामपरायणप्रीता नन्दिविा नटेश्वरी।।१४१।।

मिथ्याजगदधिष्ठाना मुक्तिदा मुक्तिरूपिणी।
लास्यप्रिया लयकरी लज्जा (७४०) रम्भादिवन्दिता।।१४२।।

भवदावसुधावृष्टिः पापारण्यदवानला।
दौभाग्यतूलवातूला जराध्वान्तरविप्रभा।।१४३।।

भाग्याब्धिचन्द्रिका भक्तचित्तकेकिघनाघना।
रोगपर्वतदम्भोलिर्मृत्युदारुकुठारिका।।१४४।।

महेश्वरी (७५०) महाकाली महाग्रासा महाशना।
अपर्णा चण्डिका चण्डमुण्डासुरनिषूदिनी।।१४५।।

क्षाराक्षरात्मिका सर्वलोकेशी विश्वधारिणी।
त्रिवर्गदात्री (७६०) सुभगा त्र्यम्बका त्रिगुणात्मिका।।१४६।।

स्वर्गापवर्गदा शुद्धा जपापुष्पनिभाकृतिः।
ओजोवती द्युतिधरा यज्ञरूपा प्रियव्रता (७७०)।।१४७।।

दुराराध्या दुराधर्षा पाटलीकुसुमप्रिया।
महती मेरुनिलया मन्दारकुसुमप्रिया।।१४८।।

वीराराध्या विराड्रूपा विरजा विश्वतोमुखी (७८०)।
प्रत्यग्रूपा पराकाशा प्राणदा प्राणरूपिणी।।१४९।।

मार्ताण्डभैरवाराध्या मन्त्रिणीन्यस्तराज्यधूः।
त्रिपुरेशी जयत्सेना निस्त्रैगुण्या परापरा(७९०)।।१५०।।

सत्यज्ञानानन्दरूपा सामरस्यपरायणा।
कपर्दिनी कलामाला कामधुक् कामरूपिणी॥१५१॥

कलानिधिः काव्यकला रसज्ञा रसशेवधिः(८००)।
पुष्टा पुरातना पूज्या पुष्करा पुष्करेक्षणा॥१५२॥

परं ज्योतिः परं धाम परमाणुः परात्परा।
पाशहस्ता (८१०) पाशहन्त्री परमन्त्रविभेदिनी॥१५३॥

मूर्तामूर्ता नित्यतृप्ता मुनिमानसहंसिका।
सत्यव्रता सत्यरूपा सर्वान्तर्यामिणी सती (८२०)॥१५४॥

ब्रह्माणी ब्रह्मजननी बहुरूपा बुधार्चिता।
प्रसवित्री प्रचण्डाज्ञा प्रतिष्ठा प्रकटाकृतिः (८३०)॥१५५॥

प्राणेश्वरी प्राणदात्री पञ्चाशत्पीठरूपिणी।
विश्रृङ्खला विविक्तस्था वीरमाता वियत्प्रसूः॥१५६॥

मुकुन्दा मुक्तिनिलया मूलविग्रहरूपिणी(८४०)।
भावज्ञा भवरोगघ्नी भवचक्रप्रवर्तिनी॥१५७॥

छन्दःसारा शास्त्रसारा मन्त्रसारा तलोदरी।
उदारकीर्तिरुद्दामवैभवा वर्णरूपिणी(८५०)॥१५८॥

जन्ममृत्युजरातप्तजनविश्रान्तिदायिनी।
सर्वोपनिषदुद्घुष्टा शान्त्यतीतकलात्मिका॥१५९॥

गम्भीरा गगनान्तःस्था गर्विता गानलोलुपा।
कल्पनारहिता काष्ठा कान्ता (८६०) कान्तार्धविग्रहा॥१६०॥

कार्यकारणनिर्मुक्ता कामकेलितरङ्गिता।
कनत्कनकताटङ्का लीलाविग्रहधारिणी॥१६१॥

अजा क्षयविनिर्मुक्ता मुग्धा क्षिप्रप्रसादिनी।
अन्तर्मुखसमाराध्या (८७०) बहिर्मुखसुदुर्लभा॥१६२॥

त्रयी त्रिवर्गनिलया त्रिस्था त्रिपुरमालिनी।
निरामया निरालम्बा स्वात्मारामा सुधासृतिः॥१६३॥

संसारपङ्कनिर्मग्नसमुद्धरणपण्डिता(८८०)
यज्ञप्रिया यज्ञकर्त्री यजमानस्वरूपिणी॥१६४॥

धर्माधारा धनाध्याक्षा धनधान्यविवर्धिनीं।
विप्रप्रिया विप्ररूपा विश्वभ्रमणकारिणी॥१६५॥

विश्वग्रासा (८९०) विद्रुमाभा वैष्णवी विष्णुरूपिणी।
अयोनिर्योनिनिलया कूटस्था कुलरूपिणी॥१६६॥

वीरगोष्ठीप्रिया वीरा नैष्कर्म्या (९००) नादरूपिणी।
विज्ञानकलना कल्या विदग्धा बैन्दवासना॥१६७॥

तत्वाधिका तत्त्वमयी तत्त्वमर्थस्वरूपिणी।
सामगानप्रिया सौम्या (९१०) सदाशिवकुटुम्बिनी॥१६८॥

सव्यापसव्यमार्गस्था सर्वापद्विनिवारिणी।
स्वस्था स्वभावनधुरा धीरा धीरसमार्चिता॥१६९॥

चैतन्यार्यसमाराध्या चैतन्यकुसुमप्रिया।
सदोदिता (९२०) सदा तुष्टा तरुणादित्यपाटला॥१७०॥

दक्षिणादक्षिणाराध्या दलस्मेरमुखाम्बुजा।
कौलिनीकेवलानर्घ्यकैवल्यपददायिनी।।१७१।।

स्तोत्रप्रिया स्तुतिमती श्रुतिसंस्तुतवैभवा।
मनस्विनी (९३०) मानवती महेशी मङ्गलाकृतिः।।१७२।।

विश्वमाता जगद्धात्री विशालाक्षी विरागिणी।
प्रगल्भा परमोदारा परामोदा (९४०) मनोमयी।।१७३।।

व्योमकेशी विमानस्था वज्रिणी वामकेश्वरी।
पञ्चयज्ञप्रिया पञ्चप्रेतमञ्चाधिशायिनी।।१७४।।

पञ्चमी पञ्चभूतेशी पञ्चसंख्योपचारिणी (९५०)
शाश्वती शाश्वतैश्वर्या शर्मदा शंभुमोहिनी।।१७५।।

धरा धरसुता धन्या धर्मिणी धर्मवर्धिनी।
लोकातीता (९३०) गुणातीता सर्वातीता शमात्मिका।।१७६।।

बन्धूककुसुमप्रख्या बाला लीलाविनोदिनी।
सुमङ्गली सुखकरी सुवेषाढ्या सुवासिनी(९७०)।।१७७।।

सुवासिन्यर्चनप्रीता शोभना शुद्धमानसा।
बिन्दुतर्पणसंतुष्टा पूर्वजा त्रिपुराम्बिका।।१७८।।

दशमुद्रासमाराध्या त्रिपुराश्री वशङ्करी।
ज्ञानमुद्रा ज्ञानगम्या ज्ञानज्ञेयस्वरूपिणी।।१७९।।

योनिमुद्रा त्रिखण्डेशी त्रिगुणाम्बा त्रिकोणगा।
अनवद्याऽद्भुतचारित्र वाञ्छितार्थ प्रदायिनी।।१८०।।

अभ्यासातिशयज्ञाता षडध्वातीतरूपिणी।
अव्याजकरूणामूर्तिरज्ञानध्वान्त दीपिका॥१८१॥

आबालगोपविदिता सर्वानुल्लङ्घ्यशासना॥
श्रीचक्रराजनिलया श्रीमत्रिपुरसुन्दरी॥१८२॥

श्री शिवा शिवशक्त्यैक्यरूपिणी ललिताम्बिका।
एवं श्री ललितादेव्या नाम्नां साहस्त्रकं जगु:॥१८३॥

श्रीललितासहस्त्रनामस्तोत्रकथनं नाम द्वितीयोध्याय:॥

उत्तरभाग:

तृतीयोऽध्याय:।

फलश्रुति:

इत्येतन्नामसाहस्त्रं कथितं ते घटोद्भव।
रहस्यानां रहस्यं च ललिताप्रीतिदायकम्॥१॥

अनेन सदृशं स्तोत्रं न भूतं न भविष्यति।
सर्वरोगप्रशमनं सर्वसंपत्प्रवर्धनम्॥२॥

सर्वापमृत्युशमनं कालमृत्युनिवारणम्।
सर्वज्वरार्तिशमनं दीर्घायुष्यप्रदायम्॥३॥

पुत्रप्रदमपुत्राणां पुरुषार्थप्रदायकम्।
इदं विशेषाच्छ्रीदेव्या: स्तोत्रं प्रीतिविधायकम्॥४॥

जपेन्नित्यं प्रयत्नेन ललितोपास्तितत्पर:।
प्रात: स्नात्वा विधानेन संध्याकर्म समाप्य च॥५॥

पूजागृहं ततो गत्वा चक्रराजं समर्चयेत्।
विद्यां जपेत् सहस्रं वा त्रिशतं शतमेव वा॥६॥

रहस्यनामसाहस्रमिदं पश्चात् पठेन्नरः।
जन्ममध्ये सकृच्चापि य एतत् पठते सुधीः॥७॥

तस्य पुण्यफलं वक्ष्ये श्रृणु त्वं कुम्भसंभव।
गङ्गादिसर्वतीर्थेषु यः स्नायात् कोटिजन्मसु॥८॥

कोटिलिङ्गप्रतिष्ठा च यः कुर्यादविमुक्तके।
कुरुक्षेत्रे तु यो दद्यात् कोटिवारं रविग्रहे॥९॥

कोटि सुवर्णभाराणां श्रोत्रियेषु द्विजन्मसु।
यः कोटिं हयमेधानामाहरेद् गाङ्गरोधसि॥१०॥

आचरेत् कूपकोटीर्यो निर्जले मरुभूतले।
दुर्भिक्षे यः प्रतिदिनं कोटिब्राह्मणभोजनम्॥११॥

श्रद्धया परया कुर्यात् सहस्रपरिवत्सरान्।
तत्पुण्यकोटिगुणितं लभेत् पुण्यमनुत्तमम्॥१२॥

रहस्यनामसाहस्रे नाम्नेऽप्येकस्य कीर्तनात्।
रहस्यनामसाहस्रे नामैकमपि यः पठेत्॥१३॥

तस्य पापानि नश्यन्ति महान्त्यपि न संशयः।
नित्यकर्माननुष्ठानान्निषिद्धकरणादपि॥१४॥

यत् पापं जायते पुंसां तत् सर्वं नश्यति द्रुतम्।
बहुनात्र किमुक्तेन श्रृणु त्वं कलशीसुत॥१५॥

अत्रैकनाम्नो या शक्तिः पातकानां निवर्तने।
तन्निवर्त्यमघं कर्तुं नालं लोकाश्चतुर्दश॥१६॥

यस्त्यक्त्वा नामसाहस्रं पापहानिमभीप्सति।
स हि शीतनिवृत्त्यर्थं हिमशैलं निषेवते॥१७॥

भक्तो यः कीर्तयेन्नित्यमिदं नामसहस्रकम्।
तस्मै श्रीललितादेवी प्रीताभीष्टं प्रयच्छति॥१८॥

अकीर्तयन्निदं स्तोत्रं कथं भक्तो भविष्यति।
नित्यं संकीर्तनाशक्तः कीर्तयेत् पुण्यवासरं॥१९॥

संक्रान्तौ विषुवे चैव स्वजन्मत्रितयेऽयने।
नवम्यां वा चतुर्दश्यां सितायां शुक्रवासरे॥२०॥

कीर्तयेन्नामसाहस्रं पौर्णमास्यां विशेषतः।
पौर्णमास्यां चन्द्रबिम्बे ध्यात्वा श्रीललिताम्बिकाम्॥२१॥

पञ्चोपचारैः संपूज्य पठेन्नामसहस्रकम्॥
सर्वे रोगाः प्रणश्यन्ति दीर्घायुष्यं च विन्दति॥२२॥

अयमायुष्करो नाम प्रयोगः कल्पचो (नो)दितः।
ज्वरार्तं शिरसि स्पृष्ट्वा पठेन्नामसहस्रकम्॥२३॥

तत्क्षणात् प्रशमं याति शिरस्तोदो ज्वरोऽपि च।
सर्वव्याधिनिवृत्त्यर्थं स्पृष्ट्वा भस्म जपेदिदम्॥२४॥

तद्भस्मधारणादेव नश्यन्ति व्याधयः क्षणात्।
जलं संमन्त्र्य कुम्भस्थं नामसाहस्रतो मुने॥२५॥

अभिषिञ्चेद् ग्रहग्रस्तान् ग्रहा नश्यन्ति तत्क्षणात्।
सुधासागरमध्यस्थां ध्यात्वा श्रीललिताम्बिकाम्॥२६॥

यः पठेन्नामसाहस्रं विषं तस्य विनश्यति।
वन्ध्यानां पुत्रलाभाय नामसाहस्रमन्त्रितम्॥२७॥

नवनीतं प्रदद्यात्तु पुत्रलाभो भवेद् ध्रुवम्।
देव्याः पाशेन संबद्धामाकृष्टामङ्कुशेन च॥२८॥

ध्यात्वाभीष्टां स्त्रियं रात्रौ जपेन्नामसहस्रकम्।
आयाति स्वसमीपं सा यद्यप्यन्तःपुरं गता॥२९॥

राजाकर्षणकामश्चेद् राजावसथदिङ्मुखः।
त्रिरात्रं यः पठेदेतच्छ्रीदेवीध्यानतत्परः॥३०॥

स राजा पारवश्येन तुरङ्गं वा मतङ्गजम्।
आरुह्यायाति निकटं दासवत् प्रणिपत्य च॥३१॥

तस्मै राज्यं च कोशं च ददात्येव वशं गतः।
रहस्यनामसाहस्रं यः कीर्तयति नित्यशः॥३२॥

तन्मुखालोकमात्रेण मुह्येल्लोकत्रयं मुने।
यस्त्विदं नामसाहस्रं सकृत् पठति भक्तिमान्॥३३॥

तस्य ये शत्रवस्तेषां निहन्ता शरभेश्वरः।
यो वाभिचारं कुरुते नामसाहस्रपाठके॥३४॥

निर्वर्त्य तत्क्रियां हन्यात् तं वै प्रत्यङ्गिरा स्वयम्।
ये क्रूरदृष्ट्या वीक्षन्ते नामसाहस्रपाठकम्॥३५॥

तानन्धान् कुरुते क्षिप्रं स्वयं मार्ताण्डभैरवः।
धनं यो हरते चौरैःनामसाहस्रजापिनः॥३६॥

यत्र कुत्र स्थितं वापि क्षेत्रपालो निहन्ति तम्।
विद्यासु कुरुते वादं यो विद्वान्नामजापिना॥३७॥

तस्य वाक्स्तम्भनं सद्यः करोति नकुलेश्वरी।
यो राजा कुरुते वैरं नामसाहस्रजापिना॥३८॥

चतुरङ्गबलं तस्य दण्डिनी संहरेत् स्वयम्।
यः पठेन्नामसाहस्रं षण्मासं भक्तिसंयुतः॥३९॥

लक्ष्मीश्चाञ्चल्यरहिता सदा तिष्ठति तद्गृहे।
मासमेकं प्रतिदिनं त्रिवारं यः पठेन्नरः॥४०॥

भारती तस्य जिह्वाग्रे रङ्गे नृत्यति नित्यशः।
यस्त्वेकवारं पठति पक्षमात्रमतन्द्रितः॥४१॥

मुह्यन्ति कामवशगा मृगाक्ष्यस्तस्य वीक्षणात्।
यः पठेन्नामसाहस्रं जन्ममध्ये सकृन्नरः॥४२॥

तद्दृष्टिगोचराः सर्वे मुच्यन्ते सर्वकिल्बिषैः।
यो वेत्ति नामसाहस्रं तस्मै देयं द्विजन्मने॥४३॥

अन्नं वस्त्रं धनं धान्यं नान्येभ्यस्तु कदाचन।
श्रीमन्त्रराजं यो वेत्ति श्रीचक्रं यः समर्चति॥४४॥

यः कीर्तयति नामानि तं सत्पात्रं विदुर्बुधाः।
तस्मै देयं प्रयत्नेन श्रीदेवीप्रीतिमिच्छता॥४५॥

न कीर्तयति नामानि मन्त्रराजं न वेत्ति यः।
पशुतुल्यः स विज्ञेयस्तस्मै दत्तं निरर्थकम्॥४६॥

परीक्ष्य विद्याविषये तेभ्यो दद्याद् विचक्षणः।
श्रीमन्त्रराजसदृशो यथा मन्त्रो न विद्यते॥४७॥

देवता ललितातुल्या यथा नास्ति घटोद्भव।
रहस्यनामसाहस्रतुल्या नास्ति तथा स्तुतिः॥४८॥

लिखित्वा पुस्तके यस्तु नामसाहस्रमुत्तमम्।
समर्चयेत् सदा भक्त्या तस्य तुष्यति सुन्दरी॥४९॥

बहुनात्र किमुक्तेन श्रुणु त्वं कुम्भसंभव।
नानेन सदृशं स्तोत्रं सर्वतन्त्रेषु दृश्यते॥५०॥

तस्मादुपासको नित्यं कीर्तयेदिदमादरात्।
एभिर्नामसहस्रैस्तु श्रीचक्रं योऽर्चयेत् सकृत्॥५१॥

पद्मैर्वा तुलसीपुष्पैः कल्हारैर्वा कदम्बकैः।
चम्पकैर्जातिकुसुमैर्मल्लिकाकरवीरकैः॥५२॥

उत्पलैर्बिल्वपत्रैर्वा कुन्दकेसरपाटलैः।
अन्यैः सुगन्धिकुसुमैः केतकीमाधवीमुखैः॥५३॥

तस्य पुण्यफलं वक्तुं न शक्नोति महेश्वरः।
सा वेत्ति ललितादेवी स्वचक्रार्चनजं फलम्॥५४॥

अन्ये कथं विजानीयुर्ब्रह्माद्याः स्वल्पमेधसः।
प्रतिमासं पौर्णमास्यामेभिर्नामसहस्रकैः॥५५॥

रात्रौ यश्चक्रराजस्थामर्चयेत् परदेवताम्।
स एव ललितारूपस्तद्रूपा ललिता स्वयम्।।५६।।

न तयोर्विद्यते भेदो भेदकृत् पापकृद् भवेत्।
महानवम्यां यो भक्तः श्रीदेवीं चक्रमध्यगाम्।।५७।।

अर्चयेन्नामसाहस्रैस्तस्य मुक्तिः करे स्थिता।
यस्तु नामसाहस्रेण शुक्रवारे समर्चयेत्।।५८।।

चक्रराजे महादेवीं तस्य पुण्यफलं श्रुणु।
सर्वान् कामानवाप्येह सर्वसौभाग्यसंयुतः।।५९।।

पुत्रपौत्रादिसंयुक्तो भुक्त्वा भोगान् यथोप्सितान्।
अन्ते श्रीललितादेव्याः सायुज्यमतिदुर्लभम्।।६०।।

प्रार्थनीयं शिवाद्यैश्च प्राप्नोत्येव न संशयः।
यः सहस्रं ब्राह्मणानामेभिर्नामसाहस्रकैः।।६१।।

समर्च्य भोजयेद् भक्त्या पायसापूपषड्रसैः।
तस्मै प्रीणाति ललिता स्वसाम्राज्यं प्रयच्छति।।६२।।

न तस्य दुर्लभं वस्तु त्रिषु लोकेषु विद्यते।
निष्कामः कीर्तयेद्यस्तु नामसाहस्रमुत्तमम्।।६३।।

ब्रह्मज्ञानमवाप्नोति येन मुच्येत बन्धनात्।
धनार्थी धनमाप्नोति यशोऽर्थी चाप्नुयाद्यशः।।६४।।

विद्यार्थी चाप्नुयाद् विद्यां नामसाहस्रकीर्तनात्।
नानेन सदृशं स्तोत्रं भोगमोक्षप्रदं मुने।।६५।।

कीर्तनीयमिदं तस्माद् भोगमोक्षार्थिभिर्नरैः।
चतुराश्रमनिष्ठैश्च कीर्तनीयमिदं सदा॥६६॥

स्वधर्मसमनुष्ठानवैकल्यपरिपूर्तये।
कलौ पापैकबहुले धर्मानुष्ठानवर्जिते॥६७॥

नामसंकीर्तनं मुक्त्वा नृणां नान्यत् परायणम्।
लौकिकाद् वचनान्मुख्यं विष्णुनामानुकीर्तनम्॥६८॥

विष्णुनाममसहस्राच्च शिवनामैकमुत्तमम्।
शिवनामसाहस्राच्च देव्या नामैकमुत्तमम्॥६९॥

देवीनामसहस्राणि कोटिशः सन्ति कुम्भज।
तेषु मुख्यं दशविधं नामसाहस्रमुच्यते॥७०॥

रहस्यनामसाहस्रमिदं शस्तं दशस्वपि।
तस्मात् संकीर्तयेन्नित्यं कलिदोषनिवृत्तये॥७१॥

मुख्यं श्रीमातृनामेति न जानन्ति विमोहिताः।
विष्णुनामपराः केचिच्छिवनामपराः परे॥७२॥

न कश्चिदपि लोकेषु ललितानामतत्परः।
येनान्यदेवतानाम कीर्तितं जन्मकोटिषु॥७३॥

तस्यैव भवति श्रद्धा श्रीदेवीनामकीर्तने।
चरमे जन्मनि यथा श्रीविद्योपासको भवेत्॥७४॥

नामसाहस्रपाठश्च तथा चरमजन्मनि।
यथैव विरला लोके श्रीविद्याचारवेदिनः॥७५॥

तथैव विरला गुह्यनामसाहस्रपाठकाः।
मन्त्रराजजपश्चैव चक्रराजार्चनं तथा॥७६॥

रहस्यनामपाठश्च नाल्पस्य तपसः फलम्।
अपठन्नामसाहस्रं प्रीणयेद् यो महेश्वरीम्॥७७॥

स चक्षुषा विना रूपं पश्येदेव विमूढधीः।
रहस्यनामसाहस्रं त्यक्त्वा यः सिद्धिकामुकः॥७८॥

स भोजनं विना नूनं क्षुन्निवृत्तिमभीप्सति।
यो भक्तो ललितादेव्याः स नित्यं कीर्तयेदिदम्॥७९॥

नान्यथा प्रीयते देवी कल्पकोटिशतैरपि।
तस्माद् रहस्यनामानि श्रीमातुः प्रयतः पठेत्॥८०॥

इति ते कथितं स्तोत्रं रहस्यं कुम्भसंभव।
नाविद्यावेदिने ब्रूयान्नाभक्ताय कदाचन॥८१॥

यथैव गोप्या श्रीविद्या तथा गोप्यमिदं मुने।
पशुतुल्येषु न ब्रूयाज्जनेषु स्तोत्रमुत्तमम्॥८२॥

यो ददति विमूढात्मा श्रीविद्यारहिताय च।
तस्मै कुप्यन्ति योगिन्यः सोऽनर्थः सुमहान् स्मृतः॥८३॥

रहस्यनामसाहस्रं तस्मात् संगोपयेदिदम्।
स्वतन्त्रेण मया नोक्तं तवापि कलशीसुत॥८४॥

ललिताप्रेरणेनैव मयोक्तं स्तोत्रमुत्तमम्।
कीर्तनीयमिदं भक्त्या कुम्भयोने निरन्तरम्॥८५॥

तेन तुष्टा महादेवी तवाभीष्टं प्रदास्यति।

श्रीसूत उवाच–

इत्युक्त्वा श्रीहयग्रीवो ध्यात्वा श्रीललिताम्बिकाम्॥८६॥

आनन्दमग्नहृदयः सद्यः पुलकितोऽभवत्॥८७॥

इति श्रीब्रह्माण्डपुराणे उत्तरखण्डे श्रीहयग्रीवागस्त्यसंवादे
श्रीललितानामसहस्रफलनिरूपणं नाम
तृतीयोऽध्यायः
ललितासहस्रनामस्तोत्रं संपूर्णम्

The Vagdevatas who were responsible for the composition of Lalita-sahasra-nama-stotra, are located in the inner enclosure of Sri-chaktra; the innemost circle represents the residence of Goddess Lalit.

ललितासहस्त्रनामवली

ॐ श्रीमात्रे नमः।

ॐ श्रीमहाराज्ञ्यै नमः।

ॐ श्रीमत्सिंहासनेश्वर्यै नमः।

ॐ चिदग्निकुण्डसम्भूतायै नमः।

ॐ देवकार्यसमुद्यतायै नमः।

ॐ उद्यद्भानुहस्त्राभायै नमः।

ॐ चतुर्बाहुसमन्वितायै नमः।

ॐ रागस्वरूपपाशाढ्यायै नमः।

ॐ क्रोधाकाराङ्कुशोज्ज्वलायै नमः।

ॐ मनोरूपेक्षुकोदण्डायै नमः ॥१०॥

ॐ पञ्चतन्मात्रसायकायै नमः।

ॐ निजारुणप्रभापूरमज्जद्ब्रह्माण्डमण्डलायै नमः।

ॐ चम्पकाशोकपुन्नागसौगन्धिकलसत्कचायै नमः।

ॐ कुरुविन्दमणिश्रेणीकनत्कोटीरमण्डितायै नमः।

ॐ अष्टमीचन्द्रविभ्राजदलिकस्थलशोभितायै नमः।

ॐ मुखचन्द्रकलङ्काभमृगनाभिविशेषकायै नमः।

ॐ वदनस्मेरमाङ्गल्यगृहतोरणचिल्लिकायै नमः।

ॐ वक्त्रलक्ष्मीपरीवाहचलन्मीनाभलोचनायै नमः।

ॐ नवचम्पकपुष्पाभनासादण्डविराजितायै नमः।

ॐ ताराकान्तितिरस्कारिनासाभरणभासुरायै नमः ॥२०॥
ॐ कदम्बमञ्जरीक्लृप्तकर्णपूरमनोहरायै नमः।
ॐ ताटकङ्कयुगलीभूततपनोडुपमण्डलायै नमः।
ॐ पद्मरागशिलादर्शपरिभाविकपोलभुवे नमः।
ॐ नवविद्रुमबिम्बश्रीन्यक्कारिदशनच्छायै नमः।
ॐ शुद्धविद्याङ्कुराकारद्विजपङ्क्तिद्वयोज्ज्वलायै नमः।
ॐ कर्पूरवीटिकामोदसमाकर्षद्दिगन्तरायै नमः।
ॐ निजसंल्लापमाधुर्यविनिर्भर्त्सितकच्छप्यै नमः।
ॐ मन्दस्मितप्रभापूरमज्जत्कामेश मानसायै नमः।
ॐ अनाकलितसादृश्यचिबुकश्रीविराजितायै नमः।
ॐ कामेशबद्धमाङ्गल्यसूत्रशोभितकन्धरायै नमः ॥३०॥
ॐ कनकाङ्गदकेयूरकमनीयभुजान्वितायै नमः।
ॐ रत्नग्रैवेयचिन्ताकल्लोलमुक्ताफलान्वितायै नमः।
ॐ कामेश्वरप्रेमरत्नमणिप्रतिपणस्तन्यै नमः।
ॐ नाभ्यालवालरोमालिलताफलकुचद्वय्यै नमः।
ॐ लक्ष्यरोमलताधारतासमुन्नेयमध्यमायै नमः।
ॐ स्तनभारदलन्मध्यपट्टबन्धवलित्रयायै नमः।
ॐ अरुणारुणकौसुम्भवस्त्रभास्वत्कटीतट्यै नमः।
ॐ रत्नकिङ्किणिकारम्यरशनादामभूपितायै नमः।
ॐ कामेशज्ञानसौभाग्यमार्दवोरुद्वयविराजितायै नमः ॥४०॥
ॐ इन्द्रगोपपरिक्षिप्तस्मरतूणाभजङ्घिकायै नमः।
ॐ गूढगुल्फायै नमः।
ॐ कूर्मपृष्ठजयिष्णुप्रपदान्वितायै नमः।
ॐ नखदीधितिसञ्छन्ननमज्जनतमोगुणायै नमः।

ॐ पदद्वयप्रभाजालपराकृतसरोरुहायै नमः।

ॐ सिञ्जानमणिमञ्जीरमण्डितश्रीपदाम्बुजायै नमः।

ॐ मरालीमन्दगमनायै नमः।

ॐ महालावण्यशेवधये नमः।

ॐ सर्वारुणायै नमः।

ॐ अनवद्याङ्ग्यै नमः ॥५०॥

ॐ सर्वाभरणभूषितायै नमः।

ॐ शिवकामेश्वराङ्कस्थायै नमः।

ॐ शिवायै नमः।

ॐ स्वाधीनवल्लभायै नमः।

ॐ सुमेरुश्रृङ्गमध्यस्थायै नमः।

ॐ श्रीमन्नगरनायिकायै नमः।

ॐ चिन्तामणिगृहान्तः स्थायै नमः।

ॐ पञ्चब्रह्मासनस्थितायै नमः।

ॐ महापद्माटवीसंस्थायै नमः।

ॐ कदम्बवनवासिन्यै नमः।

ॐ सुधासागरमध्यस्थायै नमः।

ॐ कामाक्ष्यै नमः।

ॐ कामदायिन्यै नमः।

ॐ देवर्षिगणसङ्घातस्तूयमानात्मवैभवायै नमः।

ॐ भण्डासुरवधोद्युक्तशक्तिसेनासमन्वितायै नमः।

ॐ सम्पत्करीसमारूढसिन्धुरव्रजसेवितायै नमः।

ॐ अश्वारूढाधिष्ठिताश्वकोटिभिरावृतायै नमः।

ॐ चक्रराजस्थारूढ सर्वायुधपरिष्कृतायै नमः।

ॐ गेयचक्ररथारूढमन्त्रिणीपरिसेवितायै नमः।

ॐ किरिचक्ररथारूढदण्डनाथपुरस्कृतायै नमः ।।७०।।

ॐ ज्वालामालिनिकाक्षिप्तवह्निप्रकारमध्यगायै नमः।

ॐ भण्डसैन्यवधोद्युक्तशक्तिविक्रमहर्षितायै नमः।

ॐ नित्यापराक्रमाटोपनिरीक्षणसमुत्सुकायै नमः।

ॐ भण्डपुत्रवधोद्युक्तबालाविक्रमनन्दितायै नमः।

ॐ मन्त्रिण्यम्बाविरचितविषङ्गवधतोषितायै नमः।

ॐ विशुक्रप्राणहरणवाराहीवीर्यनन्दितायै नमः।

ॐ कामेश्वरमुखालोककल्पितश्रीगणेश्वर्यै नमः।

ॐ महागणेशनिर्भिन्नविघ्नयन्त्रप्रहर्षितायै नमः(७८)

ॐ भण्डासुरेन्द्रनिर्मुक्तशस्त्रप्रत्यस्त्रवर्षिण्यै नमः।

ॐ कराङ्गुलिनखोत्पन्ननारायणदशाकृत्यै नमः(८०)

ॐ महापाशुपतास्त्राग्निनिर्दग्धासुरसैनिकायै नमः।

ॐ कामेश्वरास्त्रनिर्दग्धसभण्डासुरशून्यकायै नमः।

ॐ ब्रह्मोपेन्द्रमहेन्द्रादिदेवसंस्तुतवैभवायै नमः।

ॐ हरनेत्राग्निसन्दग्धकामसञ्जीवनौषध्यै नमः।

ॐ श्रीमद्वाग्भवकूटैकस्वरूपमुखपङ्कजायै नमः।

ॐ कण्ठाधः कटिपर्यन्तमध्यकूटस्वरूपिण्यै नमः।

ॐ शक्तिकूटैकतापन्नकट्यधोभागधारिण्यै नमः।

ॐ मूलमन्त्रात्मिकायै नमः।

ॐ मूलकूटत्रयकलेवरायै नमः।

ॐ कुलामृतैकरसिकायै नमः।।९०।।

ॐ कुलसंकेतपालिन्यै नमः।

ॐ कुलाङ्गनायै नमः।

ॐ कुलान्त:स्थायै नमः।

ॐ कौलिन्यै नमः।

ॐ कुलयोगिन्यै नमः।

ॐ अकुलायै नमः।

ॐ समयान्तस्थायै नमः।

ॐ समयाचारतत्परायै नमः।

ॐ मूलाधारैकनिलयायै नमः।

ॐ ब्रह्मग्रन्थिविभेदिन्यै नमः।।१००।।

ॐ मणिपूरान्तरुदितायै नमः।

ॐ विष्णुग्रन्थिविभेदिन्यै नमः।

ॐ आज्ञाचक्रान्तरालस्थायै नमः।

ॐ रुद्रग्रन्थिविभेदिन्यै नमः।

ॐ सहस्राराम्बुजारूढायै नमः।

ॐ तडिल्लतासमरुच्यै नमः।

ॐ षट्चक्रोपरिसंस्थितायै नमः।

ॐ महासक्त्यै नमः।

ॐ कुण्डलिन्यै नमः।।११०।।

ॐ बिसतन्तुतनीयस्यै नमः।

ॐ भवान्यै नमः।

ॐ भावनागम्यायै नमः।

ॐ भवारण्यकुठारिकायै नमः।

ॐ भद्रप्रियायै नमः।

ॐ भद्रमूर्तये नमः।

ॐ भक्तसौभाग्यदायिन्यै नमः।

ॐ भक्तिप्रियायै नमः।

ॐ भक्तिगम्यायै नमः।

ॐ भक्तिवश्यायै नमः।।१२०।।

ॐ भयापहायै नमः।

ॐ शाम्भव्यै नमः।

ॐ शारदाराध्यायै नमः।

ॐ शर्वाण्यै नमः।

ॐ शर्मदायिन्यै नमः।

ॐ शाङ्कर्यै नमः।

ॐ श्रीकर्यै नमः।

ॐ साध्व्यै नमः।

ॐ शरच्चन्द्रनिभाननायै नमः।

ॐ शातोदर्यै नमः।।१३०।।

ॐ शान्तिमत्यै नमः।

ॐ निराधारायै नमः।

ॐ निरञ्जनायै नमः।

ॐ निर्लेपायै नमः।

ॐ निर्मलायै नमः।

ॐ नित्यायै नमः।

ॐ निराकारायै नमः।

ॐ निराकुलायै नमः।

ॐ निर्गुणायै नमः।

ॐ निष्कलायै नमः।।१४०।।

ॐ शान्तायै नमः।

ॐ निष्कामायै नमः।

ॐ निरुपप्लवायै नमः।

ॐ नित्यमुक्तायै नमः।

ॐ निर्विकारायै नमः।

ॐ निष्प्रपञ्चायै नमः।

ॐ निराश्रयायै नमः।

ॐ नित्यशुद्धायै नमः।

ॐ नित्यबुद्धायै नमः।

ॐ निरवद्यायै नमः।।१५०।।

ॐ निरन्तरायै नमः।

ॐ निष्कारणायै नमः।

ॐ निष्कलङ्कायै नमः।

ॐ निरुपाधये नमः।

ॐ निरीश्वरायै नमः।

ॐ नीरागायै नमः।

ॐ रागमथन्यै नमः।

ॐ निर्मदायै नमः।

ॐ मदनाशिन्यै नमः।

ॐ निश्चिन्तायै नमः।।१६०।।

ॐ निरहङ्कारायै नमः।

ॐ निर्मोहायै नमः।

ॐ मोहनाशिन्यै नमः।

ॐ निर्ममायै नमः।

ॐ ममताहन्त्र्यै नमः।

ॐ निष्पापायै नमः।

ॐ पापनाशिन्यै नमः।

ॐ निष्क्रोधायै नमः।

ॐ क्रोधशमन्यै नमः।

ॐ निर्लोभायै नमः॥१७०॥

ॐ लोभनाशिन्यै नमः।

ॐ निःसंशयायै नमः।

ॐ संशययै नमः।

ॐ निर्भवायै नमः।

ॐ भवनाशिन्यै नमः।

ॐ निर्विकल्पायै नमः।

ॐ निराबाधायै नमः।

ॐ निर्भेदायै नमः।

ॐ भेदनाशिन्ये नमः।

ॐ निर्नाशायै नमः॥१८०॥

ॐ मृत्युमथन्यै नमः।

ॐ निष्क्रियायै नमः।

ॐ निष्परिग्रहायै नमः।

ॐ निस्तुलायै नमः।

ॐ नीलचिकुरायै नमः।

ॐ निरपायायै नमः।

ॐ दुर्लभायै नमः।

ॐ दुर्गमायै नमः।

ॐ दुर्गायै नमः॥१९०॥

ॐ दु:खहन्त्र्यै नमः।

ॐ सुखप्रदायै नमः।

ॐ दुष्टदूरायै नमः।

ॐ दुराचारशमन्यै नमः।

ॐ दोषवर्जितायै नमः।

ॐ सर्वज्ञायै नमः।

ॐ सान्द्रकरुणायै नमः।

ॐ समानाधिकवर्जितायै नमः।

ॐ सर्वशक्तिमय्यै नमः।

ॐ सर्वमङ्गलायै नमः।।२००।।

ॐ सद्गतिप्रदायै नमः।

ॐ सर्वेश्वर्यै नमः।

ॐ सर्वमय्यै नमः।

ॐ सर्वमन्त्रस्वरूपिण्यै नमः।

ॐ सर्वयन्त्रात्मिकायै नमः।

ॐ सर्वतन्त्ररूपायै नमः।

ॐ मनोन्मन्यै नमः।

ॐ माहेश्वर्यै नमः।

ॐ महादेव्यै नमः।

ॐ महालक्ष्म्यै नमः।।२१०।।

ॐ मृडप्रियायै नमः।

ॐ महारूपायै नमः।

ॐ महापूज्यायै नमः।

ॐ महापातकनाशिन्यै नमः।

ॐ महामायायै नमः।

ॐ महासत्त्वायै नमः।

ॐ महाशक्त्यै नमः।

ॐ महारत्यै नमः।

ॐ महाभोगायै नमः।

ॐ महैश्वर्यायै नमः।

ॐ महावीर्यायै नमः।

ॐ महाबलायै नमः।

ॐ महाबुद्ध्यै नमः।

ॐ महासिद्ध्यै नमः।

ॐ महायोगीश्वरेश्वर्यै नमः।

ॐ महातन्त्रायै नमः।

ॐ महामन्त्रायै नमः।

ॐ महायन्त्रायै नमः।

ॐ महासनायै नमः।

ॐ महायागक्रमाराध्यायै नमः।।२३०।।

ॐ महाभैरवपूजितायै नमः।

ॐ महेश्वरमहाकल्पमहाताण्डवसाक्षिण्यै नमः।

ॐ महाकामेशमहिष्यै नमः।

ॐ महात्रिपुरसुन्दर्यै नमः।

ॐ चतुःषष्ट्युपचाराढ्यायै नमः।

ॐ चतुःषष्टिकलामय्यै नमः।

ॐ महाचतुः षष्टिकोटियोगिनीगणसेवितायै नमः।

ॐ मनुविद्यायै नमः।

ॐ चन्द्रविद्यायै नमः।

ॐ चन्द्रमण्डलमध्यगायै नमः॥२४०॥

ॐ चारुरूपायै नमः।

ॐ चारुहासायै नमः।

ॐ चारुचन्द्रकलाधरायै नमः।

ॐ चराचरजगन्नाथायै नमः।

ॐ चक्रराजनिकेतनायै नमः।

ॐ पार्वत्यै नमः।

ॐ पद्मनयनायै नमः।

ॐ पद्मरागसमप्रभायै नमः।

ॐ पञ्चप्रेतासनासीनायै नमः।

ॐ पञ्चब्रह्मस्वरूपिण्यै नमः॥२५०॥

ॐ चिन्मय्यै नम.।

ॐ परमानन्दायै नमः।

ॐ विज्ञानघनरूपिण्यै नमः।

ॐ ध्यानध्यातृध्येयरूपायै नमः।

ॐ धर्माधर्मविवर्जितायै नमः।

ॐ विश्वरूपायै नमः।

ॐ जागरिण्यै नमः।

ॐ स्वपन्त्यै नमः।

ॐ तैजसात्मिकायै नमः।

ॐ सुप्तायै नमः॥२६०॥

ॐ प्राज्ञात्मिकायै नमः।

ॐ तुर्यायै नमः।

ॐ सर्वावस्थाविवर्जितायै नमः।

ॐ सृष्टिकर्त्र्यै नमः।

ॐ ब्रह्मरूपायै नभः।

ॐ गोप्त्र्यै नमः।

ॐ गोविन्दरूपिण्यै नमः।

ॐ संहारिण्यै नमः।

ॐ रुद्ररूपायै नमः।

ॐ तिरोधानकर्य्यै नमः॥२७०॥

ॐ ईश्वर्यै नमः।

ॐ सदाशिवायै नमः।

ॐ अनुग्रहदायै नमः।

ॐ पञ्चकृत्यपरायणायै नमः।

ॐ भानुमण्डलमध्यस्थायै नमः।

ॐ भैरव्यै नमः।

ॐ भगमालिन्यै नमः।

ॐ पद्मासनायै नमः।

ॐ भगवत्यै नमः।

ॐ पद्मनाभसहोदर्यै नमः॥२८०॥

ॐ उन्मेषनिमिषोत्पन्नविपन्नभुवनावल्यै नमः।

ॐ सहस्त्रशीर्षवदनायै नमः।

ॐ सहस्त्राक्ष्यै नमः।

ॐ सहस्त्रपादे नमः।

ॐ आब्रह्मकीटजनन्यै नमः।

ॐ वर्णाश्रमविधायिन्यै नमः।

ॐ निजाज्ञारूपनिगमायै नमः।

ॐ पुण्यापुण्यफलप्रदायै नमः।

ॐ श्रुतिसीमन्तदूरीकृतपादब्जधूलिकायै नमः।

ॐ सकलागमसन्दोहशुक्तिसम्पुटमौक्तिकायै नमः।।२९०।।

ॐ पुरुषार्थप्रदायै नमः।

ॐ पूर्णायै नमः।

ॐ भोगिन्यै नमः।

ॐ भुवनेश्वर्यै नमः।

ॐ अम्बिकायै नमः।

ॐ अनादिनिधनायै नमः।

ॐ हरिब्रह्मेन्द्रसेवितायै नमः।

ॐ नारायण्यै नमः।

ॐ नादरूपायै नमः।

ॐ नामरूपविवर्जितायै नमः।।३००।।

ॐ ह्रींकार्यै नमः।

ॐ ह्रींमत्यै नमः।

ॐ हृद्यायै नमः।

ॐ हेयोपादेयवर्जितायै नमः।

ॐ राजराजार्चितायै नमः।

ॐ राज्ञ्यै नमः।

ॐ रम्यायै नमः।

ॐ राजीवलोचनायै नमः।

ॐ रञ्जन्यै नमः।

ॐ रमण्यै नमः।।३१०।।

ॐ रस्यायै नमः।

ॐ रणत्किङ्किणिमेखलायै नमः।

ॐ रमायै नमः।

ॐ राकेन्दुवदनायै नमः।

ॐ रतिरूपायै नमः।

ॐ रतिप्रियायै नमः।

ॐ रक्षाकर्यै नमः।

ॐ राक्षसघ्न्यै नमः।

ॐ रामायै नमः।

ॐ रमणलम्पटायै नमः।।३२०।।

ॐ काम्यायै नमः।

ॐ कामकलारूपायै नमः।

ॐ कदम्बकुसुमप्रियायै नमः।

ॐ कल्याण्यै नमः।

ॐ जगतीकन्दायै नमः।

ॐ करुणारससागरायै नमः।

ॐ कलावत्यै नमः।

ॐ कलालापायै नमः।

ॐ कान्तायै नमः।

ॐ कादम्बरीप्रियायै नमः।।३३०।।

ॐ वरदायै नमः।

ॐ वामनयनायै नमः।

ॐ वारुणीमदविह्वलायै नमः।

ॐ विश्वाधिकायै नमः।

ॐ वेदवेद्यायै नमः।

ॐ विन्ध्याचलनिवासिन्यै नमः।

ॐ विधान्यै नमः।

ॐ वेदजनन्यै नमः।

ॐ विष्णुमायायै नमः।

ॐ विलसिन्यै नमः।।३४०।।

ॐ क्षेत्रस्वरूपायै नमः।

ॐ क्षेत्रेश्यै नमः।

ॐ क्षेत्रक्षेत्रज्ञपालिन्यै नमः।

ॐ क्षयवृद्धिविनिर्मुक्तायै नमः।

ॐ क्षेत्रपालसमर्चितायै नमः।

ॐ विजयायै नमः।

ॐ विमलायै नमः।

ॐ वन्द्यायै नमः।

ॐ वन्दारुजनवत्सलायै नमः।

ॐ वाग्वादिन्यै नमः।।३५०।।

ॐ वामकेश्यै नमः।

ॐ वह्निमण्डलवासिन्यै नमः।

ॐ भक्तिमत्कल्पलतिकायै नमः।

ॐ पशुपाशविमोचिन्यै नमः।

ॐ संहृताशेषपाषण्डायै नमः।

ॐ सदाचारप्रवर्तिकायै नमः।

ॐ तापत्रयाग्निसन्तप्तसमाह्लादन चन्द्रिकायै नमः।

ॐ तरुण्यै नमः।

ॐ तापसाराध्यायै नमः।

ॐ तनुमध्यायै नमः।।३६०।।

ॐ तमोपहायै नमः।

ॐ चित्यै नमः।

ॐ तत्पदलक्ष्यार्थायै नमः।

ॐ चिदेकरसरूपिण्यै नमः।

ॐ स्वात्मानन्दलवीभूतब्रह्माद्यानन्दसन्तत्यै नमः।

ॐ परायै नमः।

ॐ प्रत्यक्चितीरूपायै नमः।

ॐ पश्यन्त्यै नमः।

ॐ परदेवतायै नमः।

ॐ मध्यमायै नमः।

ॐ वैखरीरूपायै नमः।

ॐ भक्तमानसहंसिकायै नमः।

ॐ कामेश्वरप्राणनाड्यै नमः।

ॐ कृतज्ञायै नमः।

ॐ कामपूजितायै नमः।

ॐ श्रृङ्गाररससम्पूर्णायै नमः।

ॐ जयायै नमः।

ॐ जालन्धरस्थितायै नमः।

ॐ ओड्याणपीठनिलयायै नमः।

ॐ बिन्दुमण्डलवासिन्यै नमः।।३८०।।

ॐ रहोयागक्रमाराध्यायै नमः।

ॐ रहस्तर्पणतर्पितायै नमः।

ॐ सद्यः प्रसादिन्यै नमः।

ॐ विश्वसाक्षिण्यै नमः।

ॐ साक्षिवर्जितायै नमः।

ॐ षडङ्गदेवतायुक्तायै नमः।

ॐ षाड्गुण्यपरिपूरितायै नमः।

ॐ नित्यक्लिन्नायै नमः।

ॐ निरुपमायै नमः।

ॐ निर्वाणसुखदायिन्यै नमः।।३९०।।

ॐ नित्याषोडशिकारूपायै नमः।

ॐ श्रीकण्ठार्धशरीरिण्यै नमः।

ॐ प्रभावत्यै नमः।

ॐ प्रभारूपायै नमः।

ॐ प्रसिद्धायै नमः।

ॐ परमेश्वर्यै नमः।

ॐ मूलप्रकृत्यै नमः।

ॐ अव्यक्तायै नमः।

ॐ व्यक्ताव्यक्तस्वरूपिण्यै नमः।

ॐ व्यापिन्यै नमः।।४००।।

ॐ विविधाकारायै नमः।

ॐ विद्याविद्यास्वरूपिण्यै नमः।

ॐ महाकामेशनयनकुमुदाह्लादकौमुद्यै नमः।

ॐ भक्तहार्दतमोभेदभानुमद्भानुसन्तत्यै नमः।

ॐ शिवदूत्यै नमः।

ॐ शिवाराध्यायै नमः।

ॐ शिवमूर्त्यै नमः।

ॐ शिवङ्कर्यै नमः।

ॐ शिवप्रियायै नमः।

ॐ शिवपरायै नमः।।४१०।।

ॐ शिष्टेष्टायै नमः।

ॐ शिष्टपूजितायै नमः।

ॐ अप्रमेयायै नमः।

ॐ स्वप्रकाशायै नमः।

ॐ मनोवाचामगोचरायै नमः।

ॐ चिच्छक्त्यै नमः।

ॐ चेतनारूपायै नमः।

ॐ जडशक्त्यै नमः।

ॐ जडात्मिकायै नमः।

ॐ गायत्र्यै नमः।।४२०।।

ॐ व्याहृत्यै नमः।

ॐ सन्ध्यायै नमः।

ॐ द्विजवृन्दनिषेवितायै नमः।

ॐ तत्त्वासनायै नमः।

ॐ तस्यै नमः।

ॐ तुभ्यं नमः।

ॐ अय्यै नमः।

ॐ पञ्चकोशान्तरस्थितायै नमः।

ॐ निःसीममहिम्ने नमः।

ॐ नित्ययौवनायै नमः।।४३०।।

ॐ मदशालिन्यै नमः।

ॐ मदाघूर्णितरक्ताक्ष्यै नमः।

ॐ मदपाटलगण्डभुवे नमः।

ॐ चन्दनद्रवदिग्धाङ्ग्यै नमः।

ॐ चाम्पेयकुसुमप्रियायै नमः।

ॐ कुशलायै नमः।

ॐ कोमलाकारायै नमः।

ॐ कुरुकुल्लायै नमः।

ॐ कुलेश्वर्यै नमः।

ॐ कुलकुण्डालयायै नमः।।४४०।।

ॐ कौलमार्गतत्परसेवितायै नमः।

ॐ कुमारगणनाथाम्बायै नमः।

ॐ तुष्टयै नमः।

ॐ पुष्ट्यै नमः।

ॐ मत्यै नमः।

ॐ धृत्यै नमः।

ॐ शान्त्यै नमः।

ॐ स्वस्तिमत्यै नमः।

ॐ कान्त्यै नमः।

ॐ नन्दिन्यै नमः।।४५०।।

ॐ विघ्ननाशिन्यै नमः।

ॐ तेजोवत्यै नमः।

ॐ त्रिनयनायै नमः।

ॐ लोलाक्षीकामरूपिण्यै नमः।

ॐ मालिन्यै नमः।

ॐ हंसिन्यै नमः।

ॐ मात्रे नमः।

ॐ मलयाचलवसिन्यै नमः।

ॐ सुमुख्यै नमः।

ॐ नलिन्यै नमः।।४६०।।

ॐ सुभ्रवे नमः।

ॐ शोभनायै नमः।

ॐ सुरनायिकायै नमः।

ॐ कालकण्ठ्यै नमः।

ॐ कान्तिमत्यै नमः।

ॐ क्षोभिण्यै नमः।

ॐ सूक्ष्मरूपिण्यै नमः।

ॐ वज्रेश्वर्यै नमः।

ॐ वामदेव्यै नमः।

ॐ वयोऽवस्थाविवर्जितायै नमः।।४७०।।

ॐ सिद्धेश्वर्यै नमः।

ॐ सिद्धविद्यायै नमः।

ॐ सिद्धमात्रे नमः।

ॐ यशस्विन्यै नगः।

ॐ विशुद्धिचक्रनिलयायै नमः।

ॐ आरक्तवर्णायै नमः।

ॐ त्रिलोचनायै नमः।

ॐ खट्वाङ्गादिप्रहरणायै नमः।

ॐ वदनैकसमन्वितायै नमः।

ॐ पायसान्नप्रियायै नमः।।४८०।।

ॐ त्वक्स्थायै नमः।

ॐ पशुलोकभयङ्कर्यै नमः।

ॐ अमृतादिमहाशक्तिसंवृतायै नमः।

ॐ डाकिनीश्वर्यै नमः।

ॐ अनाहताब्जनिलयायै नमः।

ॐ श्यामाभायै नमः।

ॐ वदनद्वयायै नमः।

ॐ द्रंष्ट्रोज्ज्वलायै नमः।

ॐ अक्षमालादिधरायै नमः।

ॐ रुधिरसंस्थितायै नमः।।४९०।।

ॐ कालरात्र्यादिशक्त्यौघवृतायै नमः।

ॐ स्निग्धौदनप्रियायै नमः।

ॐ महावीरेन्द्रवरदायै नमः।

ॐ राकिण्यम्बास्वरूपिण्यै नमः।

ॐ मणिपूराब्जनिलयायै नमः।

ॐ वदनत्रयसंयुतायै नमः।

ॐ वज्रादिकायुधोपेतायै नमः।

ॐ डामर्यादिभिरावृतायै नमः।

ॐ रक्तवर्णायै नमः।

ॐ मांसनिष्ठायै नमः।।५००।।

ॐ गुडान्नप्रीतमानसायै नमः।

ॐ समस्तभक्तसुखदायै नमः।

ॐ लाकिन्यम्बास्वरूपिण्यै नमः।

ॐ स्वाधिष्ठानाम्बुजगतायै नमः।

ॐ चतुर्वक्त्रमनोहरायै नमः।

ॐ शूलाद्यायुधसम्पन्नायै नमः।

ॐ पीतवर्णायै नमः।

ॐ अतिगर्वितायै नमः।

ॐ मेदोनिष्ठायै नमः।

ॐ मधुप्रीतायै नमः।।५१०।।

ॐ बन्दिन्यादिसमन्वितायै नमः।

ॐ दध्यन्नासक्तहृदयायै नमः।

ॐ काकिनीरूपधारिण्यै नमः।

ॐ मूलाधाराम्बुजारूढायै नमः।

ॐ पञ्चवक्त्रायै नमः।

ॐ अस्थिसंस्थितायै नमः।

ॐ अङ्कुशादिप्रहरणायै नमः।

ॐ वरदादिनिषेवितायै नमः।

ॐ मुद्गौदनासक्तचित्तायै नमः।

ॐ साकिन्यम्बास्वरूपिण्यै नमः।।५२०।।

ॐ आज्ञाचक्राब्जनिलयायै नमः।

ॐ शुक्लवर्णायै नमः।

ॐ षडाननायै नमः।

ॐ मज्जासंस्थायै नमः।

ॐ हंसवती मुख्यशक्तिसमन्वितायै नमः।

ॐ हरिद्रान्नैकरसिकायै नमः।

ॐ हाकिनीरूपधारिण्यै नमः।

ॐ सहस्रदलपद्मस्थायै नमः।

ॐ सर्ववर्णोपशोभितायै नमः।

ॐ सर्वायुधधरायै नमः।।५३०।।

ॐ शुक्लसंस्थितायै नमः।

ॐ सर्वतोमुख्यै नमः।

ॐ सर्वौदनप्रीतचित्तायै नमः।

ॐ याकिन्यम्बास्वरूपिण्यै नमः।

ॐ स्वाहायै नमः।

ॐ स्वधायै नमः।

ॐ मत्यै नमः।

ॐ मेधायै नमः।

ॐ श्रुत्यै नमः।

ॐ स्मृत्यै नमः।।५४०।।

ॐ अनुत्तमायै नमः।

ॐ पुण्यकीर्त्यै नमः।

ॐ पुण्यलभ्यायै नमः।

ॐ पुण्यश्रवणकीर्तनायै नमः।

ॐ पुलोमजार्चितायै नमः।

ॐ बन्धमोचिन्यै नमः।

ॐ बन्धुरालकायै नमः।

ॐ विमर्शरूपिण्यै नमः।

ॐ विद्यायै नमः।

ॐ वियदादिजगत्प्रसवे नमः।।५५०।।

ॐ सर्वव्याधिप्रशमन्यै नमः।

ॐ सर्वमृत्युनिवारिण्यै नमः।

ॐ अग्रगण्यायै नमः।

ॐ अचिन्त्यरूपायै नमः।

ॐ कलिकल्मषनाशिन्यै नमः।

ॐ कात्यायन्यै नमः।

ॐ कालहन्त्र्यै नमः।

ॐ कमलाक्षनिषेवितायै नमः।

ॐ ताम्बूलपूरितमुख्यै नमः।

ॐ दाडिमीकुसुमप्रभायै नमः॥५६०॥

ॐ मृगाक्ष्यै नमः।

ॐ मोहिन्यै नमः।

ॐ मुख्यायै नमः।

ॐ मृडान्यै नमः।

ॐ मित्ररूपिण्यै नमः।

ॐ नित्यतृप्तायै नमः।

ॐ भक्तनिधये नमः।

ॐ नियन्त्र्यै नमः।

ॐ निखिलेश्वर्यै नमः।

ॐ मैत्र्यादिवासनालभ्यायै नमः॥५७०॥

ॐ महाप्रलयसाक्षिण्यै नमः।

ॐ पराशक्त्यै नमः।

ॐ परानिष्ठायै नमः।

ॐ प्रज्ञानघनरूपिण्यै नमः।

ॐ माध्वीपानालसायै नमः।

ॐ मत्तायै नमः।

ॐ मातृकावर्णरूपिण्यै नमः।

ॐ महाकैलासनिलयायै नमः।

ॐ मृणालमृदुदोर्लतायै नमः।

ॐ महनीयायै नमः।।५८०।।

ॐ दयामूर्त्यै नमः।

ॐ महासाम्राज्यशालिन्यै नमः।

ॐ आत्मविद्यायै नमः।

ॐ महविद्यायै नमः।

ॐ श्रीविद्यायै नमः।

ॐ कामसेवितायै नगः।

ॐ श्रीषोडशाक्षरीविद्यायै नमः।

ॐ त्रिकूटायै नमः।

ॐ कामकोटिकायै नमः।

ॐ कटाक्षकिङ्करीभूतकमलाकोटिसेवितायै नमः।।५९०।।

ॐ शिरःस्थितायै नमः।

ॐ चन्द्रनिभायै नमः।

ॐ भालस्थायै नमः।

ॐ इन्द्रधनुष्प्रभायै नमः।

ॐ हृदयस्थायै नमः।

ॐ रविप्रख्यायै नमः।

ॐ त्रिकोणान्तरदीपिकायै नमः।

ॐ दाक्षायण्यै नमः।

ॐ दैत्यहन्त्र्यै नमः।

ॐ दक्षयज्ञविनाशिन्यै नमः।।६००।।

ॐ दरान्दोलितदीर्घाक्ष्यै नमः।

ॐ दरहासोज्ज्वलन्मुख्यै नमः।

ॐ गुरुमूर्त्यै नमः।

ॐ गुणनिधये नमः।

ॐ गोमात्रे नमः।

ॐ गुहजन्मभुवे नमः।

ॐ देवेश्यै नमः।

ॐ दण्डनीतिस्थायै नमः।

ॐ दहराकाशरूपिण्यै नमः।

ॐ प्रतिपन्मुख्यराकान्ततिथिमण्डलपूजितायै नमः।।६१०।।

ॐ कलात्मिकायै नमः।

ॐ कलानाथायै नमः।

ॐ काव्यालापविनोदिन्यै नमः।

ॐ सचामररमावाणीसव्यदक्षिणसेवितायै नमः।

ॐ आदिशक्त्यै नमः।

ॐ अमेयायै नमः।

ॐ आत्मने नमः।

ॐ परमायै नमः।

ॐ पावनाकृतये नमः।

ॐ अनेककोटिब्रह्माण्डजनन्यै नमः।।६२०।।

ॐ दिव्यविग्रहायै नमः।

ॐ क्लींकार्यै नमः।

ॐ केवलायै नमः।

ॐ गुह्यायै नमः।

ॐ कैवल्यपददायिन्यै नमः।

ॐ त्रिपुरायै नमः।

ॐ त्रिजगद्वन्द्यायै नमः।

ॐ त्रिमूर्त्यै नमः।

ॐ त्रिदशेश्वर्यै नमः।

ॐ त्र्यक्षर्यै नमः।

ॐ दिव्यगन्धाढ्यायै नमः।

ॐ सिन्दूरतिलकाञ्चितायै नमः।

ॐ उमायै नमः।

ॐ शैलेन्द्रतनयायै नमः।

ॐ गौर्यै नमः।

ॐ गन्धर्वसेवितायै नमः।

ॐ विश्वगर्भायै नमः।

ॐ स्वर्णगर्भायै नमः।

ॐ अवरदायै नमः।

ॐ वागधीश्वर्यै नमः।।६४०।।

ॐ ध्यानगम्यायै नमः।

ॐ अपरिच्छेद्यायै नमः।

ॐ ज्ञानदायै नमः।

ॐ ज्ञानविग्रहायै नमः।

ॐ सर्ववेदान्तसंवेद्यायै नमः।

ॐ सत्यानन्दस्वरूपिण्यै नमः।

ॐ लोपामुद्रार्चितायै नमः।

ॐ लीलाक्लृप्तब्रह्माण्डमण्डलायै नमः।

ॐ अदृश्यायै नमः।

ॐ दृश्यरहितायै नमः।।६५०।।

ॐ विज्ञात्र्यै नमः।

ॐ वेद्यवर्जितायै नमः।

ॐ योगिन्यै नमः।

ॐ योगदायै नमः।

ॐ योग्यायै नमः।

ॐ योगानन्दायै नमः।

ॐ युगन्धरायै नमः।

ॐ इच्छाशक्तिज्ञानशक्तिक्रियाशक्ति स्वरूपिण्यै नमः।

ॐ सर्वाधारायै नमः।

ॐ सुप्रतिष्ठायै नमः।।६६०।।

ॐ सदसद्रूपधारिण्यै नमः।

ॐ अष्टमूर्त्यै नमः।

ॐ अजाजैत्र्यै नमः।

ॐ लोकयात्राविधायिन्यै नमः।

ॐ एकाकिन्यै नमः।

ॐ भूमरूपायै नमः।

ॐ निर्द्वैतायै नगः।

ॐ द्वैतवर्जितायै नमः।

ॐ अन्नदायै नमः।

ॐ वसुदायै नमः।

ॐ वृद्धायै नमः।

ॐ ब्रह्मात्मैक्यस्वरूपिण्यै नमः।

ॐ बृहत्यै नमः।

ॐ ब्राह्मण्यै नमः।

ॐ ब्राह्म्यै नमः।

ॐ ब्रह्मानन्दायै नमः।

ॐ बलिप्रियायै नमः।

ॐ भाषारूपायै नमः।

ॐ बृहत्सेनायै नमः।

ॐ भावाभावविवर्जितायै नमः॥६८०॥

ॐ सुखाराध्यायै नमः।

ॐ शुभकार्यै नमः।

ॐ शोभनासुलभागत्यै नमः।

ॐ राजराजेश्वर्यै नमः।

ॐ राज्यदायिन्यै नमः।

ॐ राज्यवल्लभायै नमः।

ॐ राजत्कृपायै नमः।

ॐ राजपीठनिवेशितनिजाश्रितायै नमः।

ॐ राज्यलक्ष्म्यै नमः।

ॐ कोशनाथायै नमः॥६९०॥

ॐ चतुरङ्गबलेश्वर्यै नमः।

ॐ साम्राज्यदायिन्यै नमः।

ॐ सत्यसन्धायै नमः।

ॐ सागरमेखलायै नमः।

ॐ दीक्षितायै नमः।

ॐ दैत्यशमन्यै नमः।

ॐ सर्वलोकवशङ्कर्यै नमः।

ॐ सर्वार्थदात्र्यै नमः।

ॐ सावित्र्यै नमः।

ॐ सच्चिदानन्दरूपिण्यै नमः।।(७००)।।

ॐ देशकालापरिच्छिन्नायै नमः।

ॐ सर्वगायै नमः।

ॐ सर्वमोहिन्यै नमः।

ॐ सरस्वत्यै नमः।

ॐ शास्त्रमय्यै नमः।

ॐ गुहाम्बायै नमः।

ॐ गुह्यरूपिण्यै नमः।

ॐ सर्वोपाधिविनिर्मुक्तायै नमः।

ॐ सदाशिवपतिव्रतायै नमः।

ॐ सम्प्रदायेश्वर्यै नमः।।७१०।।

ॐ साधुने नमः।

ॐ यै नमः।

ॐ गुरुमण्डलरूपिण्यै नमः।

ॐ कुलोत्तीर्णायै नमः।

ॐ भगाराध्यायै नमः।

ॐ मायायै नमः।

ॐ मधुमत्यै नमः।

ॐ मह्यै नमः।

ॐ गणाम्बायै नमः।

ॐ गुह्यकाराध्यायै नमः।।७२०।।

ॐ कोमलाङ्ग्यै नमः।

ॐ गुरुप्रियायै नमः।

ॐ स्वतन्त्रायै नमः।

ॐ सर्वतन्त्रेश्यै नमः।

ॐ दक्षिणामूर्तिरूपिण्यै नमः।

ॐ सनकादिसमाराध्यायै नमः।

ॐ शिवज्ञानप्रदायिन्यै नमः।

ॐ चित्कलायै नमः।

ॐ आनन्दकलिकायै नमः।

ॐ प्रेमरूपायै नमः।।७३०।।

ॐ प्रियङ्कर्यै नमः।

ॐ नामपारायणप्रीतायै नमः।

ॐ नन्दिविद्यायै नमः।

ॐ नटेश्वर्यै नमः।

ॐ मिथ्याजगदधिष्ठानायै नमः।

ॐ मुक्तिदायै नमः।

ॐ मुक्तिरूपिण्यै नमः।

ॐ लास्यप्रियायै नमः।

ॐ लयकर्यै नमः।

ॐ लज्जायै नमः।।७४०।।

ॐ रम्भादिवन्दितायै नमः।

ॐ भवदावसुधावृष्ट्यै नमः।

ॐ पापारण्यदवानलायै नमः।

ॐ दौर्भाग्यतूलवातूलायै नमः।

ॐ जराध्वान्तरविप्रभायै नमः।

ॐ भाग्याब्धिचन्द्रिकायै नमः।

ॐ भक्तचित्तकेकिघनाघनायै नमः।

ॐ रोगपर्वतदम्भोलये नमः।

ॐ मत्युदारुकुठारिकायै नमः।

ॐ महेश्वर्यै नमः।।७५०।।

ॐ महाकाल्यै नमः।

ॐ महाग्रासायै नमः।

ॐ महाशनायै नमः।

ॐ अपर्णायै नमः।

ॐ चण्डिकायै नमः।

ॐ चण्डमुण्डासुरनिषूदिन्यै नमः।

ॐ क्षराक्षरात्मिकार्य नमः।

ॐ सर्वलोकेश्यै नमः।

ॐ विश्वधारिण्यै नमः।

ॐ त्रिवर्गदात्र्यै नमः।।७६०।।

ॐ सुभगायै नमः।

ॐ त्र्यम्बकायै नमः।

ॐ त्रिगुणात्मिकायै नमः।

ॐ स्वर्गापवर्गदायै नमः।

ॐ शुद्धायै नमः।

ॐ जपापुष्पनिभाकृतये नमः।

ॐ ओजोवत्यै नमः।

ॐ द्युतिधरायै नमः।

ॐ यज्ञरूपायै नमः।

ॐ प्रियव्रतायै नमः।।७७०।।

ॐ दुराराध्यायै नमः।

ॐ दुराधर्षायै नमः।

ॐ पाटलीकुसुमप्रियायै नमः।

ॐ महत्यै नमः।

ॐ मेरुनिलयायै नमः।

ॐ मन्दारकुसुमप्रियायै नमः।

ॐ वीराराध्यायै नमः।

ॐ विराड्रूपायै नमः।

ॐ विरजायै नमः।

ॐ विश्वतोमुख्यै नमः।।७८०।।

ॐ प्रत्यग्रूपायै नमः।

ॐ पराकाशायै नमः।

ॐ प्राणदायै नमः।

ॐ प्राणरूपिण्यै नमः।

ॐ मार्तण्डभैरवाराध्यायै नमः।

ॐ मन्त्रिणीन्यस्तराज्यधुरे नमः।

ॐ त्रिपुरेश्यै नमः।

ॐ जयत्सेनायै नमः।

ॐ निस्त्रैगुण्यायै नमः।

ॐ परापरायै नमः।।७९०।।

ॐ सत्यज्ञानानन्दरूपायै नमः।

ॐ सामरस्यपरायणायै नमः।

ॐ कपर्दिन्यै नमः।

ॐ कलामालायै नमः।

ॐ कामदुधे नमः।

ॐ कामरूपिण्यै नमः।

ॐ कलानिधये नमः।

ॐ काव्यकलायै नमः।

ॐ रसज्ञायै नमः।

ॐ रसशेवधये नमः।।८००।।

ॐ पुष्टायै नमः।

ॐ पुरातनायै नमः।

ॐ पूज्यायै नमः।

ॐ पुष्करायै नमः।

ॐ पुष्करेक्षणायै नमः।

ॐ परस्मै ज्योतिषे नमः।

ॐ परस्मै ज्योतिषे नमः।

ॐ परस्मै धाम्ने नमः।

ॐ परमाणवे नमः।

ॐ परात्परायै नमः।

ॐ पाशहस्तायै नमः।।८१०।।

ॐ पाशहन्त्र्यै नमः।

ॐ परमन्त्रविभेदिन्यै नमः।

ॐ मूर्तायै नमः।

ॐ अमूर्तायै नमः।

ॐ नित्यतृप्तायै नमः।

ॐ मुनिमानसहंसिकायै नमः।

ॐ सत्यव्रतायै नमः।

ॐ सत्यरूपायै नमः।

ॐ सर्वान्तर्यामिन्यै नमः।

ॐ सत्यै नमः।।८२०।।

ॐ ब्रह्माण्यै नमः।

ॐ ब्रह्मणे नमः।

ॐ जनन्यै नमः।

ॐ बहुरूपायै नमः।

ॐ बुधार्चितायै नमः।

ॐ प्रसवित्र्यै नमः।

ॐ प्रचण्डायै नमः।

ॐ आज्ञायै नमः।

ॐ प्रतिष्ठायै नमः।

ॐ प्रकटाकृतये नमः।।८३०।।

ॐ प्राणेश्वर्यै नमः।

ॐ प्राणदात्र्यै नमः।

ॐ पञ्चाशत्पीठरूपिण्यै नमः।

ॐ विशृङ्खलायै नमः।

ॐ विविक्तस्थायै नमः।

ॐ वीरमात्रे नमः।

ॐ वियत्प्रसवे नमः।

ॐ मुकुन्दायै नमः।

ॐ मुक्तिनिलयायै नमः।

ॐ मूलविग्रहरूपिण्यै नमः।।८४०।।

ॐ भावज्ञायै नमः।

ॐ भवरोगघ्न्यै नमः।

ॐ भवचक्रप्रवर्तिन्यै नमः।

ॐ छन्दःसारायै नमः।

ॐ शास्त्रसारायै नमः।

ॐ मन्त्रसारायै नमः।

ॐ तलोदर्यै नमः।

ॐ उदारकीर्तये नमः।

ॐ उद्दामवैभवायै नमः।

ॐ वर्णरूपिण्यै नमः।।(८५०)।।

ॐ जन्ममृत्युजरातप्तजनविश्रान्तिदायिन्यै नमः।

ॐ सर्वोपनिषदुद्घुष्टायै नमः।

ॐ शान्त्यतीतकलात्मिकायै नमः।

ॐ गम्भीरायै नमः।

ॐ गगनान्तःस्थायै नमः।

ॐ गर्वितायै नमः।

ॐ गानलोलुपायै नमः।

ॐ कल्पनारहितायै नमः।

ॐ काष्ठायै नमः।

ॐ कान्तायै नमः।।८६०।।

ॐ कान्तार्धविग्रहायै नमः।

ॐ कार्यकारणनिर्मुक्तायै नमः।

ॐ कामकेलितरङ्गितायै नमः।

ॐ कनत्कनकताटङ्कायै नमः।

ॐ लीलाविग्रहधारिण्यै नमः।

ॐ अजायै नमः।

ॐ क्षयविनिर्मुक्तायै नमः।

ॐ मुग्धायै नमः।

ॐ क्षिप्रप्रसादिन्यै नमः।

ॐ अन्तर्मुखसमाराध्यायै नमः।।८७०।।

ॐ बहिर्मुखसुदुर्लभायै नमः।

ॐ त्रय्यै नमः।

ॐ त्रिवर्गनिलयायै नमः।

ॐ त्रिस्थायै नमः।

ॐ त्रिपुरमालिन्यै नमः।

ॐ निरामयायै नमः।

ॐ निरालम्बायै नमः।

ॐ स्वात्मारामायै नमः।

ॐ सुधास्त्रुत्यै नमः।

ॐ संसारपङ्कनिर्मग्नसमुद्धरण पण्डितायै नमः।।८८०।।

ॐ यज्ञप्रियायै नमः।

ॐ यज्ञकर्त्र्यै नमः।

ॐ यजमानस्वरूपिण्यै नमः।

ॐ धर्माधारायै नमः।

ॐ धनाध्यक्षायै नमः।

ॐ धनधान्यविवर्धिन्यै नमः।

ॐ विप्रप्रियायै नमः।

ॐ विप्ररूपायै नमः।

ॐ विश्वभ्रमणकारिण्यै नमः।

ॐ विश्वग्रासायै नमः॥८९०॥

ॐ विद्रुमाभायै नमः।

ॐ वैष्णव्यै नमः।

ॐ विष्णुरूपिण्यै नमः।

ॐ अयोनये नमः।

ॐ योनिनिलयायै नमः।

ॐ कूटस्थायै नमः।

ॐ कुलरूपिण्यै नमः।

ॐ वीरगोष्ठीप्रियायै नमः।

ॐ वीरायै नमः।

ॐ नैष्कर्म्यायै नमः॥९००॥

ॐ नादरूपिण्यै नमः।

ॐ विज्ञानकलनायै नमः।

ॐ कल्यायै नमः।

ॐ विदग्धायै नमः।

ॐ बैन्दवासनायै नमः।

ॐ तत्त्वाधिकायै नमः।

ॐ तत्त्वमय्यै नमः।

ॐ तत्त्वमर्थस्वरूपिण्यै नमः।

ॐ सामगानप्रियायै नमः।

ॐ सौम्यायै नमः॥९१०॥

ॐ सदाशिवकुटुम्बिन्यै नमः।

ॐ सव्यापसव्यमार्गस्थायै नमः।

ॐ सर्वापद्विनिवारिण्यै नमः।

ॐ स्वस्थायै नमः।

ॐ स्वभावमधुरायै नमः।

ॐ धीरायै नमः।

ॐ धीरसमर्चितायै नमः।

ॐ चैतन्यार्घ्यासमाराध्यायै नमः।

ॐ चैतन्यकुसुमप्रियायै नमः।

ॐ सदोदितायै नमः।।९२०।।

ॐ सदा तुष्टायै नमः।

ॐ तरुणादित्यपाटलायै नमः।

ॐ दक्षिणादक्षिणाराध्यायै नमः।

ॐ दरस्मेरमुखाम्बुजायै नमः।

ॐ कौलिनीकेवलायै नमः।

ॐ अनर्घ्यकैवल्यपददायिन्यै नम

ॐ स्तोत्रप्रियायै नमः।

ॐ स्तुतिमत्यै नमः।

ॐ श्रुतिसंस्तुतवैभावयै नमः।

ॐ मनस्विन्यै नमः।।९३०।।

ॐ मानवत्यै नमः।

ॐ महेश्यै नमः।

ॐ मङ्गलाकृत्यै नमः।

ॐ विश्वमात्रे नमः।

ॐ जगद्धात्र्यै नमः।

ॐ विशालाक्ष्यै नमः।

ॐ विरागिण्यै नमः।

ॐ प्रगल्भायै नमः।

ॐ परमोदारायै नमः।

ॐ परामोदायै नमः।।९४०।।

ॐ मनोमय्यै नमः।

ॐ व्योमकेश्यै नमः।

ॐ विमानस्थायै नमः।

ॐ वज्रिण्यै नमः।

ॐ वामकेश्वर्यै नमः।

ॐ पञ्चयज्ञप्रियायै नमः।

ॐ पञ्चप्रेतमञ्चाधिशायिन्यै नमः।

ॐ पञ्चम्यै नमः।

ॐ पञ्चभूतेश्यै नमः।

ॐ पञ्चसख्योपचारिण्यै नमः।।९५०।।

ॐ शाश्वत्यै नमः।

ॐ शाश्वतैश्वर्यायै नमः।

ॐ शर्मदायै नम.।

ॐ शम्भुमोहिन्यै नमः।

ॐ धरायै नमः।

ॐ धरसुतायै नमः।

ॐ धन्यायै नमः।

ॐ धर्मिण्यै नमः।

ॐ धर्मवर्धिन्यै नमः।

ॐ लोकातीतायै नमः॥९६०॥

ॐ गुणातीतायै नमः।

ॐ सर्वातीतायै नमः।

ॐ शमात्मिकायै नमः।

ॐ बन्धूककुसुमप्रख्यायै नमः।

ॐ बालायै नमः।

ॐ लीलाविनोदिन्यै नमः।

ॐ सुमङ्गल्यै नमः।

ॐ सुखकर्यै नमः।

ॐ सुवेषाढ्यायै नमः।

ॐ सुवासिन्यै नमः॥९७०॥

ॐ सुवासिन्यर्चनप्रीतायै नमः।

ॐ शोभानायै नमः।

ॐ शुद्धमानसायै नमः।

ॐ बिन्दुतर्पणसन्तुष्टायै नमः।

ॐ पूर्वजायै नमः।

ॐ त्रिपुराम्बिकायै नमः।

ॐ दशमुद्रासमाराध्यायै नमः।

ॐ त्रिपुराश्रीवशङ्कर्यै नमः।

ॐ ज्ञानमुद्रायै नमः।

ॐ ज्ञानगम्यायै नमः॥९८०॥

ॐ ज्ञानज्ञेयस्वरूपिण्यै नमः।

ॐ योनिमुद्रायै नमः।

ॐ त्रिखण्डेश्यै नमः।

ॐ त्रिगुणायै नमः।

ॐ अम्बायै नमः।

ॐ त्रिकोणगायै नमः।

ॐ अनघायै नमः।

ॐ अद्भूतचारित्रायै नमः।

ॐ वाञ्छितार्थप्रदायिन्यै नमः।

ॐ अभ्यासातिशयज्ञातायै नमः।।९९०।।

ॐ षडध्वातीतरूपिण्यै नमः।

ॐ अव्याजकरुणामूर्तये नमः।

ॐ अज्ञानध्वान्तदीपिकायै नमः।

ॐ आबालगोपविदितायै नमः।

ॐ सर्वानुल्लङ्घ्यशासनायै नमः।

ॐ श्रीचक्रराजनिलयायै नमः।

ॐ श्रीमत्त्रिपुरसुन्दर्यै नमः।

ॐ श्रीशिवायै नमः।

ॐ शिवशक्त्यैक्यरूपिण्यै नमः।

ॐ ऐं ह्रीं श्रीं ललिताम्बिकायै नमः।।१०००।।

1. OM śrī-mātā.
The holy mother.
(The expression 'Śrī' suggests the involvement of Śri-vidyā)

2. OM śrī-mahārājniī.
The Great Queen.
(She is the queen presiding over the Śrī-nagara, which is symbolized by Śrī-chakra representing the entire universe)

3. OM śrīmat-siṁhāsaneśvarī.
The ruler seated on the grand lion's throne.
(The lion's throne is the triangle, bindu-maṇḍala, within the Śrī-chakra)

4. chid-agnikuṇḍa-saṁbhūtā.
Born out of the altar of the fire of pure consciousness.
(The altar referred to here is the bindu or kāmakalā)

5. deva-kārya-samudyatā.
Manifesting herself to fulfill the objectives of the gods.
(The reference is to the killing of Bhaṇḍāsura)

6. udyad-bhānu-sahasraābhā.
Bright like the thousand rising suns.

7. chatur-bāhu-samanvitā.
Endowed with four arms.

8. rāga-svarūpa-pāśāḍhyā.
Holding the noose which is of the nature of desire.

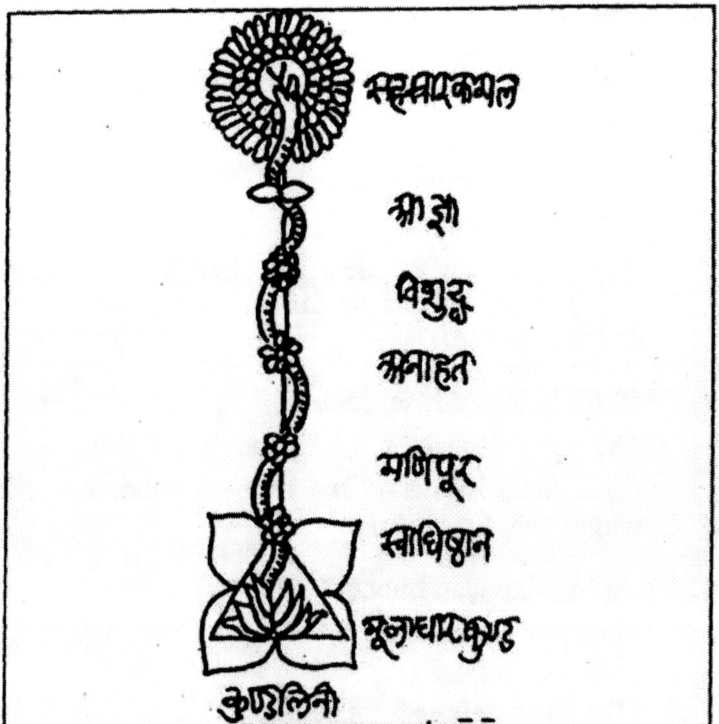

4.CHIDAGNI-KUNḌA-SAṀBHŪTĀ

9. krodhākārāṅkuśojjvalā

Resplendent with the elephant-goad of the nature of wrath.

10. manorūpeksu-kodaṇḍā.

Armed with the sugarcane-bow which is of the nature of mind.

11. pañcha-tanmātra-sāyakā.

Having the arrows which are really the five subtle elements (viz. earth, water, fire, air and ākāśa).

12. nijāruṇa-prabhā-pūra-majjad-brahmāṇḍa-maṇḍalā.

Flooding the whole universe with her own rosy effulgence.

7.CHATUR-BĀHU-SAMANVITĀ; 8.RĀGA-PĀŚA; 9.KRODHĀṄKUŚA; 10.MANO-KODAṆḌA; 11.PAÑCHA-TAVMATRA-SAYAKA

13. champākaśoka-punnāga-saugandhika-lasat-kachā.

Her hair is decorated with the (flowers of) Chaṁpaka, Punnāga and Saugandhikā.

14. kuruvinda-maṇi-sreṇi-kanat-koṭīra-maṇḍitā.

Her crown is resplendent with rows of Kuruvinda gems set in it.

15. ashṭamī-chandra-vibhrāja-dalika-sthala-śobhitā.

Her forehead is bright as the moon on the eight night of the lunar month.

16. mukha-chandra-kalaṅkābha-mṛganābhi-viśesakā.

The tiny mark of musk on the forehead is like the spot in the moon.

17. vadana-smara-māṅgalya-gṛha-toraṇa-chillikā.

Her eye brows are the entrance-arches of the mansion of Kāmarāja.

18. vaktra-lakshmī-parīvāha-chalanmīnābha-lochanā.

Her eyes are like fish sporting in the steam of the beauty of her face.

19. nava-chaṁpaka-pushpābha-nāsādaṇḍa-virājitā.

Her nose is beautiful like newly blossomed champaka flower.

20. tārā-kānti-tiraskāri-nāsābharaṇa-bhāsurā.

Shining with the jewel-ornament on her nose which excels the stars in its splendour.

21. kadaṁba-mañjarī-kḷpta-karṇapūra-manoharā.

Bedecked with clusters of the Kadaṁba flowers worn above her ears.

22. tāṭaṅka-yugalī-bhūta-tapanoḍupa-maṇḍalā.

The two ear-rings are the orbs of the sun and moon.

23. padmarāga-śilādarśa-paribhāvi-kapola-bhūh.

Her cheeks eclipse the brightness of the ruby (padmarāga).

24. nava-vidruma-biṁba-śrī-nyākkāri-radanacchadā.

Her lips put to shame the colour of fresh corals and of the Biṁba fruit.

25. śuddha-vidyāṅkurākāra-dvija-paṅkti-dvayojjvalā

She shines with the two rows of her teeth which are in the nature of the sprout of pure knowledge.

26. karpūra-vīṭikāmoda-samākarshad-digantarā.

The fragrance coming from the betel-leaves which she chews attracts the four quarters.

27. nija-sallāpa-mādhurya-vinirbhartsita-kacchhapī.

The sweet melody of her words puts to shame the music of Kacchhapī (the vīṇā of Sarasvatī).

28. manda-smita-prabhā-pūra-majjat-kāmeśa-mānasā.

The mind of Kāmeśvara is drowned in the fulness of the glory of her sweet smile.

29. nākalita-sādṛśya-chibuka-śrī-virājitā.

She is lustrous with the beauty of her chin, the equal of which cannot be found.

30. kāmeśa-baddha-māṅgalya-sūtra-śobhita-kandharā.

Adorned with the wedding string tied by Kāmeśa around her neck.

31. kanakāṅgada-keyūra-kamanīya-bhujānvitā.

Her arms are encircled with ornaments made of gold.

32. ratna-graiveya-chintāka-lola-muktāphalānvitā.

Having a pearl as pendant dangling from the necklace of gems.

30. KAMEŚA-BADDHA-MĀNGALYA-SŪTRA

33. kāmeśvara-prema-ratnamaṇi-pratipaṇa-sthanī.

Her two breasts are the price offered in exchange for that priceless gem, the love of Kāmeśvara.

34. nābhyālavāla-romāli-latā-phala-kucha-dvayā.

Her two breasts are the fruits growing on the creeper-like hair which springs from her deep navel.

35. laksya-romalatā-dhārāt-samunneya-madhyamā.

Her waist is only to be conjectured from the group of creeper-like hair.

36. stana-bhāra-dalan-madhya-paṭṭa-bandha-vali-trayā.

A golden girdle supports her waist which bends under the burden of her breasts and makes visible the three folds of the skin of the stomach below the bosom.

37. aruṇāruṇa-kausuṁbha-vastra-bhāsvat-kaṭī-taṭī.

Her waist is bright with a rosy tinted garment.

38. ratna-kiṅkiṇikā-ramya-rasanādāma-bhūṣitā.

Decked in a belt, beautiful with be-jewelled jingle-bells.

39. kāmeśa-jñāta-saubhāgya-mārdavoru-dvayānvitā.

The splendour and softness of her thighs are known (only) to Kāmeśa.

40. māṇikya-makuṭākāra-jānudvaya-virājitā.

Her knees are like two bejewelled crowns.

41. indragopa-parikṣipta-smara-tūṇābha-jaṅghikā.

The calves of her legs are like the sapphire-studded quiver of the God of Love.

42. gūḍha-gulphā.

With hidden ānkles.

43. kūrma-pṛshṭha-jayishṇu-prapadānvitā.

Possessing the insteps, which are arched like the back of a tortoise.

44. nakha-dīdhiti-saṁchhanna-nimajjana-tamoguṇā.

The bright rays from her nails dispel the darkness in the hearts of the worshippers.

45. pada-dvaya-prabhā-jāla-parākṛta-saroruhā.

The soles of her feet by their beauty put to shame the lotus.

46. śiñjāna-maṇi-mañjīra-maṇḍita-śrī-padāṁbujā.

Her lotus-like feet are adorned with jewelled anklets that tinkle.

47. marāḷī-manda-gamanā.

Her gait is slow and graceful like that of the swan.

48. mahā-lāvaṇya-śevadhih.

The treasure-house of beauty.

49. sarvāruṇā

All rosy hued.

50. anavadyāṅgī.

With limbs faultless.

51. sarvābharaṇa-bhūshitā.

Adorned with every ornament.

52. śiva-kāmeśvarāṅkasthā.

Sitting on the lap of Śiva who is Kāmeśvara. (who symbolizes the support of the whole world according to *Jnānārṇava* :

कामेश्वरस्य रूपं तत् विश्वाधारस्वरूपकम्।

52. ŚIVA-KĀMEŚVARĀṄKASTHĀ

53. śivā.

The beneficient.

54. svādhīna-vallabhā.

She has won over her Lord.

55. sumeru-madhya-śṛṅgasthā.

Dwelling on the central peak of Mount Sumeru.

56. śrīman-nagara-nāyikā.

Ruler of the resplendent city (which is Śrī-chakra)

56. ŚRĪMAN-NAGARA

57. chintāmaṇi-gṛhāntahsthā.

Residing inside the house known as the wish-fulfilling gem (Chintāmaṇi)

58. pañcha-brahmāsana-sthitā.

Sitting upon a seat formed by five brahmas (Brahmā,

Vishṇu, Rudra and Īśāna as the four legs of the cot and Sadāśiva as the mattress).

58. PAÑCHA-BRAHMĀSANA-STHITĀ.

59. maha-padmāṭavī-saṁsthā.

Residing in the great forest of lotuses.

60. kadaṁba-vana-vāsinī.

Living in a grove of kadamba trees.

61. sudhā-sāgara-madhyasthā.

Residing in the centre of the ocean of nectar.

62. kāmākshī.

Lovely eyed.

63. kāma-dāyinī.

The bestower of all that the devotees desire.

64. devarshi-gaṇa-saṁghāta-stūyamānātmavaibhavā.

Her glory is sung by the assembly of gods and sages.

65. bhaṇḍāsura-vadhodyukta-śakti-senā-samanvitā.

She is accompanied by a host of śaktis for the sake of slaying the demon Bhaṇḍāsura.

66. sampatkarī-samārūḍha-sindhūra-vraja-sevitā.

Attended by herds of elephants conducted by the attendant, Sampatkarī.

67. aśvārūḍhādhiṣṭhitāśva-koṭi-koṭibhir-āvṛtā.

Surrounded by many crores of horses conducted by another attendant, Aśvārūḍhā.

68. chakrarāja-rathārūḍha-sarvāyudha-parishkṛtā.

Seated in the chariot named Chakrarāja, she is armed with all the weapons.

69. geyachakra-rathārūḍha-mantriṇī-parisevitā.

She is attended by Mantriṇī (Śyāmalā) who rides the chariot called Geyachakra.

69. MANTRIṆĪ (ŚYĀMALĀ)

70. kirichakra-rathāruḍha-daṇḍanāthā-puraskṛtā.

She is heralded by Daṇḍanāthā (Vārāhi) who rides on the chariot known as Kirichakra.

70. Daṇḍanāthā (Vārāhi)

71. jvālāmālinikākshipta-vahni-prākāra-madhyagā.

She dwells in the centre of the fortress of fire constructed by Jvālāmālinī.

72. bhaṇḍa-sainya-vadhodyukta-śakti-vikrama-harshitā.

She is delighted with the work of attendant goddesses (śaktis) that are engaged in destroying the army of Bhaṇḍāsura.

73. nityā-parākramāṭopa-nirīkshaṇa-samutsukā.

She rejoices at beholding the rising valour of the nityā-deities.

74. bhaṇḍa-putra-vadhodyukta-bālā-vikrama-nanditā.

She rejoices in the valour of Bālā displayed while slaying the sons of Bhaṇḍāsura.

74. Bala

75. mantriṇyaṁbā-virachita-vishaṅga-vadha-toshitā.

She is delighted at the destruction of Vishaṅga (the minister of Bhaṇḍāsura) effected by the mother-goddess Mantriṇī (Śyāmalā).

76. viśukra-prāṇa-haraṇa-vārāhī-vīrya-nanditā.

She is happy with the strength of Vārāhī, (her commander of the army) who forced the life out of Viśukra (commander of Bhaṇḍāsura).

77. kāmeśvara-mukhāloka-kalpita-śrī-gaṇeśvarā.

Śrī-Gaṇeśvara (viz. Gaṇapati) was formed by her glances at Kāmeśvara.

78. mahāgaṇeśa-nirbhinna-vighna-yantra-praharshitā.

She is delighted at Gaṇeśa shattering the magic circle of obstacles.

79. bhaṇḍāsurendra-nirmukta-śastra-pratyastra-varshiṇī.

She is showering missiles in response to the weapon thrown by Bhaṇḍāsura.

80. karāṅguli-nakhotpanna-nārāyaṇa-daśākṛtih.

From the nails of her (ten) fingers sprang the ten forms of Nārāyaṇa.

81. mahāpāśupatāstrāgni-nirdagdhāsura-sainikā

She burnt the army of the demons with the fire coming out cf the missile called Mahāpāśupata.

82. kāmeśvarāstra-nirdagdha-sabhaṇḍāsura-śūnyaka

Bhāṇḍasura and his city called Śūnyakā were reduced to ashes by the fire coming out of the weapon of Kāmeśvara.

83. brahmopendra-mahendrādideva-samstuta-vaibhavā.

Her supreme power is praised by Brahmā, Vishṇu, Mahendra and all the gods.

84. hara-netrāgni-saṁdagdha-kāma-saṁjīvanaushadhih.

She was the reviving herb to Manmatha who was burnt up by the fire emanating from the eyes of Śiva.

85. śrīmad-vāgbhava-kūṭaika-svarūpa-mukha-paṅkajā.

Her lotus-like face represents the divine "vāgbhava" group (the first group of seed-syllables in the mantra Pañchadaśī).

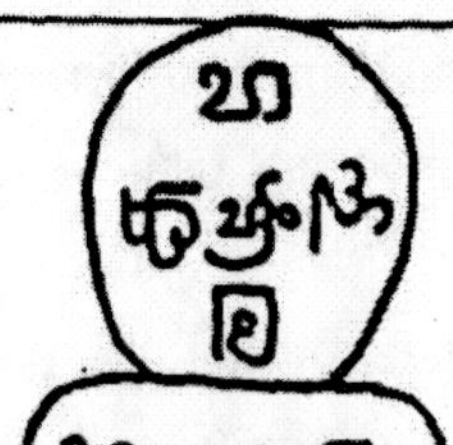

85-87. THE THREE-KŪṬAS

86. kaṇṭhādhah-kaṭiparyanta-madhyakūṭa-svarūpiṇī.

From the neck downwards till the waist she represent madhyakūṭa (the second group of the seed-syllables in the same mantra).

87. śakti-kūṭaikatāpanna-kaṭyadhobhāga-dhāriṇī.

From the waist downwards she represent śaktikūṭa (the final group of seed-syllables in the same mantra)

88. mūla-mantrātmikā.

She is verily the nature of the root mantra (the fifteen-syllabled mantra, Pañcha-daśī)

89. mūla-kūṭa-traya-kalevarā.

The three divisions of the syllables of the mantra Pañchadaśī constitute her physical body.

90. kulāmṛtaika-rasikā.

She has the special taste of the nectar that oozes out of the kula (the mystic family, represented by the brahma-randhra on top of the skull).

91. kula-saṁketa-pālinī.

She is the guardian of the mystic conventions of the 'family'.

92. kulāṅganā.

The lady belonging to the sacred 'family'.

93. kulāntah-sthā.

Residing within the 'family'; known only by the inner and esoteric scriptures.

94. kaulinī.

Belonging to the mystic 'family'; of the nature of the esoteric scriptures; the kula also means Kāma-kāla.

95. kula-yoginī.

Abiding in conjunction with the 'family' (or the esoteric scriptures).

96. akulā.

Out of 'family' or lineage; beyond the esoteric scriptures.

97. samayāntah-sthā

Within the sacred and secret conventions or pledges of mystic practice (viz. internal worship).

98. samayāchāra-tatparā

Devoted to the conduct determined by the sacred conventions (of internal worship).

99. mūlādhārika-nilayā.

Chiefly residing in the mulạdhāra centre.

100. brahma-granthi-vibhedinī.

Severing the mystic knot known as Brahma-granthi.

101. maṇipūrāntar-uditā.

Appearing in the Maṇipūra.

102. vishṇu-granthi-vibhedinī.

Severing the mystic knot known as Vishṇu-granthi.

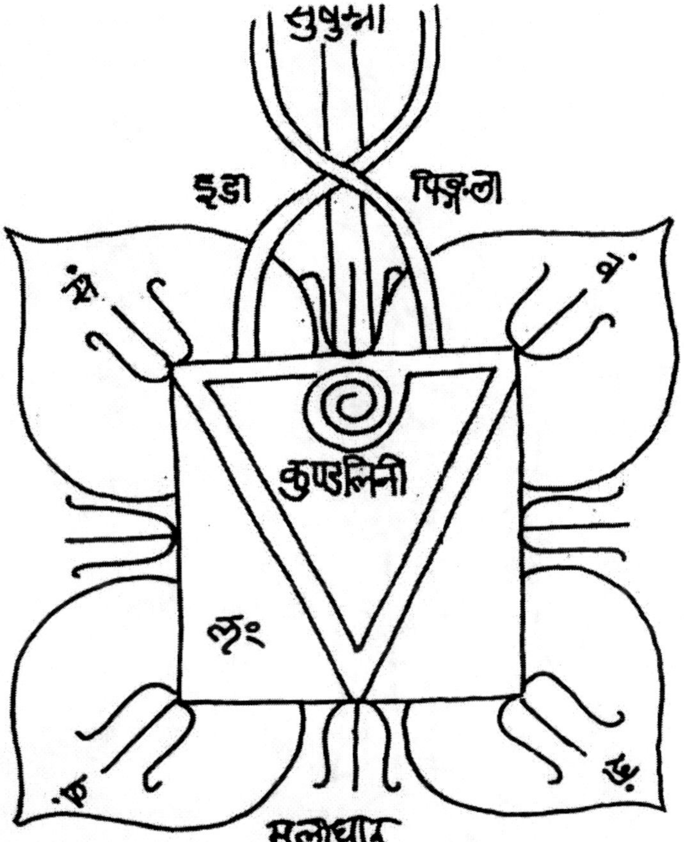

99. MŪLĀDHĀRA

103. āj̃ñā-chakrāntarāla-sthā.

Residing in the centre of the Ājñāchakra.

104. rudra-granthi-vibhedinī.

Severing the mystic knot known as Rudra-granthi.

105. sahasrārāṁbujārūḍhā.

She has ascended the thousand-petalled lotus (viz. Sahasrāra-chakra).

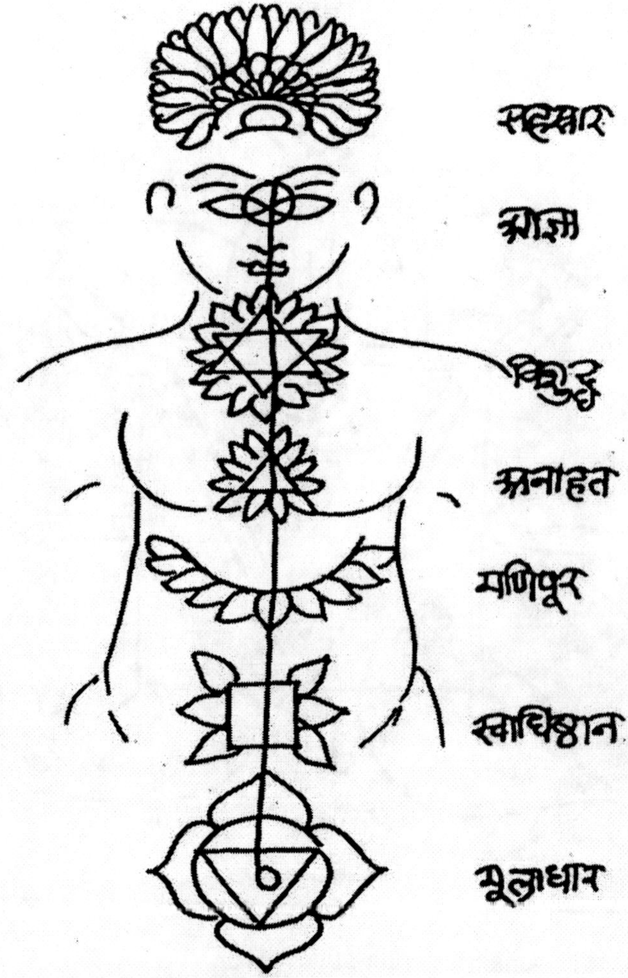

105. SAHASRĀRĀMBUJA

106. sudhā-dhārābhivarshiṇī.

Showering the torrents of ambrosia down (on the devotee's inner body)

107. taṭil-latā-samaruchih.
Brilliant as a flash of lightning.

108. shaṭ-chakropari-saṁsthitā.
Residing above the six chakras (mentioned above).

108. SHAṬ-CHAKRA

109. mahtāśaktih.

Delighting greatly in ceremonials and festivals.

110. kuṇḍalinī.

Whose nature is that of Kuṇḍalini.

111. bisa-tantu-tanīyasī.

Extremely fine and subtle like the fibre within the lotus-stalk.

112. bhavānī.

The spouse of Śiva (Bhava) and the giver of life of him.

113. bhāvanā-gamyā.

She is to be attained by deep meditation.

114. bhavāraṇya-kuṭhārikā.

She is the axe that cuts down the forest of phenomenal existence.

115. bhadra-priyā.

Delighting in benevolence.

116. bhadra-mūrtih.

Of benevolent appearance.

117. bhakta-saubhāgya-dāyinī.

Conferring prosperity on the devotees.

118. bhakti-priyā.

Delighting in devotion.

119. bhakti-gamyā.

To be approached by devotion.

120. bhakti-vaśyā.

Controlled by devotion.

121. bhayāpahā.

Remover of fear.

122. śāṁbhavī.

The wife of Śaṁbhu (viz. Śiva)

123. śāradārādhyā.

Worshipped by Śāradā (viz Sarasvatī, the Goddess of learning).

124. śarvāṇī.

The wife of Śiva, whose body is earth.

125. śarma-dāyinī.

Conferring happiness.

126. śaṁkarī.

The consort of Śaṁkara; the provider of welfare.

127. śrīkarī.

The provider of prosperity.

128. sādhvī.

Chaste.

123. ŚĀRADĀ

129. sarat-chandra-nibhānanā.

Having face like the full moon in the spring season.

130. śātodarī.

Slender-waisted.

131. śāntimatī.
Peaceful.

132. nirādhārā.
Without dependence.

133. nirañjanā.
Stainless; devoid of associations.

134. nirlepā.
Without impurity, arising out of karmas.

135. nirmalā
Devoid of stains.

136. nityā.
Eternal.

137. nirākārā.
Formless.

138. nirākulā.
Unagitated and undecaying.

139. nirguṇā.
Without attributes and definitions.

140. nishkalā.
Without parts.

141. śāntā.
Tranquil; composed.

142. nishkāmā.

Devoid of desires.

143. nirupaplavā.

Indestructible.

144. nitya-muktā.

Ever free.

145. nirvikārā

Unchanging.

146. nishprapañchā.

Unproliferating; independent of the spreading phenomena.

147. nirāśrayā.

Without support.

148. nitya-śuddhā.

Ever pure.

149. nitya-buddhā.

Ever wise.

150. niravadyā.

Blameless.

151. nirantarā.

Compact.

152. nishkāraṇā.

Without cause; uncaused

153. nishkalaṅkā.

Faultless.

154. nirupādhih.

Without limitations that are caused by primal ignorance or avidyā

155. nirīśvarā.

Having none as a ruler or superior.

156. nīrāgā.

Utterly bereft of passion.

157. rāga-mathanā.

Destroying desire and hate.

158. nirmadā.

Lacking pride or arrogance.

159. mada-nāśinī.

Destroying pride.

160. niśchintā.

Without care.

161. nirahaṁkārā.

Without egoism.

162. nirmohā.

Without confusion and indecision.

163. moha-nāśinī.

The destroyer of confusion.

164. nirmamā.

Unselfish.

165. mamatā-hantrī.

The destroyer of selfishness

166. nishpāpā.

Free from sins.

167. pāpa-nāśinī.

The destroyer of sins.

168. nishkrodhā.

Without anger.

169. krodha-śamanī.

The destroyer of the anger.

170. nirlobhā.

Without greed.

171. lobha-nāśinī.

The destroyer of greed.

172. nih-saṁśayā.

Free from doubt.

173. saṁśayaghnī.

The destroyer of doubts.

174. nirbhavā.

Unoriginated.

175. bhava-nāśinī.

The destroyer of phenomenal existence.

176. nirvikalpā.

Devoid of confabulations and constructions

177. nirābādhā.

Undistrubed.

178. nirbhedā.

Without differences and distinctions.

179. bheda-nāśinī.

The destroyer of all differences and distinctions

180. nirnāśā.

Imperishable.

181. mṛtyu-mathanī.

The destroyer of death itself.

182. nishkriyā.

Without action.

183. nishparigrahā.

Receiving nothing.

184. nistulā.

Incomparable.

185. nīla-chikurā.

Possessed of dark blue curls of hair on the forehead.

186. nirapāyā.

Free from decay and destruction.

187. niratyayā.

Without transgression.

188. durlabhā.

Hard to attain.

189. durgamā.

Difficult of approach.

190. durgā.

The Goddess who removes all evil states.

191. duhkha-hantrī.

The destroyer of sorrow and pain.

192. sukha-pradā.

One who bestows happiness.

193. dushṭa-dūrā.

Unattainable by the wicked folk.

194. durāchāra-śamanī.

One who suppresses evil conduct and customs.

195. dosha-varjitā.

Devoid of faults

196. sarvajñā.

Omniscient.

197. sāndra-karuṇā.

Intensely compassionate.

198. samānādhika-varjitā.

Having neither equals nor any superior.

199. sarva-śakti-mayī.

Possessing all powers.

200. sarva-maṅgalā.

One whose nature is all good fortune.

201. sad-gati-pradā.

Leading into the right path.

202. sarveśvarī.

Ruler of all.

203. sarva-mayī.

All.

204. sarva-mantra-svarūpiṇī.

She is of the very nature of all mantras.

205. sarva-yantrātmikā.

She is of the nature of all yantras (magical devices)

206. sarva-tantra-rūpā.

She is the spirit of all tantras (occult and esoteric practices)

207. manonmanī.

(Manonmanī is the eighth place from the centre between the eyebrows, just below the Brahma-randhra).

208. maheśvarī.

The great ruler of all.

210. MAHĀLAKSHMĪ

209. mahādevī.

The great goddess.

210. mahālakṣmī.

Of the form of the great Lakshmī.

211. mṛḍa-priyā.

Beloved of Mṛḍa (viz. Śiva)

212. mahā-rūpā

Having all shapes.

213. mahā-pūjyā.

Mighty object of worship.

214. mahā-pātaka-nāśinī.

The destroyer of grave sins.

215. mahā-māyā.

The great deluder; it is also the popular name of Devī.

216. mahā-sattvā.

The grant reality.

217. mahā-śaktih.

The great energy.

218. mahā-ratih.

The great delight.

219. mahā-bhogā.
The great enjoyment.

220. mahaiśvaryā.
The great sovereignty.

221. mahā-vīryā.
The great strength.

222. mahā-balā.
The great might.

223. mahā-buddhih.
The great intelligence.

224. mahā-siddhih.
Possessed of all great attainments.

225. mahā-yogīśvareśvarī.
The ruler of the great yoga-masters.

226. mahā-tantrā.
Of the nature of the great tantras.

227. mahā-mantrā.
Of the form of the great mantras.

228. mahā-yantrā.
Of the nature of the great yantras.

229. mahāsanā.
Having the great seat.

230. mahāyāga-kramārādhyā.

Worshipped by the method of mahāyāga.

231. mahābhairava-pūjitā.

Worshipped by Mahābhairava.

232. maheśvara-mahākalpa-mahātāṇḍava-sākshiṇī.

The witness to the great dance of Maheśvara in the final cycle of existence.

233. mahākāmeśa-mahishī.

The consort of Mahākāmeśvara (viz. Śiva, whose śakti she is)

234. mahā-tripurasundarī.

The great Tripurasundarī.

(The three realms are those of sun, moon and fire which are said to evolve from bindu. If the bindu is Lalitā, three deities Bhaga-mālini, Kāmeśvarī and Vajreśvarī represent the three realms respectively).

235. chatuhshashṭyupachārāḍhyā.

Adored by sixty-four ceremonies of worship.

236. chatuhshaṣṭi-kalāmayī.

Of the nature of all the sixty-four branches of learning.

237. mahā-chatuhshashṭi-koṭi-yoginī-gaṇa-sevitā.

Attended by the sixty-four crores of the grand assemblies of Yoginīs.

238. manu-vidyā.

The tradition communicated by Manu, one of the twelve masters of Śrī-vidyā.

मनुश्चन्द्रः कुबेरश्च लोपामुद्रा च मन्मथः।

अगस्तिरग्निश्च इन्द्रः स्कन्दः शिवस्तथा।

क्रोधभट्टारको देव्या द्वादशामी उपासकाः।।

239. chandra-vidyā.

Worshipped by Chandra (another originator of the Śrī-vidyā tradition).

240. chandra-maṇḍala-madhyagā,

Residing in the centre of the lunar orb. (served by the tithinityā deities each of whom represents a lunar day; and they are fifteen in number, pañchadaśī; the goddess is the sixteenth, shoḍaśī or Śrī).

241. chāru-rūpā.

Whose form is exceedingly charming.

242. chāru-hāsā.

One with an engaging smile on her face.

243. chāru-chandra-kalādharā.

Wearing a lovely crescent moon on her head.

244. charāchara-jagannāthā.

Ruler of all the animate and inanimate worlds.

245. chakra-rāja-niketanā.

Abiding in the Śrī-Chakra. (The goddess transforms

herself into the Śrīchakra. *Kāma-kalā-vilāsa,* 36, says) :

The goddess transforms herself into the srichakra. Kāma-kala-vilāsa, 36, says

सेयं परा महेशी चक्राकारेण परिणमेत यदा।

तद्देहावयवानां परिणतिरावरणदेवताः सर्वाः।।

246. Pārvatī.

The daughter of the Mountain (Himavān).

247. padma-nayanā.

Lotus-eyed.

248. padma-rāga-sama-prabhā.

Shining like a ruby.

249. PAÑCHA-PRETĀSANĀ

249. pañcha-pretāsanāsīnā.

Seated on the cot made of the five 'corpses' (viz, the five Brahmas, who are inert : Brahmā, Vishṇu, Rudra, Īśvara and Sadāśiva).

250. pañcha-brahma-svarūpiṇī.

Of the nature of the the five brahmās (the five brahmās are Brahmā, Vishṇu, Rudra, Īśvara and Sadāśiva).

251. CHINMAYĪ

251. chinmayī.

Consciousness itself.

(Represented by the bindu inside the triangle in Śrīchakra).

252. paramānandā.

Who is supremely blissful.

253. vijñāna-ghana-rūpiṇī.

Of the nature of the mass of pure consciousness.

254. dhyāna-dhyātṛ-dhyeya-rūpā.

Of the nature of meditation, meditator and the object of meditation.

255. dharmādharma-vivarjitā.

Devoid of both virtue and vice.

256. viśva-rūpā.

Of the nature of all things.

257. jāgariṇī.

She is wakefulness.

258. svapantī.

She is the dream.

259. taijasātmikā.

She is verily the tejas (which is responsible for dream)

260. suptā.

She is the sleep.

261. prājñātmikā.

She is verily the prājñā (responsible for sleep)

262. turyā.

She is the fourth state.

263. sarvāvasthā-vivarjitā.

She is not involved in any of the states.

264. sṛshṭi-kartrī.

The creator.

265. brahma-rūpā.

Of the form of Brahmā.

266. goptrī.

The Protectress

267. govinda-rūpiṇī.

Of the form of Govinda.

268. saṁhāriṇī.

The destroyer.

269. rudra-rūpā.

Of the form of Rudra.

270. tirodhāna-karī.

She is the cause of obscuration and disappearance.

271. Īśvarī.

The Ruler.

272. sadāśivā.

She is of the nature of Sadā-śiva (preponderantly sattva)

273. anugraha-dā.

One who bestows grace and blessing on the devotees.

274. pañcha-kṛtya-parāyaṇā.

She is engaged in the pentad of cosmic functions (creation, preservation, destruction, obscuration and grace).

275. bhānu-maṇḍala-madhyasthā.

Dweller in the midst of the solar orb.

276. bhairavī

Consort of Bhairava (i.e. Paramaśiva.)

277. bhaga-mālinī.

The second nityā-deity, called Bhaga-mālinī.

278. padmāsanā.

Seated on the lotus.

279. bhagavatī.

The Goddess possessed of the six great merits (sovereignty, valour, celebrity, wealth, gnosis and dispassion).

280. padmanābha-sahodarī.

Sister of Vishṇu, whose navel is the lotus on which the creator is stationed

281. unmeṣa-nimishotpanna-vipanna-bhuvanāvalih.

The endless chain of worlds arise and dissappear, with the opening and closing of her eyes.

282. sahasra-śīrsha-vadanā.

Thousand-headed and thousand-faced.

283. sahasrākshī.

Thousand-eyed.

284. sahasra-pād.

Thousand-footed.

285. ābrahma-kīṭa-jananī.

Mother of all creatures from Brahmā down to the smallest worm.

286. varṇāśrama-vidhāyinī.

The establisher of the castes and orders.

287. nijājñā-rūpa-nigamā.

The Vedas are verily the expression of Her command.

288. puṇyāpuṇya-phala-pradā.

The dispenser of the fruits of merit and demerit.

289. śruti-sīmanta-sindūrī-kṛta-pādābja-dhulikā.

The dust of Her lotus feet forms the vermilion mark on the parting of the hair on the head of the Vedas (personified as goddesses)

290. sakalāgama-sandoha-śuktisaṁpuṭa-mauktikā.

She is the pearl which is enclosed in the shell (constituted by the host of scriptures).

291. purushārtha-pradā.

One who fulfils the objectives of human existence.

292. pūrṇā.

The fullness.

294. BHUVANEŚVARĪ

293. bhoginī.

The enjoyer.

294. bhuvaneśvarī.

Ruler of the universe.

295. aṁbikā.

The mother.

296. anādi-nidhanā.

Having neither beginning nor end.

297. hari-brahmendra-sevitā.
Served by Vishnu, Brahmā and Indra.

298. nārāyaṇī.
Consort of Nārāyaṇa.

299. nādarūpā.
Of the form of sound.

300. nāmarūpa-vivarjitā.
Bereft of names and forms.

301. hrīṁ-kārī.
The sacred syllable hrīṁ.

302. hrī-matī.
Possessor of Hrī (sense of modesty).

303. hṛdyā.
Abiding in the heart

304. heyopādeya-varjitā.
Free from acceptances and rejections.

305. rājarājārchitā.
Worshipped by the ruler of rulers (Kubera)

306. rājñī.
The Queen.

307. ramyā.
The Charmer.

308. rājīva-lochanā.

The lotus-eyed.

309. rañjanī.

The delighter.

310. ramaṇi.

The gladdener.

311. rasyā.

The to-be-tasted.

312. ranat-kinkini-mekhalā.

The wearer of the girdle, to which tinkling bells are fastened.

313. ramā.

She is of the form of Lakshmī.

314. rākendu-vadanā.

Having a face like the full moon.

315. ratirūpā.

In the form of Rati, consort of Manmatha.

316. rati-priyā.

The lover of enjoyments.

317. rakshā-karī.

The protectress.

322. KĀMAKALĀ

318. rākṣasa-ghnī

The slayer of demons.

319. rāmā.

The enchantress.

320. ramana-lampaṭā.

Devoted to her lover.

321. kāmyā.

Who is desired by all.

322. kāmakalā-rūpā.

She is of the form of Kāmakalā.

322. KĀMAKALEŚVARĪ

323. kadaṁba-kusuma-priyā.

Fond of Kadamba flowers.

324. Kalyāṇī.

Auspicious and benevolent.

325. jagatī-kandā.

The root of the world.

326. karuṇā-rasa-sāgarā.

The ocean of the sentiment of compassion.

327. kalāvatī.

Possessed of all sciences and art (sixty-four in number)

328. kalālāpā.

Sweet in speech.

329. kāntā.

The charmer.

330. kādaṁbarī-priyā.

Fond of mead.

331. vara-dā.

The granter of boons.

332. vāma-nayanā.

Beautiful-eyed.

333. vāruṇīmada-vihvalā.

Inebriated with liquor.

334. viśvādhikā.

Transcending the universe.

335. veda-vedyā.

Known only by the Vedas.

336. vindhyāchala-nivāsinī.

Residing in tiie Vindhyā mountains.

337. vidhātrī.

The supporter of the universe.

338. veda-jananī.

The mother of the Vedas.

339. vishṇu-māyā.

The creative and deluding power of all-pervading Vishnu.

340. vilāsinī.

The playful one.

341. kshetra-svarūpā

Of the nature of sacred spots or planes of existence.

342. kshetreśī.

The ruler of all planes of existence.

343. kshetra-kshetrajña-pālinī.

The protector of the planes of existence and of the souls inhabting them.

344. kshaya-vṛddhi-vinirmuktā.

Untouched by decay and growth.

345. kshetrapāla-samarchitā.

Worshipped by Kshetrapāla.

346. vijayā.

The Ever-victorious.

347. vimalā.

The Unsullied.

348. vandyā.

The Adorable.

349. vandāru-jana-vatsalā.

Fond of the worshipping folk.

350. vāg-vādinī.

The speaker of the word.

351. vāma-keśī.

Having beautiful hair.

352. vahni-maṇḍala-vāsinī.

Residing in the circle of Fire (one of the three spheres of phenomenal existence, others being Sūrya-maṇḍala and Chandra-maṇḍala, circles of sun and moon).

353. bhaktimat-kalpa-latikā.

The wish-fulfilling creeper for the devotees.

354. paśu-pāśa-vimochinī.

The liberator of the ignorant from bondage.

355. samhṛtāśesha-pāshaṇḍā,

The destroyer of all heretics.

356. sadāchāra-pravartikā.

The prompter of correct conduct.

357. tāpa-trayāgni-samtapta-samāhlādana-chandrikā.

She is like the moonlight, delighting those who are burned by the triple fire of misery (ādhibhautika, ādhidaivika and ādhyātmika).

358. taruṇī.

The ever youthful.

359. tāpasārādhyā,

Worshipped by the ascetics.

360. tanu-madhyā.

The slender-waisted.

361. tamopahā.

The remover of darkness.

362. chitih.

Pure consciousness.

363. tat-pada-laksyārthā.

She is the meaning intended by the expression "tat".

364. chideka-rasa-rūpiṇī.

The one essence of pure consciousness.

365. svātmānanda-lavī-bhūta-brahmādy-ānanda-samtatih.

The totality of the bliss of Brahmā and others is but a minute portion of Her own bliss.

366. parā.

The highest consciousness which is transcendental.

367. pratyak-chitī-rūpā.

Inner consciousness.

368. paśyantī.

The consciousness which is of the nature of Paśyantī ('seeing')

369. parā-devatā.

The supreme (transcendental) deity.

370. madhyamā.

The consciousness which is of the nature of Madhyamā.

371. vaikharīrūpa

The consciousness which is explicit (of the nature of Vaikhari)

372. bhakta-mānasa-haṁsikā.

The swan that moves about in the minds of the devotees.

373. kāmeśvara-prāṇa-nāḍī.

The vital current of Kāmeśvara.

374. kṛta-jñā.

The knower of all actions.

375. kāma-pūjitā.

Worshipped by Kāma (or Manmatha, one of the twelve original devotees of Śrī-vidyā)

376. sṛṅgāra-rasa-sampūrṇā.

Filled with the essence of amorous sentiment.

377. jayā.

victorious.

378. jālandhara-sthitā.

Abiding in the jālandhara seat.

379. oḍyāṇa-pīṭha-nilayā.

Abiding in the centre known as Oḍyāṇa.

380. bindu-maṇḍala-vāsinī.

Dwelling in the centre of Bindu.

381. raho-yāga-kramārādhyā.

One who is worshipped in the secret rituals (of internal worship)

382. rahas-tarpaṇa-tarpitā.

Gratified by the secrect oblations.

383. sadyah-prasādinī.

The bestower of immediate grace.

384. viśva-sākshiṇī.

The witness of the entire universe.

385. sākshi-varjitā.

Herself unwitnessed.

386. shaḍaṅga-devatā-yuktā.

Accompanied by the deities of six limbs (in nyāsa)

387. shāḍ-guṇya-paripūritā.

Possessing the six qualities (sovereignty, valour, celebrity, wealth, gnosis and dispassion).

388. nitya-klinnā.

Ever compassionate.

389. nirupamā.

Without equal.

390. nirvāṇa-sukha-dāyinī.

One who confers the bliss of highest emancipation.

391. nityā-shoḍaśikā-rūpā.

Of the form of the sixteen tithi-nityā deities (of the lunar cult, chandra-jñāna).

392. śrīkaṇṭhārdha-śarīriṇī.

Possessing half the body of Śrīkaṇṭa (viz. Śiva)

393. prabhāvatī.

The lustrous one.

394. prabhā-rūpā.

Of the form of brightness.

392. ŚRĪKANṬHĀRDHA-ŚARĪRIṆĪ.

395. prasiddhā.
The celebrated one.

396. parameśvarī.
The supreme ruler.

397. mūla-prakṛtiḥ.
The primordial nature.

398. avyaktā.

The unmanifest one.

399. vyaktāvyakta-svarūpiṇī.

Of the form of the manifest as well as the unmanifest.

400. vyāpinī.

The all-pervasive principle.

401. vividhākārā.

Of various forms.

402. vidyāvidyā-svarūpiṇī.

Of the nature of both knowledge leading to liberation and ignorance leading to bondage.

403. mahākāmeśa-nayana-kumudāhlada-kaumudī.

The moonlight which gladdens the kumuda flowers of the eyes of Mahākāmeśa.

404. bhakta-hārda-tamo-bheda-bhānumad-bhānu-saṁtatih.

She is the sunbeam which drives out the darkness from the heart of her devotees.

405. śiva-dūtī,

One who has Śiva as her messenger.

406. śivārādhyā.

Worshipped by Śiva.

407. śiva-mūrtih.

Of the form of the benign Śiva.

408. śivam-karī.

The giver of happiness.

409. śiva-priyā.

The beloved of Śiva.

410. śiva-parā.

Devoted to Śiva; beyond Śiva.

411. śishṭeshṭā.

Desired by the folk who are correct in their conduct.

412. śishṭa-pūjitā.

Worshipped by the people whose behaviour is proper.

413. aprameyā.

Immeasurable.

414. svaprakāśā.

Self-luminous.

415. mano-vāchām-agocharā.

She is beyond mind and speech.

416. chit-śaktih.

She is the power of pure consciousness.

417. chetanā-rūpā.

She is the form of active consciousness.

418. jaḍa-śaktiḥ.

She is the power of inanimate creation (inert energy).

419. jaḍātmikā.

She is the objective and inert world.

420. gāyatrī.

She is the metre consisting of 24 syllables, regarded as the goddess of Vedic lore.

420. GĀYATRĪ.

421. vyāhṛtih.

She is the three sacred ejaculations: Bhūh, Bhuvah and Svah.

422. sandhyā.

She is the deity presiding over the twilight-ritual.

423. dvija-bṛnda-nishevitā.

Worshipped by all the twice-born.

424. tattvāsanā,

Having the primal categories of reality as her seat.

425. tat.

'That'

426. tvam.

'Thou'.

427. ayī

'Oh'.

428. pañcha-kośāntara-sthitā.

Dwelling within the five sheaths of the individual (anna-maya, praṇa-maya, mano-maya, vijñāna-maya and ānanda-maya)

429. nihsīma-mahimā

Hers is glory without limits.

430. nitya-yauvanā.

Ever young.

431. mada-śālinī.

Resplendent with the rapture of delight.

432. mada-ghūrṇita-raktākshī.

With reddened eyes rolling with inebriated rapture.

433. mada-pāṭala-gaṇḍa-bhūh.

With cheeks blushing with rapture.

434. chandana-drava-digdhāṅgī.

Her body smeared with sandal paste.

435. chāṁpeya-kusuma-priyā.

Fond of Champaka flower.

436. kuśalā.

Skilful.

437. komalākārā.

Of graceful appearance.

438. kurukullā.

The name of the deity distinguished by the power of vimarśā.

439. kuleśvarī.

The ruler of the mystic 'family'.

440. kulakuṇḍālayā.

Abiding in the mūlādhāra centre.

441. kaula-mārga-tatpara-sevitā.

Worshipped by those who are devoted to the Kaula path.

442. kumāra-gaṇanāthāṁbā.

Mother of Kumāra and Gaṇanātha (viz. Kārthikeya and Gaṇapati).

443. tushṭih.

Contentment.

444. pushṭih.

Nourishment.

445. matih.

Intelligence.

446. dhṛtih

Fortitude.

447. śāntih

Tranquillity.

448. svasti-matī

The secure and prosperous.

449. kāntih

Effulgence.

450. nandinī.

The delighter

451. vighnanāśinī.
the destroyer of obstacles.

452. tejovatī.
Filled with splendour.

453. tri-nayanā.
Three-eyed.

454. lolākshī-kāma-rūpiṇī.
Of the nature of the desire in women.

455. mālinī.
Wearing garlands.

456. haṁsinī.
Swan.

457. mātā.
Mother.

458. malayāchala-vāsinī.
Residing in the Malaya mountains.

459. sumukhī.
Pretty-faced

460. nalinī.
Lotus.

461. su-bhrūh.
With beautiful eye-brows.

462. śobhanā.

Handsome.

463. sura-nāyikā.

Leader of the Gods.

464. kālakaṇṭhī.

Wife of Kālakaṇṭha (viz. Śiva, who is poison-throated)

465. kāntimatī.

Radiant.

466. kshobhiṇī.

Causing emotion.

467. sūkshma-rūpiṇī.

Of subtle form.

468. vajreśvarī.

The sixth tithi-nityā deity; also presiding over the vajrāyudha of Indra.

469. vāmadevī.

The wife of Vāmadeva.

470. vayovasthā-vivarjitā.

Exempt from the changing states of life.

471. siddheśvarī.

Ruler of the siddhas

472. siddha-vidyā

Of the nature of the adept's lore.

473. siddha-mātā.

The mother of the adepts (yogins who have accomplished their ends)

474. yaśasvinī.

Celebrated.

475. viśuddhi-chakra-nilayā.

Abiding in the visuddhi centre.

476. ārakta-varṇā.

Of rosy complexion

477. trilochanā.

Three-eyed.

478. khaṭvāṅgādi-praharaṇā.

Armed with missiles and weapons like the khaṭ vāṅga.

479. vadanaika-samanvitā.

Possessed of one face.

480. pāyasānna-priyā.

Fond of milk porridge.

481. tvak-sthā.

The deity of the organ of touch.

482. paśu-loka-bhayaṁkarī.

Terrifying to the ignorant.

482. PAŚULOKA-BHAYAṀKARĪ.

483. amṛtādi-mahā-śakti-saṁvṛtā.

Surrounded by Amrta and other Śaktis.

484. ḌĀKINĪ

484. ḍākinīsvarī.

The deity known as Ḍākinyamba (Ḍākinī is also a yoginī)

485. anāhatābja-nilayā.

Abiding in the anāhata-lotus.

486. śyamābhā.

Black in hue.

487. vadana-dvayā.

Two-faced.

488. daṁṣṭrojjvalā.

With shining tusks.

489. aksha-mālādi-dharā.

Wearing a garland of Aksha beads and other ornaments.

490. rudhira-saṁsthitā.

Residing in the blood.

491. kalārātryādi-śaktyaugha-vṛtā.

Attended by hosts of Śaktis, Kālarātri, etc.

492. snigdhaudana-priyā.

Fond of greasy food.

494. RĀKINĪ

493. mahā-vīrendra-varadā.

Granting boons to great warriors.

494. rākinyambā-svarūpiṇī.

Assuming the form of the mother Rākinī (one of the principal yoginis).

495. maṇipūrābja-nilayā.

Abiding in the Manipūra-lotus.

496. vadana-traya-samyutā.

Three-faced (The reference is to the three units of the Śrīvidyā : Vāgbhava, Kāmaraja and Śakti).

497. vajrādikāyudhopetā.

Armed with the thunderbolt and other weapons.

498. ḍāmaryādibhir-āvrtā.

Surrounded by Ḍāmarī and other śaktis.

499. rakta-varṇā.

Red-coloured.

500. māṁsa-nishṭhā.

Presiding over flesh.

501. guḍānna-prīta-mānasā.

Fond of rice mixed with jaggery.

502. samasta-bhakta-sukhadā.

Conferring happiness on all her devotees.

503. lākinyambā-svarūpiṇī.

Assuming the form of the mother Lākinī.

504. svādhishṭhānāmbuja-gatā.

Residing in the Svādhishṭhāna-lotus.

505. chatur-vaktra-manoharā.

Four-faced and fascinating, (like Brahmā)

503. LĀKINĪ

506. śūlādyāyudha-sampannā.

Armed with the spear and other weapons.

507. pīta-varṇā.

Yellow-complexioned.

508. ati-garvitā.

Exceedingly arrogant.

509. medo-nishṭhā.

Presiding over the bodily constituent fat.

510. madhu-prītā.

Fond of mead.

511. bandinyādi-samanvitā

Attended by Bandinī and others.

512. dadhyannāsakta-hṛdayā.

Fond of rice mixed with curds.

513. kākinī-rūpa-dhāriṇī.

Assuming the form of Kākinī.

514. mūlādhārāṁbujārūḍhā.

Mounting the Mūlādhāra-lotus.

515. pañcha-vaktrā.

Five-faced, (like Śiva)

516. asthi-saṁsthitā.

Presiding over the bodily constituent, bone.

517. aṅkuśādi-praharaṇā.

Armed with elephant goad and other weapons.

518. varadādi-nishevitā.

Attended by Varadā and others.

519. mudgaudanāsakta-chittā.

Fond of food mixed with mudga-beans

520. śākinyaṁbā-svarūpiṇī.

Assuming the form of Śākinī.

521. ājñā-chakrābja-nilayā.

Residing in the Ājñā centre-lotus.

517 AṄKUŚĀDI-PRAHARAṆĀ

522. śukla-varṇā.

White-complexioned

523. shaḍānanā.

Six-faced, (like Kārtikeya)

524. majjā-saṁsthā.

Presiding over the bodily constituent, marrow.

525. haṁsavatī-mukhya-śakti-samanvitā.

Attended by Haṁsavatī and other śaktis.

526. haridrānnaika-rasikā.

Fond of saffron-flavoured food.

527. hākinī-rūpa-dhāriṇī.

Assuming the form of Hākinī.

528. sahasra-dala-padma-sthā.

Residing in the thousand-petalled lotus.

529. sarva-varṇopaśobhitā.

Decorated with all colours.

530. sarvāyudha-dharā.

Armed with all weapons.

531. śukla-saṁsthitā.

Residing in the bodily constitutent, semen.

530. SARVĀYUDHA-DHARĀ

532. sarvato-mukhī.

Facing every side.

533. sarvaudana-prīta-chittā

Fond of all kinds of food.

534. yākinyaṁbā-svarūpiṇī.

Assuming the form of Yākinī.

535. Svāhā.

The carrier of offerings to the gods.

536. Svadhā.

The carrier of offerings to the manes.

537. matih.

Of the nature of mind.

538. medhā.

Intelligence.

539. śrutih.

The Vedic corpus.

540. smṛtih.

The scriptural lore based on the Vedic corpus.

541. anuttamā.

The best (viz. without anything better)

542. puṇya-kīrtih.

Celebrity for virtue (merit)

543. puṇya-labhyā
Attained through virtuous living.

544. puṇya-śravana-kīrtanā.
Whose greatness is praised with songs which are meritorious.

545. pulomajārchitā.
Worshipped by Indra's wife, Śachī-devi.

546. BANDHA-MOCHANĪ

546. bandha-mochanī.
The releaser from fetters.

547. barbarālakā.

The wavy-haired.

548. vimarśā-rūpiṇī.

Of the vimarśā form.

549. VIDYĀDEVI

549. vidyā.

The wisdom which leads to liberation

550. viyadādi-jagat-prasūh.

The mother of the universe composed of ether and other elements.

551. sarva-vyādhi-praśamanī.

The remover of all ailments.

552. sarva-mṛtyu-nivāriṇī.

The deliverer from all forms of death.

553. agra-gaṇyā.

The fore-most to be noticed.

554. achintya-rūpā.

Of unthinkable form.

555. kali-kalmasha-nāśinī.

The destroyer of sins in the present age of evil.

556. kātyāyanī.

The daughter of the sage named Katya.

557. kāla-hantrī.

The destroyer of time.

558. kamalākṣa-nishevitā.

Worshipped by Kamalāksha (viz. Vishṇu, who is lotus-eyed)

556. KATYAYANI

559. tāmbūla-pūrita-mukhī.
Her mouth is filled with betel leaves.

560. dāḍimī-kusuma-prabhā.
Of the hue of pomegranate flower.

561. mṛgākshī.
The fawn-eyed.

562. MOHINĪ

562. mohinī.
The enchantress.

563. mukhyā.
The most important one.

564. mṛḍāṇī.
The wife of Mṛḍa (viz. Śiva)

565. mitra-rūpiṇī.
Of the form of the friend.

566. nitya-tṛptā.
The ever-content.

569. NIKHILEŚVARĪ

567. bhakta-nidhih.

The treasure for the devotees.

568. niyantrī

The regulator.

569. nikhileśvarī.

Ruler of all.

570. maitryādi-vāsanā-labhyā.

To be attained through the sentiments like friendliness.

571. mahā-pralaya-sākshiṇī.

The witness of the great dissolution

572. parā-śaktih.

The supreme power.

573. parā-nishṭhā.

The final place of rest.

574. prajñāna-ghana-rūpiṇī.

Of the nature of the mass of knowledge.

575. mādhvī-pānālasā.

Languid by drinking wine.

576. mattā.

The inebriated.

577. mātṛkā-varṇa-rūpiṇī.

Of the form of the sacred mātṛkā letters (matrices) 'a', to 'ksha', of the Sanskrit alphabet.

गणेशग्रहनक्षत्रयोगिनीराशिरूपिणीं।
देवीं मन्त्रमयीं नौमि मातृकां पीठरूपिणीम्।।
Nityā-shodasikārnava

578. mahā-kailāsa-nilayā.
Residing in the great Kailāsa.

579. mṛṇāla-mṛdu-dorlatā.
Her creeper-like arms are soft as the lotus stem.

580. mahanīyā.
Illustrious.

581. dayā-mūrtih.
The personification of mercy.

582. mahā-sāṁrājya-śālinī.
Resplendent with wide dominion.

583. ātma-vidyā.
The self-gnosis.

यज्ञविद्या महाविद्या गुह्यविद्या च शोभने।
आत्माविद्या च देवि त्वं विमुक्तिफलदायिनी।।

cf. Linga-purāna
आत्माकारेण संवित्तिः बुधैः विद्येति गीयते।।

584. mahā-vidyā.
cf. This refers to shoḍasī-vidyā
वर्णितुं नैव शक्येऽयं श्रीविद्या षोडशाक्षरी।
ब्रह्मविद्यास्वरूपा हि भुक्तिमुक्तिफलप्रदा।।

The exalted science

Vāmakesvara-Tantra : सर्वदेवमयी विद्या।

585. śrī-vidyā.

The sacred and mystic science.

तन्त्रेषु ललितादेव्यास्तेषु मुख्यमिदं मुने।
श्रीविद्यैव तु मन्त्राणां तत्र कादिर्यथा परा।।

cf. also मोक्षैकहेतुर्विद्या तु श्रीविद्या नात्र संशय:

586. kāma-sevitā.

Served by Manmatha (the god of love)

one of the twelve originators of Sri-vidyā tradition, especially of the fifteen-syllables mantra, panchadasī

काम्यते योगिभिरिति काम:।

587. śrī-shoḍaśakshārī-vidyā.

The science of sixteen-syllabled mantra.

कामराजाख्यमन्त्रान्ते श्रीबीजेन समन्विता।
षोडशाक्षरविद्येति प्रकीर्तिता।।

Jñānārṇava

588. tri-kūṭā.

Three-peaked (viz. the three groups of syllables in the above mantra, known as the kūṭās : Vāgbhava, Kāmarāja and Śakti).

589. kama-koṭikā.

The deity of the sacred site, Kāma-kotī.

586. KAMA

590. kaṭāksha-kiṁkarī-bhūta-kamalā-koṭi-sevitā.

Served by millions of Lakshmīs, who are won over merely by her side glances

591. śirah-sthitā.

Residing in the head.

592. chandra-nibhā.

Moon-like.

593. phāla-sthā.

Situated in the forehead.

594. indra-dhanush-prabhā.

Rainbow-hued.

595. hṛdaya-sthā.

Abiding in the heart.

596. ravi-prakhyā.

Resembling the sun.

597. trikoṇāntara-dıpikā.

The light shining within the triangle (in the Śrī-chakra)

598. dākshāyaṇī.

The daughter of Daksha-prajāpati.

599. daitya-hantrī.

The slayer of demons.

600. daksha-yajna-vināśinī.

The destroyer of the sacrifice of Daksha-prajāpati.

601. darāndolita-dīrghākshī.

Wide-eyed and shiftly-eyed.

602. dara-hāsojjvalan-mukhī.

Face lit up with slight smile.

599. DAITYA-HANTRĪ

603. guru-mūrtih.

Assuming the form of the teacher.

आदिनाथो महादेवि महाकालो हि यः स्मृतः।
गुरुः स एव देवेशि सर्वमन्त्रेषु नापरः।।

also Kulachūdāmani

अहं विशामि त्वद्देहे शक्त्या युक्तोऽभवत्प्रभुः।
तस्माद् भव गुरुर्नाथ शिष्योऽहं परमेश्वर।।

604. guṇa-nidhih.

The treasure-house of great qualities.

605. gōmātā.

The Mother of kine.

606. guha-janma-bhūh.

The mother of Guha (viz.Kārtikeya)

607. deveśī.

The ruler of all the gods.

608. daṇḍanīti-sthā.

Dwelling in order and justice.

609. daharākāśa-rūpiṇī.

The subtle ether within the heart.

610. pratipad-mukhya-rākānta-tithi-maṇḍala-pūjitā.

Worshipped by the group of tithi-nityā deities, representing the fifteen days of the lunar month from the pratipad to the full-moon.

611. kalātmikā.

Of the form of kalā.

612. kalā-nāthā.

The ruler of the kalās.

613. kāvyālāpa-vinodinī.

Delighting in the poetical forms of speech.

614. sachāmara-ramā-vāṇī-savya-dakshiṇa-sevitā.

Attended on either side by Lakshmī and Sarasvatī, bearing flywhisks.

615. ādi-śaktih.

The primordial power.

616. ameyā.

Immeasurable.

617. Ātman.

Of the nature of self in all beings.

618. paramā.

The supreme spirit.

619. pāvanākṛtih.

Of pure form.

620. aneka-koṭi-brahmāṇḍa-jananī.

The mother of many millions of worlds.

619. PĀVANĀKṚTI

621. divya-vigrahā.

Divinely shaped.

622. klīṁ-kārī.

Of the form of the mystic syllable, klīṁ.

623. kevalā.

The absolute.

624. guhyā.

The secret.

625. kaivalya-pada-dāyinī.

The bestower of the liberated status.

626. tripurā.

The deity presiding over the first enclosure in Śrī-chakra.

627. tri-jagad-vandyā.

Adored by the three worlds.

628. tri-mūrtih.

The triple-formed;of the nature of the three gods Brahmā, Vishṇu and Rudra.

629. tridaśeśvarī

The ruler of the gods.

630. tryaksharī.

The three-syllabled mantra, 'Aim Hrīm Śrīm'; or alternately 'Aim klīm sauh'.

631. divya-gandhādhyā.

Endowed with the divine fragrance.

632. sindūra-tilakāñchitā.

Decorated with the red mark on the forehead.

633. Umā.

The goddess who performed austerities for obtaining Śiva as her consort.

635.GAURĪ

634. śailendra-tanayā.

Daughter of the king of mountains (viz. The Himalayas)

635. gaurī.

The fair-complexioned one.

636. gandharva-sevitā.

Served by the celestial denizens known as Gandharvas.

637. viśva-garbhā.

Having the entire universe in her womb.

638. svarṇa-garbhā.

Of the nature of the golden egg, which brought forth the universe.

639. avaradā.

One who punishes the wicked.

640. vāgadhīśvarī

Ruler of all speech.

641. dhyāna-gamyā.

To be reached only by deep meditation.

cf. Kulārnava पूजाकोटिसमं स्तोत्रं स्तोत्रकोटिसमो जपः।
जपकोटिसमं ध्यानं ध्यानकोटिसमो लयः।।

also उत्तमो ब्रह्मसद्भावो ध्यानभावस्तु मध्यमः।
जपपूजाधमा प्रोक्ता बाह्यपूजाधमाधमा।।

642. aparicchhedyā.

Not fragmented by space and time.

643. jñāna-dā.

Bestower of knowledge.

644. jñāna-vigrahā.

Whose form is pure knowledge.

645. sarva-vedānta-samvedyā.

To be known fully through all the Upanishads.

646. satyānanda-svarūpiṇī.

One whose nature is reality and bliss.

647. lopāmudrārchitā.

Worshipped by Lopāmudra, the wife of Agastya.

648. līlā-klpta-brahmāṇḍa-maṇḍalā.

One for whom the creation of world systems is but sport.

649. adṛśyā

Invisible.

650. dṛśya-rahitā.

Beyond the visible objects.

651. vijñātrī.

The all-knower.

652. vedya-varjitā.

Transcending the knowable; she has nothing to be known.

653. yoginī.

Engaged in yoga.

654. yoga-dā.

Bestower of Yoga.

655. Yogyā.

The object of yoga.

656. yogānandā.

Delighting in yoga; the bliss of yoga.

657. yugaṁdharā.

The bearer of the yoke; the bearer of the ages(yugas), kṛta, tretā, dvāpara and kali.

658. icchhā-śakti-jñāna-śakti-kriyā-śakti-svarūpiṇī.

Of the form of the three energies of desire, gnosis and action.

659. sarvādhārā,

Supporter of all.

(cf. Durgā-sapta-śatī, 11, 4, 4:

आधारभूता जगतस्त्वमेका)

660. supratishṭhā.

Firmly established.

661. sad-asad-rūpa-dhāraṇī.

The foundation for all forms, real as well as unreal.

662. ashṭa-mūrtih.

The goddess who personifies eight forms (categories of existence : earth, water, fire, air and ākāśa; manas, ahaṁkāra and prakṛti)

663. ajā-jaitrī.

The conqueror of primal ignorance(avidyā)

664. loka-yātrā-vidhāyinī.

The director of the course of the worlds, their origination preservation and dissolution.

665. ekākinī.

The one, without a second.

(cf. Devī-bhāgavata, 1, 15, 52

सर्वं खल्विदमेवाहं नान्यदस्ति सनातनम्।)

666. bhūma-rūpā.

The aggregate of all existing things; the highest form; the Brahman.

667. nirdvaitā.

Devoid of plurality and differentiation.

668. dvaita-varjitā.

Transcending duality.

(cf. Devī-bhāgavata, 3, 6, 2

सदैकत्वं न भेदोऽस्ति सर्वदैव।)

669. anna-dā.

The giver of food.

675. BRĀHMĪ

670. vasu-dā.

The giver of wealth.

671. vṛddhā.

The ancient one; the primaeval spirit.

672. brahmātmaikya-svarūpiṇī.

The nature of the oneness of Brahman and ātman (the individual soul)

673. bṛhatī.

The great one.

673. brāhmaṇī.

The consort of Brāhmaṇa.

675. brāhmī.

The consort or power (śakti) of Brahmā.

676. brahmānandā.

The bliss of Brahman.

677. bali-priyā.

Delighting in the offerings made by the devotees.

678. bhāshā-rūpā.

Of the form of languages which human beings use.

679. bṛhat-senā.

With a mighty army.

680. bhavābhāva-vivarjitā.

Devoid of both existence and non-existence.

681. sukhārādhyā.

Easily worshipped.

682. śubha-karī.

The performer of good deeds.

683. śobhanā-sulabhā-gatih.

The happy and right path, which is also easily attained, viz. the liberation.

684. rāja-rajeśvarī.

The ruler of the king of kings (or Kubera)

(Kubera is one of the twelve promulgators of Śrī-vidyā)

685. rājya-dāyinī.

The bestower of dominion.

686. rājya-vallabhā.

Delighting in dominion.

687. rājat-kṛpā.

Radiating compassion.

688. rājapīṭha-niveśita-nijaśritā.

Her dependants are established on thrones.

689. rājya-lakshmīh.

The royal wealth and splendour

(The reference is to the five Lakshmīs : (1) Śrī-vidyā, (2) Ekāksharī (3) Mahā (4) Sāṁrājya and (5) Tri-śakti)

690. kośa-nāthā.

The sovereign of the treasures.

(Five treasures are mentioned in the text (1) Śrī-vidyā (2) Param-jyothi (3) Pari-nishkalā-śāṁbhavī (4) Ajapā and (5) Mātṛka, and the goddess is described as Pañcha-kośeśvarī).

691. chaturaṅga-baleśvarī.

The ruler of the four-fold army of kings (elephants, horses, foot-soldiers and chariots)

692. sāṁrajya-dāyinī.

The bestower of empires.

693. satya-sandhā.

Devoted to truth.

694. sāgara-mekhalā.

Girdled by the oceans.

695. dīkshitā.

Initiated into the mystic lore.

696. daitya-śamanī.

The suppressor of the demons.

697. sarva-loka-vaśaṁkarī.

One who conquers all the worlds and keeps them under her control.

698. sarvārtha-dātrīi.

The bestower all objects that one desires.

(cf. Siddheśvara-tantra

सर्वसिद्धिप्रदा देवी हेलयापि च चिन्तिता।

ततः सा दक्षिणा नाम्ना त्रिषु लोकेषु गीयते।।)

699. sāvitrī.

The solar deity.

700. sat-chid-ānanda-rūpiṇī.

The form of existence, consciousness and bliss.

701. deśa-kālāparicchhinnā.

Unlimited by space and time.

702. sarvagā.

Omnipresent.

703. SARVA-MOHINĪ

704. SARASVATĪ

703. sarva-mohinī.

Bewitching all creatures.

704. sarasvatī.

The goddess of speech and learning.

705. śāstramayī.

The nature of scriptural lore.

706. guhāmbā.

The mother of Guha (viz. Kārtikeya); guha also represents the peak-syllable 'Hrīm' in Pañchadaśī.

707. guhya-rūpiṇī.

One whose real form is altogether hidden

708. sarvopādhi-vinirmuktā.

Free from all limitations and dependences.

709. sadāśiva-pati-vratā.

The devoted spouse of her husband Sadāśiva.

710. sampradāyeśvarī.

The lady presiding over traditional wisdom.

711. sādhu.

The proper one and the most gentle goddess.

712. kāmakalā.

Of the form of kāma-kalā.

713. guru-maṇḍala-rūpiṇī.

Of the nature of the lineage of spritual masters from Sadāśiva till one's own teacher.

714. kulottīrṇā.

Transcending the sense-functions.

715. bhagārādhyā.

One who is to be worshipped in the solar orb.

716. māyā.

The power of delusions and projections (symbolized by the syllable 'Hrīṁ')

717. madhumatī.

The goddess named Madhumatī; the spirit who is sweet like honey. (Madhu-vidyā is referred to here).

718. mahī.

The earth (represented in the outermost enclosure in Śrīchakra, bhūpura)

719. gaṇāmbā.

The Mother of the hosts of attendants (viz. the yoginīs)

(The gaṇas of the devī are the seven well-known mātṛkas; nine kula-devis viz. Nārasiṁhī, Chāmuṇḍā, Vāruṇī, Kalāpī, Kurukullā, Nārāyaṇī, Kaumāri, Parājitā and Aparājitā; and the eight nāyikās Balinī, Kāmeśvarī, Vimalā, Aruṇā, Medinī, Jayantī, Sarveśvarī and Kauleśī).

720. guhyakārādhyā.

Worshipped by the guhyakas (a class of celestial beings)

721. komalāṅgī.

The tender-limbed one.

722. guru-priyā

Beloved of the spritual masters.

(cf. मन्त्ररूपा भवेद्देवी देवरूपो गुरुर्भवेत्।
गुरूरूपा भवेदात्मा आत्मरूपी मनुर्भवेत्॥)

723. svatantrā

The Independent one.

724. sarva-tantreśī.

The ruler of all Tantras.

725. dakshiṇāmūrti-rūpiṇī.

Of the form of Dakshiṇāmūrti.

726. sanakādi-samārādhyā.

Worshipped by the sages Sanaka and others.

727. śiva-jñāna-pradāyinī.

The bestower of the knowledge of Śiva.

728. chitkalā.

An aspect of pure consciousness.

729. ānanda-kalīka.

An aspect of bliss.

729. ĀNANDA-KALIKĀ

733 NANDI-VIDYĀ

730. prema-rūpā.

Of the form of love.

731. priyaṁ-karī.

The performer of what is good and desired.

732. nāma-pārāyaṇa-prītā.

One who delights in the repetition of (Her) names by the devotees.

733. nandi-vidyā.

The branch of knowledge taught by Nandi.

734. naṭeśvarī.

Wife of Naṭarāja.

735. mithyā-jagad-adhiṣṭhānā.

The ground of this illusory universe.

736. mukti-dā.

The giver of emancipation.

737. mukti-rūpiṇī.

Of the form of emancipation.

738. lāsya-priyā.

Fond of the feminine variety of dancing.

739. laya-karī.

Causing dissolution.

738. LĀSYAPRIYĀ

740. LAJJĀ

740. lajjā.

The principle of modesty (hrī).

741. raṁbhādi-vanditā.

Adored by the heavenly nymphs Raṁbhā and others.

742. bhava-dāva-sudhā-vṛshṭih.

The rain of nectar in the forest of wordly existence.

743. pāpāraṇya-dāvānalā.

The forest-fire (consuming) the forest of sins.

744. daurbhāgya-tūla-vātūlā.

The gale blowing away misfortune like thistledown.

745. jarādhvānta-ravi-prabhā.

The sunshine (dispelling) the darkness of decay.

746. bhāgyābdhi-chandrikā.

The moonlight (illuminating) the ocean of good fortune.

747. bhakta-chitta-keki-ghanāghanā.

The cloud that (nourishes) the peacocks which are the minds of her devotees.

748. roga-parvata-dambholih.

The thunderbolt which shatters the mountain of diseases.

749. mṛtyu-dāru-kuṭhārikā.

The axe that cuts down the tree of death.

751 MAHĀKĀLĪ

750. maheśvarī.

The great ruler.

751. mahākālī.

The consort of Mahā-kāla.

752. mahā-grāsā.

The great devourer.

753. mahāśanā.

The great consumer.

754. aparṇā.

Pārvati who performed severe austerities, without having even a leaf for her garment.

755. CHAṆḌIKĀ

755. chaṇḍikā.

The goddess who is violent of aspect.

756. chaṇḍa-muṇḍāsura-nishūdinī.

The destroyer of demons Chaṇḍa and Muṇḍa.

757. ksharā-ksharātmikā.

One who comprehends both what is perishable and what is not.

758. sarva-lokeśī

The ruler of all worlds.

759. viśva-dhāriṇī.

The supporter of the universe.

760. tri-varga-dātrī.

The giver of the threefold values of life (virtue, wealth and pleasures).

761. subhagā

Good fortune.

762. tryaṁbakā.

The three-eyed one.

763. triguṇātmikā.

Possessed of the three qualities (sattva, rajas and tamas).

764. svargāpavarga-dā.

The bestower of heavens as well as emancipation. (cf Durgā-sapta-śatī, 13, 5,

आराधिता सैव नृणां भोगस्वर्गापवर्गदा)

765. śuddhā.

The pure one.

766. japā-pushpa-nibhākṛtih.

One whose body is like the hibiscus flower.

767. ojovatī.

Full of vitality.

768. dyuti-dharā.

The light-bearer.

769. yajña-rūpā.

Of the nature of sacrifice.

770. priya-vratā.

Fond of vows.

771. durārādhyā.

One who is difficult to worship.

772. durādharshā.

One who is difficult to be taken possession of.

773. pāṭalī-kusuma-priyā.

Fond of pāṭali flowers.

774. mahatī.

The great one.

775. meru-nilayā.

Residing on the mount Meru; or in Śrī-chakra.
श्रीचक्रमपि देवेशि मेरूरूपं न संशयः। -Jñānārṇava)

776. mandāra-kusuma-priyā.

Fond of the Mandāra flowers.

777. vīrārādhyā.

Worshipped by the valiant ones (viz. those who have strong minds and firm will).

778. virāḍ-rūpā.

One whose form is immense and wise-spread, comprehending all that is moving and all that is stationary

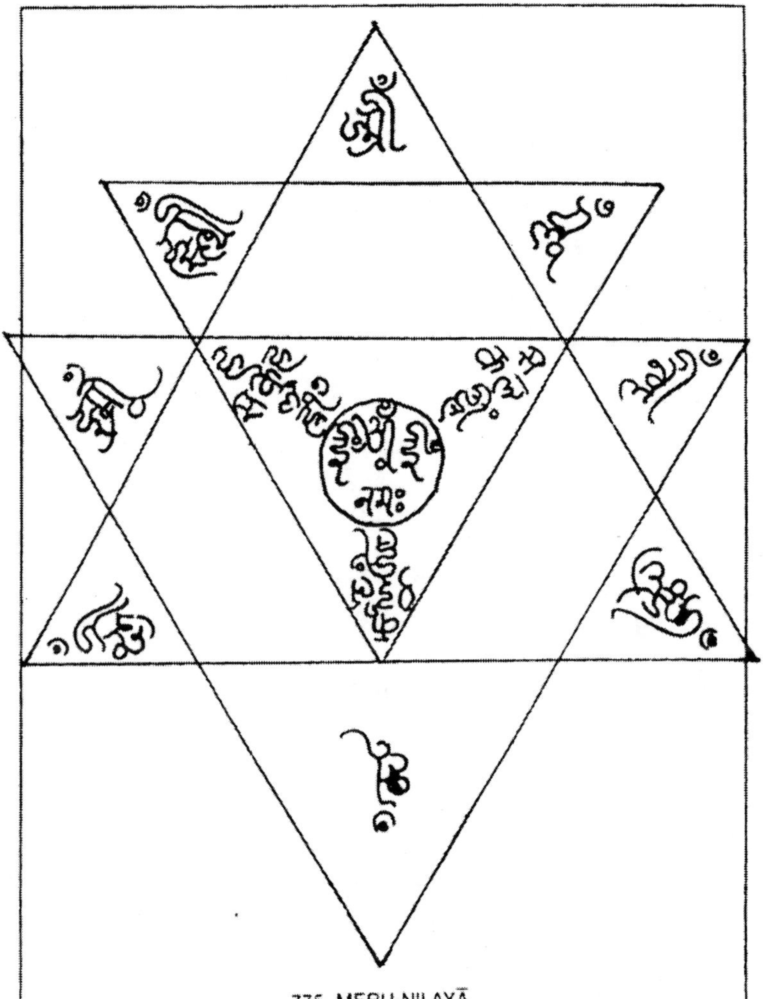

775. MERU-NILAYĀ

779. virajāh.

Without the stains of passion.

780. viśvato-mukhī.

With her countenance on all sides.

781. pratyag-rūpā.

The interior nature of all beings.

782. parākāśā

The supreme akāśa.

783. prāṇa-dā.

The giver of life.

784. prāṇa-rūpiṇī.

The form of life in all beings.

785. mārtāṇḍabhairavāradhyā.

Worshipped by Mārtāṇḍa-bhairava.

786. mantriṇī-nyasta-rājya-dhūh.

One who has entrusted the administration of her kingdom to Mantriṇī (Śyāmalā).

787. tripureśī.

The ruler of the three realms (the heavens, the mid-region and the earth).

(cf. also Yoginī-hṛdaya-

त्रिपुरेशी महामन्त्रं पिण्डाण्डात्मकमीश्वरि।

यो जानाति स योगीन्द्रः स शंभुः स हरिर्विधिः॥

788. jayat-senā.

With a victorious army.

789. nistraiguṇyā

Devoid of the effect of the three qualities (sattva, rajas and tamas).

790. parāparā.

One who is both superior and inferior.

791. satya-jñānānanda-rūpā.

One whose nature is truth, wisdom and bliss.

792. sāmarasya-parāyaṇā.

The final plane of the union of Śiva and Śakti

The reference is to the mantra which is masculine and vidyā which is feminine being identical. Bhāskara-raya says.

(सामरस्यरूपत्वात् उभयात्मतेति द्योतयितुं मन्त्राणां मध्ये विद्येत्युक्तम्।)

793. kapardinī.

The consort of Kapardi (viz. Śiva).

794. kalā-mālā.

The garland of the aspects of existence and experience (kalās).

795. kāma-dhuk.

The cow of plenty.

(The reference is to the five kāma-dudhā : (1) Śrī-vidyā, (2) Amṛta-pīṭheśī, (3) Sūdha-sū, (4) Amṛteśī and (5) Anna-pūrṇā).

796. KĀMA-RŪPIṆĪ

796. kāma-rūpiṇī.

One who assumes whatever form she desires; one whose form is desire.

797. kalā-nidhih.

The treasure-house of all learning.

798. kāvya-kalā.

The art of poetry.

799. rasa-jñā.

The knower of literary relish.

800. rasa-śevadhih.

The store-house of relish and sentiment.

801. pushṭā.

The nourished one.

802. purātanā.

The ancient one.

803. pūjyā.

The adorable one.

804. pushkarā.

The lotus.

805. pushkarekshaṇā.

The lotus-eyed one.

806. paraṁ-jyotih.

The supreme light.

807. param-dhāma.

The supreme abode.

808. paramaṇuh.

The ultimate atom.

809. pārāt-parā.

One who is above the highest.

810. pāśa-hastā.

One who holds a noose in her hand.

811. pāśa-hantrī.

The destroyer of the fetters of phenomenal existence.

812. para-mantra-vibhedinī.

The destroyer of the charms and spells cast by the enemies; Pratyaṅgirā.

813. mūrtā.

One who has a material form.

814. amūrtā.

One who is bereft of material forms.

815. anitya-tṛptā.

One who is content even with the perishable offerings.

816. muni-mānasa-haṁsikā.

The swan of the Mānasa lake (the mind of sages).

817. satya-vratā.

Of fixed vows.

818. satya-rūpā.

Of the nature of reality.

819. sarvāntaryāminī.

The inner controller of all beings.

820. satī.

The wife of Śiva, who immolated herself in the sacrificial fire of her father, Daksha.

821. brahmāṇī.

The giver of life of Brahmā.

822. brahmā.

The supreme Brahman.

(Devyatharvaśīrsha :

अहं ब्रह्मस्वरूपिणी मत्तः प्रकृतिपुरुषात्मकं जगत्।

Vāmakeśvara-tantra :

परब्रह्मस्वरूपा च।)

823. jananī.

The mother.

824. bahu-rūpā.

Of manifold form.

825. budhārchitā.

Worshipped by the wise ones.

826. prasavitrī.

The creator of all the worlds.

827. prachaṇḍā.

The violent and cruel goddess.

828. ājñā.

The command.

829. pratishṭhā.

The foundation.

830. prakaṭākṛtih.

One whose forms are manifest for all.

831. prāṇeśvarī.

The ruler of the vital currents.

832. prāṇa-dhātrī.

The nourisher of the vital currents.

833. pañchāshat-pīṭha rūpiṇī.

One who assumes the form of the fifty centres of Śakti (which correspond to the fifty letters of the Sanskrit alphabet, beginning with 'a', kāma-rūpa-pīṭ ha).

834. viśṛṅkhalā.

The unfettered one.

835. vivikta-sthā.

Abiding in lonely spots.

836. vīra-mātā.

The mother of the valiant ones.

837. viyat-prasūh.

The producer of the subtle element, ākāsa.

838. mukundā.

The nature of Vishnu; the giver of salvation.

839. mukti-nilayā.

The abode of emancipation.

840. mūla-vigraha-rūpiṇī.

One whose form is that of the primary idol.

841. bhāva-jñā.

The knower of the inmost thoughts of all beings.

842. bhava-roga-ghnī.

The destroyer of the disease that is earthly existence.

843. bhava-chakra-pravartinī.

One who sets into motion the wheel of earthly existence.

844. chhandah-sārā.

The essence of all the Vedas.

845. śāstra-sārā.

The essence of all the scriptures.

846. mantra-sārā.

The essence of all the mantras.

847. talodarī.

The flat-bellied one.

848. udāara-kīrtih.

Of high celebrity.

849. uddāma-vaibhavā.

Whose glory is exalted.

850. varṇa-rūpiṇī.

Of the nature of the letters of the alphabet.

851. jamma-mṛtyu-jarā-tapta-jana-viśrānti-dāyinī.

The bringer of peace to the beings who are burning in the fires of birth death and decay.

852. sarvopanishad-udghushṭā.

Proclaimed by all the Upanishads.

853. śāntyātīta-kalātmikā.

She is the nature of the kalā called Śāntyātīta.

854. gaṁbhīrā.

The fathomless one.

855. gaganāntah-sthā.

Residing in the interior of the sky.

856. garvitā.

The proud one.

857. gāna-lolupā.

Delighting in music.

857. GĀNA-LOLUPĀ

861. KĀNTĀRDHA-VIGRAHĀ

858. kalpanā-rahitā.

Free from mental constructions.

859. kāshṭhā.
The final end; the goal.

860. kāntā.
One who is delightful.

861. kāntārdha-vigrahā.
Having half of the body of her consort.

862. kārya-kāraṇa-nirmuktā.
Free from cause and effect.

863. kāma-keli-taraṅgitā.
Overflowing with erotic desire and pleasure.

864. kanat-kanaka-tāṭaṅkā.
Wearing gold ear-rings, which are lustrous.

865. līlā-vigraha-dhāraṇī.
Having a form only for the sake of sport.

866. ajā.
The unborn one.

867. kshaya-vinirmuktā.
Free from decay.

868. mugdhā.
The lovely maiden.

869. kshipra-prasādinī.
One who is easily pleased.

870. antar-mukha-samārādhyā.

Worshipped well by those who turn inward (viz. interested in the antaryāga or bhāvanā, contemplation).

871. bahir-mukha-sudurlabhā.

Difficult of attainment by those who are outward-oriented (viz. devoted to external objects).

872. trayī.

The triple revelation (the three vedas: Ṛig, Yajus and Sāma)

873. tri-varga-nilayā.

Abode of the three values of life (dharma, artha and kāma)

874. tri-sthā.

Residing in the three factors (viz. the three Vedas, the three worlds, the three fires, the three values, the three gunas and so on)

cf. (also refers to Śrī-Vidyā :

त्रिकलाढ्यां त्रिहृल्लेखां त्रिहृस्वस्वरभूषितां।

यो जपत्यम्ब ते विद्यां सोऽक्षर: परम: स्वराट्॥

875. tripura-mālini.

The goddess of the inner ten sided figure of Śrī-chakra.

876. nirāmayā.

Free from disease

877. nirālambā.

Without support.

878. svātmārāmā.

Rejoicing in herself.

879. sudhā-srutih.

The stream of nectar.

880. saṁsāra-paṅka-nirmagna-samuddharaṇa-paṇḍitā.

Skilled in lifting those who are sunk in the mire of phenomenal life.

881. yajña-priyā.

Fond of sacrifices.

882. yajña-kartrī.

The performer of sacrifices.

883. yajamāna-svarūpiṇī.

Of the nature of the sacrificer.

884. dharmādhārā.

The supporter of dharma.

885. dhanādhyaksha.

The ruler of all wealth.

886. dhana-dhānya-vivardhinī.

One who promotes wealth in the shape of money and grains.

887. vipra-priyā.

Fond of the wise ones.

888. vipra-rūpā.

Manifesting herself as the wise ones.

889. viśva-bhramaṇa-kāriṇī.

Causing the universe to revolve in cycles.

890. viśva-grāsā.

The consumer of the universe (during pralaya or the great dissolution).

891. vidrumābhā.

Of the colour of coral.

892. vaishṇavī.

The power of Vishṇu.

893. vishṇu-rupiṇī.

Of the form of Vishṇu.

(cf. Muṇḍa-mālā-tantra-

यथा शिवस्तथा दुर्गा या दुर्गा विष्णुरेव सः।

अत्र यः कुरुते भेदं स नरो मूढ दुर्मतिः।।

894. ayonih.

Without origin.

895. yoni-nilayā.

The ultimate place of origin; the dweller in the triangle called Kāma-kalā.

892. VAISHNAVI

898. VIRĀ

896. kūṭasthā.

One who abides in the three kūṭas (Vagbhava, Kāma-rāja and Śakti).

897. kula-rūpiṇī.,

Of the nature of conventional conduct.

898. vīra-goshṭhi-priyā.

Fond of the assembly of the valiant ones.

899. vīrā.

The valiant one.

900. naishkarmyā.

Abstaining from actions.

901. nādā-rūpiṇī.

Of the form of sound.

902. vijñāna-kalanā.

Causing perception and gnosis.

903. kalyā.

Skilful; early dawn.

904. vidagdhā.

Artful; skilled

905. baindavāsanā.

Seated in the bindu (inside the triangle in Śrī-chakra)

(cf. Jñānārṇava : त्रिकोणरूपयोनिस्तु बिन्दुना बैन्दवं भवेत्।)

906. tattvādhikā.

Transcending the categories of existence and experience.

and Chatuś-śatī

तत्वातीतस्वभावा च विद्यैषा भाष्यते सदा।।)

(cf. Liṅga-purāṇa :

विकल्परहितं तत्वं परमित्यभिधयिते।

907. tattva-mayī.

Reality itself.

(cf. Āgama-kalpa-druma :

तत्वात् ब्रह्माण्डमुन्पत्रं तत्वेन परिवर्धते।

तत्वे विलीयते देवि तत्वाद् ब्रह्माण्डनिर्णय:।।)

908. tat-tvam-artha-svarūpiṇī.

Whose nature consists of the meaning of the words, "that" and "Thou"

909. sāma-gāna-priyā.

Fond of Sāma songs.

910. saumyā.

Benign.

911. sadāśiva-kuṭumbinī.

The spouse in the household of Sadāśiva.

912. savyāpasavya-mārga-sthā.

Abiding in the right as well as the left paths.

913. sarvāpad-vinivāriṇī.

The remover of all misfortunes.

911. SADĀŚIVA-KUṬUMBINĪ

914. svasthā.

Self-contained.

915. svabhāva-madhurā.

Sweet by her very nature.

916. dhīrā.

The wise one.

917. dhīra-samarchitā.

Worshipped by the wise ones.

918. chaitanyārghya-samārādhyā.

Worshipped with consciousness as the oblation offered.

919. chaitanya-kusuma-priyā.

Fond of the Chaitanya-flower as a decoration and as an offering.

920. sadoditā.

Ever sublime.

921. sadā-tushṭā.

Ever contented.

922. taruṇāditya-pāṭalā.

Ruddy like the rising sun.

923. dakshiṇādakshiṇārādhyā.

Adored by the right hand and left hand worshippers.

924. dara-smera-mukhāṁbujā.

Whose lotus-like face is wreathed with sweet smiles.

925. kaulinī-kevalā.

Worshipped as the sole deity by the devotees of the mystic lineage who are emancipated even while they are alive 'jivan-muktāś cha kaulikāh')

926. anarghya-kaivalya-pada-dāyinī.

The bestower of the abode of invaluable emancipation.

927. stotra-priyā.

Fond of praise.

928. stuti-matī.

Recipient of praise.

929. śruti-samstuta-vaibhavā.

Whose glory is celebrated in the scriptures.

930. manasvinī.

Having mind under her control.

931. mānavatī

High-minded.

932. maheśī.

Consort of Mahesa; the great sovereign.

933. maṅgalākṛtih.

Of beneficial appearance.

933. MAṄGALĀKṚTI

934. viśva-mātā.

The mother of the universe.

935. jagat-dhātrī.

The supporter of the world.

936. viśālākshi.

The wide-eyed one.

937. virāgiṇī.

The dispassionate one.

938. pragalbhā.

The mature and talented lady.

939. paramodārā.

Supremely generous.

940. parāmodā.

Supremely delightful.

941. manomayī.

Dominated by mind.

942. vyoma-keśī.

Whose hair is ākāśa.

943. vimāna-sthā.

Riding the celestial chariot.

944. vajriṇī.

945. VĀMAKEŚVARĪ

One who carries the weapon known as vajra.

945. vāmakeśvarī.

Of the nature of the tantra by that name (Vāmakeśvaratantra).

946. pañcha-yajña-priyā.

Fond of five sacrifices prescribed for the householder (deva, pitr, manushya bhūta and brahma).

947. pañcha-preta-mañchādhiśāyinī.

Recumbent upon a couch formed of five'corpses'. (the pañcha-brahmās : Vishṇu, Rudra, Iśvara and Sadāśiva)

948. pañchamī.

The fifth one (viz. Vārāhi)

949. pañcha-bhūteśī

Ruler of the five elements (earth, water, fire, air and ākāśa)

950. pañcha-saṁkhyopachāriṇī.

Worshipped with five offerings : gandha, pushpa, dhūpa, dīpa and naivedya.

951. śāsvatī

The eternal one.

952. śāsvat-aiśvaryā.

Possessing eternal dominion.

953. śarmadā.

The giver of happiness.

954. śaṁbhu-mohinī.

One who bewitched Śaṁbhu (viz. Śiva)

955. dharā.

The earth.

956. dhara-sutā,

The daughter of Himavān.

957. dhanyā.

The fortunate one.

958. dhārmiṇī.

The righteous one.

959. dharma-vardhinī.

The promoter of righteousness.

960. lokātītā.

Transcending the worlds.

961. guṇātītā.

Transcending the qualities (the three guṇas)

962. sarvātītā.

Transcending all.

963. śamātmikā.

Of the nature of tranquility.

964. bandhūka-kusuma-prakhyā.

Resembling the Bandhūka flower.

965. BĀLĀ

965. bālā.

The young maiden (the goddess Bālā.)

कामेशि ललिता बाला महत्रिपुरसुन्दरी।
त्रिपुरा भैरवी ह्येता ऊर्ध्वाम्नायं समाश्रिता:।।

966. līlā-vinodinī.

Delighting in sport.

967. sumaṅgalī.

Very auspicious.

968. sukha-karī.

One who makes for happiness.

969. suveshāḍhyā.

Bedecked with beautiful raiment.

970. suvāsinī.

In auspicious married state.

971. suvāsinyarchana-prītā.

Pleased by the worship conducted by married woman.

972. āśobhanā.

Ever beautiful.

973. śuddha-mānasā.

The pure-minded.

974. bindu-tarpaṇa-santushṭā

Pleased by offerings in the bindu.

975. pūrva-jā.

The first-born.

976. tripurāmbikāa.

The goddess presiding over the eighth enclosure in Sri-chakra.

977. daśa-mudrā-samārādhyā.

Worshipped by ten mudrā-devatās located in the inner line of the 'bhūpura' enclosure of Śrī-chakra; Saṁkshobhiṇī, Vidrāviṇī, Ākarshaṇī, Vaśaṁkarī, unmādinī, Mahāṅkuśā, Khecharī, Bījā, Yonī and Iśvarī.

(cf. योनिं लिंगं च सुरभि हेतिमुद्राचतुष्टयम्।

वनमालां महामुद्रां नभोमुद्रामपि क्रमात्।

The four heti-mudrās (viz. weapons) mentioned above are

पुस्तकं ज्ञानशूलं च कपालं चेति च क्रमात्।)

The mudrās (hand-gestures) are also shown immediately after dhyāna of the divine form. The ten powers of the deity to overcome obstacles respresented by weapons are also called mudrās or hand-gestures: triśūla, makarī, padma, dhenu, āvāhana, sthāpana, namaskāra, parigha, ghaṭa and mṛgī.

978. tripurā-śrī-vasaṁkarī.

The ruler of Tripurā.

979. jñāna-mudrā.

Whose form is the gesture of gnosis.

980. jñāna-gamyā.

To be attained by supreme gnosis.

981. jñāna-jñeya-svarūpiṇī.

Of the form of knowledge and the object of knowledge.

982. yoni-mudrā.

Whose form is the gesture of Yoni.

983. trikhaṇḍeśī.

The ruler of the three units of the mantra.

(The three kāṭas are Vāgbhava, Kāma-rāja and Śakti), to be invoked in the three points of the devotee's body : navel, heart and between the eyebrows respectively).

The Khaṇḍas are

1) क ए ई ल ह्रीं।।

2) ह स क ह ल ह्रीं।। and

3) सकल ह्रीं

984. tri-guṇā.

Endowed with the three qualities (sattva, rajas and tamas)

985. aṁbā.

The mother.

986. trikoṇa-gā.

Residing in the triangle (kāma-kalā)

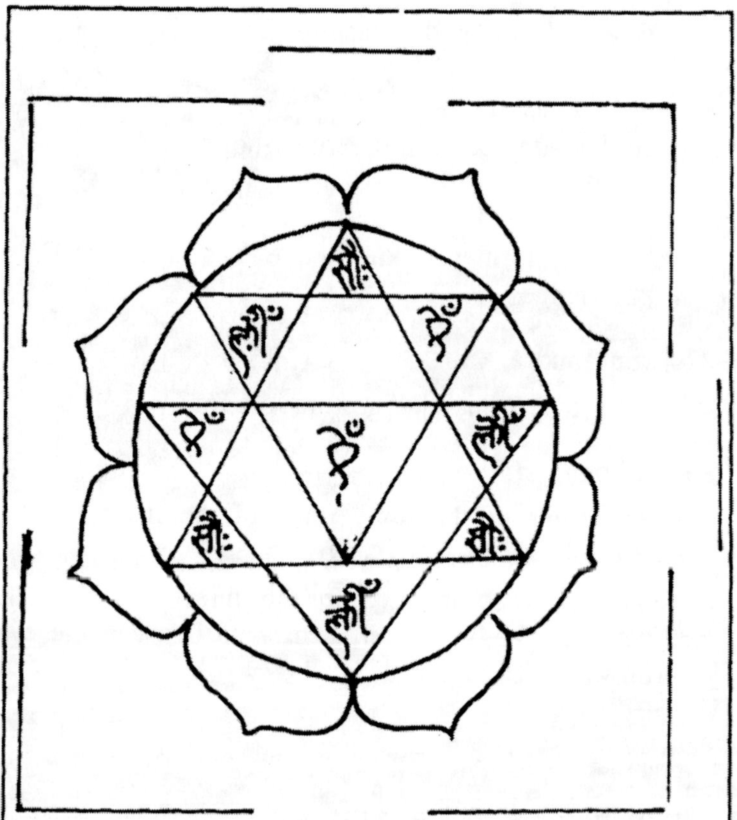

987. anaghā.

The sinless one.

988. adbhuta-chāritrā.

One whose deeds are marvellous.

989. vāñchhitārtha-pradāyinī.

The bestower of all the desired objects.

990. abhyāsātiśaya-jñātā.

Known through constant, continued and intense devotion.

991. shaḍ-adhvātīta-rūpiṇī.

Transcending the six pathways: tattva, pāda, varṇa, bhuvana, mantra and kalā.

992. avyāja-karuṇā-mūrtih.

Personification of compassion without a reason.

993. ajñā-dhvānta-dīpikā.

The lamp that dispels the darkness of ignorance.

994. ābāla-gopa-viditā.

Known even to small children and ignorant cowherds.

995. sarvānullanghya-śāsanā.

One whose commands are never disobeyed by any one.

996. śrī-chakra-rāja-nilayā.

Abiding in the great Śrī-chakra.

997. śrīmat-tripura-sundarī.

The great goddess tripura-sundarī.

998. śrī-śivā.

The great and benevolent goddess.

999. śiva-śaktyaika-rūpiṇī.

The united form of Śiva and Śakti.

(The reference is to the Śrī-chakra, where the Śiva-units and the Śakti-units combine to produce the Chakra).

चतुर्भिः शिवचक्रैश्च शक्तिक्रैश्च पंचभिः।

नवचक्रैश्च संसिद्धं श्रीचक्रं शिवयोर्वपुः॥)

1000. lalitāṁbikā.

The Mother Lalitā

॥ श्री ॥

॥ ललितात्रिशतीस्तोत्रम्॥

In the Introductory portion, Agastya tells Hayagrīva that his mind is not at rest even after receiving the Stotra containing the thousand names, and begs him to communicate the further wisdom about Lalitā. Agastya held the feet of Hayagrīva in supplication and continued in this position for three full years. Hayagrīva did not know what further wisdom was held back from Agastya, and was wrapt in thought about it. At length Lalitā herself appeared with her consort, Kameśvara, before Hayagrīva, and revealed to him the Triśatī, which she herself had composed along with Kameśvara, and directed Hayagrīva to communicate this to Agastya, and this would set his mind at rest. Hayagrīva thereupon asked Agastya to rise and gave him the wisdom contained in Triśatī-stotra.

अगस्त्य उवाच–

हयग्रीव दयासिन्धो भगवन् शिष्यवत्सल।
त्वत्तः श्रुतमशेषेण श्रोव्यं यद्यदस्ति तत्॥१॥

रहस्यनामसाहस्त्रमपि त्वत्तः श्रुतं मया।
इतः परं मे नास्त्येव श्रोतव्यमिति निश्चयः॥२॥

तथापि मम चित्तस्य पर्याप्तिर्नैव जायते।
कात्स्न्यार्थः प्राप्य इत्येव शोचयिष्याम्यहं प्रभो॥३॥

किमिदं कारणं ब्रूहि ज्ञातव्यांशोऽस्ति वा पुनः।
अस्ति चेन्मम तद्ब्रूहि ब्रूहीत्युक्त्वा प्रणम्य तम्।।४।।

सूत उवाच–

समाललम्बे तत्पादयुगलं कलशोद्भवः।
हयाननो भीतभीतः किमिदं किमिदं त्विति।।५।।

मुञ्च मुञ्चेति तं चोक्त्वा चिन्ताक्रान्तो बभूव सः।
चिरं विचार्य निश्चिन्वन्वक्तव्यं न मयेत्यसौ।।६।।

तूष्णीं स्थितः स्मरन्नाज्ञां ललिताम्बाकृतं पुरा।
प्रणम्य विप्रं स मुनिस्तत्पादावत्यजन्स्थितः।।७।।

वर्षत्रयावधि तथा गुरुशिष्यौ तथा स्थितौ।
तच्छृण्वन्तश्च पश्यन्तः सर्वलोकाः सुविस्मिताः।।८।।

ततः श्रीललितादेवी कामेश्वरसमन्विता।
प्रादुर्भूय हयग्रीवं रहस्येवमचोदयत्।।९।।

श्रीदेव्युवाच–

अश्वाननावयोः प्रीतिः शास्त्रविश्वासिनि त्वयि।
राज्यं देयं शिरो देयं न देया षोडशाक्षरी।।१०।।

स्वमातृजारवद्गोप्या विद्यैषेत्यागमा जगुः।
ततोऽतिगोपनीया मे सर्वपूर्तिकरी स्तुतिः।।११।।

मया कामेश्वरेणापि कृता संगोपिता भृशम्।
मदाज्ञया वचो देव्यश्चक्रुर्नामसहस्रकम्।।१२।।

आवाभ्यां कथितां मुख्यं सर्वपूर्तिकरी स्तुतिः।
सर्वक्रियाणां वैकल्यपूर्तिर्यज्जपतो भवेत्।।१३।।

सर्वपूर्तिकरं तस्मादिदं नाम कृतं मया।
तद्ब्रूहि त्वमगस्त्याय पात्रमेव न संशयः॥१४॥

पत्न्यस्य लोपामुद्राख्या मामुपास्तेऽतिभक्तितः।
अयं च नितरां भक्तस्तस्मादस्य वदस्व तत्॥१५॥

अमुञ्चमानस्त्वत्पादौ वर्षत्रयमसौ स्थितः।
एतज्ज्ञातुमतो भक्त्या हीदमेव निदर्शनम्॥१६॥

चित्तपर्याप्तिरेतस्य नान्यथा संभविष्यति।
सर्वपूर्तिकरं तस्मादनुज्ञातो मया वद॥१७॥

सूत उवाच–

इत्युक्त्वान्तरधादम्बा कामेश्वरसमन्विता।
अथोत्थाप्य हयग्रीवः पाणिभ्यां कुम्भसंभवम्॥८॥

संस्थाप्य निकटे वाचमुवाच भृशविस्मितः।

हयग्रीव उवाच–

कृतार्थोऽसि कृतार्थोऽसि कृतार्थोऽसि घटोद्भव॥

त्वत्समो ललिताभक्तो नास्ति नास्ति जगत्त्रये।
येनागस्त्य स्वयं देवी तव वक्तव्यमन्वशात्॥२०॥

सच्छिष्येण त्वया चाहं द्रष्टवानस्मि तां शिवाम्।
यतन्ते दर्शनार्थाय ब्रह्मविष्णवीशपूर्वकाः॥२१॥

अतः परं ते वक्ष्यामि सर्वपूर्तिकरं स्तवम्।
यस्य स्मरणमात्रेण पर्याप्तिस्ते भवेद्धृदि॥२२॥

रहस्यनामसाहस्रादपि गुह्यतमं मुने।
आवश्यकं ततोऽप्येतल्ललितां समुपासितुम्॥२३॥

तदहं संप्रवक्ष्यामि ललिताम्बानुशासनात्।
श्रीमत्पञ्चदशाक्षर्याः कादिवर्णान्क्रमान्मुने।।२४।।

पृथिग्वंशतिनामानि कथितानि घटोद्भव।
आहत्य नाम्नां त्रिशती सर्वसंपूर्तिकारिणी।।२५।।

रहस्यातिरहस्यैषा गोपनीय प्रयत्नतः।
तां श्रुष्णुष्व महाभाग सावधानेन चेतसा।।२६।।

केवलं नामबुद्धिस्ते न कार्या तेषु कुम्भज।
मन्त्रात्मकत्वमेतेषां नाम्नां नामात्मतापि च।।२७।।

तस्मादेकाग्रनमसा श्रोतव्यं च त्वया सदा।

सूत उवाच–

इत्युक्त्वा तं हयग्रीवः प्रोचे नामशतत्रयम्।।२८।।

हयग्रीव उवाच–

ककाररूपा कल्याणी कल्यणगुणशलिनी।
कल्याणशैलनिलया कमनीया कलावती।।

कमलाक्षी कल्मषघ्नी करुणामृतसागरा।
कदम्बकाननावासा कदम्बकुसुमप्रिया।।१।।

कंदर्पविद्या कंदर्पजनकापाङ्गवीक्षणा।
कर्पूरवीटीसौरभ्यकल्लोलितककुप्तटा।।३।।

कलिदोषहरा कंजलोचना कम्रविग्रहा।
कर्भादिसाक्षिणी कारयित्री कर्मफलप्रदा।।४।।

ॐ एतत्तदित्यनिर्देश्या चैकानन्दचिदाकृतिः।।५।।

एतत्तदित्यनिर्देश्या चैकानन्दचिदाकृतिः।।८।।

एकाग्रचित्तनिर्ध्याता चैषणारहितादृता।।६।।

एकाग्रचित्तनिर्ध्याता चैषणारहितादृता।।
एकभोगा चैकरसा चैकैश्वर्यप्रदायिनी।।७।।

एकातपत्रसाम्राज्यप्रदा चैकान्तपूजिता।
एधमानप्रभा चैजदनेकजगदीश्वरी।।७।।

एकभोगा चैकरसा चैकैश्वर्गप्रदायिनी।।८।।

एकवीरादिसंसेव्या चैकप्रभवशालिनी।
ईकाररूपा चेशित्री चेप्सितार्थप्रदायिनी।।९।।

ईदृगित्य निर्देश्या चेश्वरत्वविधायिनी।
ईशानादिब्रह्ममयी चेशित्वाद्यष्टसिद्धिदा।।१०।।

ईक्षित्रीक्षणसृष्टाण्डकोटिरीश्वरवल्लभा।
ईडिता चेश्वरार्धाङ्गशरीरेशाधिदेवता।।११।।

ईश्वरप्रेरणकरी चेशताण्डवसाक्षिणी।
ईश्वरोत्सङ्गनिलया चेतिबाधाविनाशिनी।।१२।।

ईहाविरहिता चेशशक्तिरीषत्स्मितानना।
लकाररूपा ललिता लक्ष्मीवाणीनिषेविता।।१३।।

लाकिनी ललनारूपा लसद्दाडिमपाटला।
ललन्तिकालसत्फाला ललाटनयनार्चिता।।१४।।

लक्षणोज्ज्वलदिव्याङ्गी लक्षकोट्यण्डनायिका।
लक्ष्यार्था लक्षणागम्या लब्धकामा लतातनुः।।१५।।

ललामराजदलिका लम्बिमुक्तालताञ्चिता।
लम्बोदरप्रसूर्लभ्या लज्जाढ्या लयवर्जिता।।१६।।

ह्रींकाररूपा ह्रींकारनिलया ह्रींपदप्रिया।
ह्रींकारबीजा ह्रींकारमन्त्रा ह्रींकारलक्षणा।।१७।।

ह्रींकारजपसुप्रीता ह्रींमती ह्रींविभूषणा।
ह्रींशीला ह्रींपदारध्या ह्रींगर्भा ह्रींपदाभिधा॥१८॥

ह्रींकारवाच्या ह्रींकारपूज्या ह्रींकारपीठिका।
ह्रींकारवेद्या ह्रींकारचिन्त्या ह्रीं ह्रींशरीरिणी॥१९॥

हरप्रिया हराराध्या हरिब्रह्मेन्द्रवन्दिता॥२०॥

हयारूढासेविताङ्घ्रिर्हयमेधसमर्चिता।
हर्यक्षवाहना हंसवाहना हतदानवा॥२१॥

हत्यादिपापशमनी हरिदश्वादिसेविता।
हस्तिकुम्भोत्तुङ्गकुचा हस्तिकृत्तिप्रियाङ्गना॥२२॥

हरिद्राकुङ्कुमादिग्धा हर्यश्वाद्यमरार्चिता।
हरिकेशसखी हादिविा हालामदोल्लसा॥२३॥

सकाररूपा सर्वज्ञा सर्वेशी सर्वमङ्गला।
सर्वकर्त्री सर्वभर्त्री सर्वहन्त्री सनातना॥२४॥

सर्वानवद्या सर्वाङ्गसुन्दरी सर्वसाक्षिणी।
सर्वात्मिका सर्वसौख्यदात्री सर्वविमोहिनी॥२५॥

सर्वाधारा सर्वगता सर्वावगुणवर्जिता।
सर्वारुण सर्वमाता सर्वभूषणभूषिता॥२६॥

ककारार्था कालहन्त्रीं कामेशी कामितार्थदा।
कामसंजीवनी कल्या कठिनस्तनमण्डला॥२७॥

करभोरु: कलानाथमुखी कचजिताम्बुदा।
कटाक्षस्यन्दिकरुणा कपालिप्राणनायिका:॥२८॥

कारुण्यविग्रहा कान्ता कान्तिधूतजपावलि:।
कलालापा कम्बुकण्ठी करनिर्जितपल्लवा॥२९॥

कल्पवल्लीसमभुजा कस्तूरीतिलकाञ्चिता।
हकारार्था हंसगतिर्हाटकाभरणोज्ज्वला॥३०॥

हारहारिकुचाभोगा हाकिनी हल्यवर्जिता।
हरित्पतिसमाराध्या हठात्कारहतासुरा॥३१॥

हर्षप्रदा हविर्भोक्त्री हार्दसंतमसापहा।
हल्लीसलास्यसंतुष्टा हंसमन्त्रार्थरूपिणी॥३२॥

हानोपादाननिर्मुक्ता हर्षिणी हरिसोदरी।
हाहाहूहूमुखस्तुत्या हानिवृद्धिविवर्जिता॥३३॥

हय्यङ्गवीनहृदया हरिगोपारुणांशुका।
लकाराख्या लतापूज्या लयस्थित्युद्भवेश्वरी॥३४॥

लास्यदर्शनसंतुष्टा लाभालाभविवर्जिता।
लङ्घ्येतराज्ञा लावण्यशालिनी लघुसिद्धिदा॥३५॥

लाक्षारससवर्णाभा लक्ष्मणाग्रजपूजिता।
लभ्यतरा लब्धभक्तिसुलभा लाङ्गलायुधा॥३६॥

लग्नचामरहस्तश्रीशारदापरिवीजिता।
लज्जापदसमाराध्या लंपटा लकुलेश्वरी॥३७॥

लब्धमाना लब्धरसा लब्धसंपत्समुन्नतिः
ह्रींकारिणी च ह्रींकाराद्या ह्रींमध्या ह्रींशिखामणिः॥३८॥

ह्रींकारकुण्डाग्निशिखा ह्रींकारशशिचन्द्रिका।
ह्रींकारभास्कररुचि ह्रींकाराम्भोदचञ्चला॥३९॥

ह्रींकारकन्दाङ्कुरिका ह्रींकारैकपरायणा।
ह्रींकारदीर्घिकाहंसी ह्रींकारोनकेकिनी॥४०॥

ह्रींकारारण्यहरिणी ह्रींकारालवालवल्लरी।
ह्रींकारपञ्जरशुकी ह्रींकाराङ्गणदीपिका॥४१॥

ह्रींकारकन्दरासिंही ह्रींकाराम्भोजभृङ्गिका।
ह्रींकारसुमनोमाध्वी ह्रींकारतरुमञ्जरी।।४२।।

सकाराख्या समरसा सकलागमसंस्तुता।
सर्ववेदान्ततात्पर्यभूमि: सदसदाश्रया।।४३।।

सकला सच्चिदानन्दा साध्या सद्गतिदायिनी।
सनकादिमुनिध्येया सदाशिवकुटुम्बिनी।।४४।।

सकलाधिष्ठानरूपा सत्यरूपा समाकृति:।
सर्वप्रपञ्चनिर्मात्री समानाधिकवर्जिता।।४५।।

सर्वोत्तुङ्गा संगहीना सद्गुणा सकलेष्टदा
ककारिणी काव्यलोला कामेश्वरमनोहरा।।४६।।

कामेश्वरप्रणानाडी कामेशोत्सङ्गवासिनी।
कामेश्वरालिङ्गिताङ्गी कामेश्वरसुखप्रदा।।४७।।

कामेश्वरप्रणयिनी कामेश्वरविलासिनी।
कामेश्वरतप:सिद्धि: कामेश्वरमन:प्रिया।।४८।।

कामेश्वरप्राणनाथा कामेश्वरविमोहिनी।
कामेश्वरब्रह्मविद्या कामेश्वरगृहेश्वरी।।४९।।

कामेश्वराह्लादकरी कामेश्वरमहेश्वरी।
कामेश्वरी कामकोटिनिलया काङ्क्षितार्थदा।।५०।।

लकारिणी लब्धरूप: लब्धधीर्लब्धवाञ्छिता।
लब्धपापमनोदूरा लब्धाहंकारदुर्गमां।५१।।

लब्धशक्तिर्लब्धदेहा लब्धैश्वर्यसमुन्नति:।
लब्धवृद्धिर्लब्धलीला लब्धयौवनशालिनी।।५२।।

लब्धातिशयसर्वाङ्गसौन्दर्या लब्धविभ्रमा।
लब्धरागा लब्धपतिर्लब्धनानागमस्थिति:।।५३।।

लब्धभोगा लब्धसुखा लब्धहर्षाभिपूरिता।
ह्रींकारमूर्तिर्ह्रींकारसौधशृङ्गकपोतिका॥५४॥

ह्रींकारदुग्धाब्धिसुधा ह्रींकारकमलेन्दिरा।
ह्रींकारमणिदीपार्चिर्ह्रींकारतरुशारिका॥५५॥

ह्रींकारपेटकमणिर्ह्रींकारादर्शबिम्बिता।
ह्रींकारकोशासिलता ह्रींकारास्थाननर्तकी॥५६॥

ह्रींकारशुक्तिकामुक्तामणिर्ह्रींकारबोधिता।
ह्रींकारमयसौवर्णस्तम्भविद्रुमपुत्रिका॥५७॥

ह्रींकारवेदोपनिषद्ह्रींकाराध्वरदक्षिणा।
ह्रींकारनन्दनारामनवकल्पकवल्लरी॥५८॥

ह्रींकारहिमवद्गङ्गा ह्रींकारार्णवकौस्तुभा।
ह्रींकारमन्त्रसर्वस्वा ह्रींकारपरसौख्यदा॥५९॥

इत्येवं ते मयाख्यातं देव्या नामशतत्रयम्
रहस्यातिरहस्यत्वाद्गोपनीयं त्वया मुने॥१॥

शिववर्णानि नामानि श्रीदेव्या कथितानि हि।
शक्त्यक्षराणि नामानि कामेशकथितानि च॥२॥

उभयाक्षरनामानि ह्युभाभ्यां कथितानि वै।
तदन्यैर्ग्रथितं स्तोत्रमेतस्य सदृशं किमु॥३॥

नानेन सदृशं स्तोत्रं श्रीदेवीप्रीतिदायकम्।
लोकत्रयेऽपि कल्याणं संभवेन्नात्र संशयः॥४॥

इति हयमुखगीतं स्तोत्रराजं निशम्य
प्रगलितकलुषोऽभूच्चित्तपर्याप्तिमेत्य।
निजगुरुमथ नत्वा कुम्भजन्मा तदुक्तं
पुनरधिकरहस्यं ज्ञातुमेवं जगाद॥५॥

अगस्त्य उवाच–

अश्वानन महाभाग रहस्यमपि मे वद।
शिववर्णानि कान्यत्र शक्तिवर्णानि कानि हि।।६।।

उभयोरपि वर्णानि कानि वा वद देशिक।
इति पृष्टः कुम्भजेन हयग्रीवोऽवदत्पुनः।।७।।

तव गोप्यं किमस्तीह साक्षादम्बानुशासनात्।
इदं त्वतिरहस्यं ते वक्ष्यामि श्रुणु कुम्भज।।८।।

एतद्विज्ञानमात्रेण श्रीविद्या सिद्धिदा भवेत्।
कत्रयं हद्वयं चैव शैवो भागः प्रकीर्तितः।।९।।

शक्त्यक्षराणि शेषाणि ह्रींकार उभयात्मकः।
एवं विभागमज्ञात्वा ये विद्याजपशालिनः।।१०।।

न तेषां सिद्धिदा विद्या कल्पकोटिशतैरपि।
चतुर्भिः शिवचक्रैश्च शक्तिचक्रैश्च पञ्चभिः।।११।।

नवचक्रैश्च संसिद्धं श्रीचक्रं शिवयोर्वपुः।
त्रिकोणमष्टकोणं च दशकोणद्वयं तथा।।१२।।

चतुर्दशारं चैतानि शक्तिचक्राणि पञ्च च।
बिन्दुश्चाष्टदलं पद्मं पद्मं षोडशपत्रकम्।।१३।।

चतुरश्रं च चत्वारि शिवचक्राण्यनुक्रमात्।
त्रिकोणे बैन्दवं श्लिष्टं अष्टारेऽष्टदलाम्बुजम्।।१४।।

दशारयोः षोडशारं भूगृहं भुवनाश्रके।
शैवानामपि शाक्तानां चक्राणां च परस्परम्।।१५।।

अविनाभावसंबन्धं यो जानाति सा चक्रवित्।
त्रिकोणरूपिण शक्तिर्बिन्दुरूपपरः शिवः।।१६।।

अविनाभावसंबंन्धं तस्माद्बिन्दुत्रिकोणयोः।
एवं विभागमज्ञात्वा श्रीचक्रं यः समर्चयेत्।।१७।।

न तत्फलमवाप्नोति ललिताम्बा न तुष्यति।
ये च जानन्ति लोकेऽस्मिन्श्रीविद्याचक्रवेदिनः।।१८।।

सामान्यवेदिनः सर्वे विशेषज्ञोऽतिदुर्लभः।
स्वयंविविशेषज्ञो विशेषज्ञं समर्चयेत्।।१९।।

तस्मै देयं ततो ग्राह्यमशक्तस्तस्य दापयेत्।
अन्धंतमः प्रविशन्ति येऽविद्यां समुपासते।।२०।।

इति श्रुतिरपाहैतानविद्योपासकान्पुनः।
विद्यान्योपासकानेव निन्दत्यारुणिंकीश्रुतिः।।२१।।

अश्रुताः सुश्रुताये च यज्वानो येऽप्ययज्वनः।
स्वर्यन्तो नापेक्षन्ते इन्द्रमग्निं च ये विदुः।।२२।।

सिकात इव संयन्ति रश्मिभिः समुदीरिताः।
अस्माल्लोकादमुष्माच्चेत्याह चारण्यकश्रुतिः।।२३।।

यस्म नो पश्चिमं जन्म यदि वा शंकर स्वयम्।
तेनैव लभ्यते विद्या श्रीमत्पञ्चदशाक्षरी।।२४।।

इति मन्त्रेषु बहुधा विद्याया महिमोच्यते।
मोक्षैकहेतुविा तु श्रीविद्या नात्र संशयः।।२५।।

न शिल्पादिज्ञानयुक्ते विद्वच्छब्दः प्रयुज्यते।
मोक्षैकहेतुविद्या सा श्रीविद्यैव न संशयः।।२६।।

तस्माद्विद्याविदेवात्र विद्वाविन्वद्वानितीर्यते।
स्वयं विद्याविदे दद्यात्क्ष्यापयेत्तद्गुणान्सुधीः।।२७।।

स्वयंविद्यारहस्यज्ञो विद्यामाहात्म्यवेपि।
विद्याविदं नार्चयेच्चेत्को वा तं पूजयेज्जनः।।२८।।

प्रसङ्गादिदमुक्तं ते प्रकृतं श‍ृणु कुम्भज।
यः कीर्तयेत्सकृद्भक्त्या दिव्यनामशतत्रयम्।।२९।।

तस्य पुण्यमहं वक्ष्ये श‍ृणु त्वं कुम्भसंभव।
रहस्यनामसाहस्रपाठे यत्फलमीरितम्।।३०।।

तत्फलं कोटिंगुणितमेकनामजपाद्भवेत्।
कामेश्वरीकामेशाभ्यां कृतं नामशतत्रयम्।।३१।।

नान्येन तुलयेदेतत्स्तोत्रेणान्यकृतेन च।
श्रियः परम्परा यस्य भावि वा चोत्तरोत्तरम्।।३२।।

तेनैव लभ्यते चैतत्पश्चाच्छ्रेयः परीक्षयेत्।
अस्या नाम्नां त्रिशत्यास्तु महिमा केन वर्ण्यते।।३३।।

या स्वयं शिवयोर्वक्त्रपद्माभ्यां परिनिःसृता।
नित्यं षोडशसंख्याकान्विप्रानादौ तु भोजयेत्।।३४।।

अभ्यक्तांस्तिलतैलेन स्नातानुष्णेन वारिणा।
अभ्यर्च्य गन्धपुष्पाद्यैः कामेश्वर्यादिनामाभिः।।३५।।

सूपापूपैः शर्कराद्यैः पायसैः फलसंयुतैः।
विद्याविदो विशेषेण भोजयेत्षोडश द्विजान्।।३६।।

एवं नित्यार्चनं कुर्यादादौ ब्राह्मणभोजनम्।
त्रिशतीनामाभिः पश्चाद्ब्राह्मणान्क्रमशोऽर्चयेत्।।३७।।

तैलाभ्यङ्गादिकं दत्वा विभवे सति भक्तितः।
शुक्लप्रतिपदारभ्य पौर्णमास्यवधि क्रमात्।।३८।।

दिवसे दिवसे विप्रा भोज्या विंशतिसंख्यया।
दशभिः पञ्चविर्भापि त्रिभिरेकेन वा दिनैः।।३९।।

त्रिंशत्षष्टिः शतंविप्राः संभोज्यास्त्रिशतं क्रमात्
एवं यः कुरुते भक्त्या जन्ममध्ये सकृन्नरः।।४०।।

तस्यैव सफलं जन्म मुक्तिस्तस्य करे स्थिरा।
रहस्यनामसाहस्रभोजनेऽप्येवमेव हि।।४१।।

आदौ नित्यबलिं कुर्यात्पश्चाद्ब्राह्मणभोजनम्।
रहस्यनामसाहस्रमहिमा यो मयोदितः।।४२।।

सशीकराणुरत्नैकनाम्नो महिमवारिधेः।
वाग्देवीरचिते नामसाहस्रे यद्यदीरितम्।।४३।।

तत्फलं कोटिगुणितं नाम्नोऽप्येकस्य कीर्तनात्।
एतदन्यैर्जपैः स्तोत्रैरर्चनैर्यत्फलं भवेत्।।४४।।

तत्फलं कोटिगुणितं भवेन्नामशतत्रयात्।
वाग्देवीरचितास्तोत्रे तादृशो महिमा यदि।।४५।।

साक्षात्कामेशकामेशीकृतेऽस्मिन्गृह्यतामिति।
सकृत्संकीर्तनादेव नाम्नामास्मिञ्शतत्रये।।४६।।

भवेच्चित्तस्य पर्याप्तिर्नूनमन्यानपेक्षिणी।
न ज्ञातव्यमितोऽप्यन्यत्र जप्तव्यं च कुम्भज।।४७।।

यद्यात्साध्यतमं कार्यं तत्तदर्थमिदं जपेत्।
तत्तत्फलमवाप्नोति पश्चात्कार्यं परीक्षयेत्।।४८।।

ये ये प्रयोगास्तन्त्रेषु तैस्तैर्यत्साध्यते फलम्।
तत्सर्वं सिध्यति क्षिप्रं नामत्रिशतकीर्तनात्।।४९।।

आयुष्करं पुष्टिकरं पुत्रदं वश्यकारकम्।
विद्याप्रदं कीर्तिकरं सुकवित्वप्रदायकम्।।५०।।

सर्वसंपत्प्रदं सर्वभोगदं सर्वसौख्यदम्।
सर्वाभीष्टप्रदं चैव देव्या नामशतत्रयम्।।५१।।

एतज्जपपरो भूयान्नान्यदिच्छेत्कदाचन।
एतत्कीर्तनसंतुष्टा श्रीदेवी ललिताम्बिका।।५२।।

भक्तस्य यदिष्टं स्यात्तत्तत्पूरयते ध्रुवम्।
तस्मात्कुम्भोद्भव मुने कीर्तय त्वमिदं सदा॥५३॥

नापरं किंचिदपि ते बोद्धव्यं नावशिष्यते।
इति ते कथितं स्तोत्रं ललिताप्रीतिदायकम्॥५४॥

नाविद्यावेदिने ब्रूयान्नाभक्ताय कदाचन।
न शठाय न दुष्टाय नाविश्वासाय कर्हिचित्॥५५॥

यो ब्रूयात्त्रिंशती नाम्नां तस्यानर्थो महान्भवेत्।
इत्याज्ञा शंकरी प्रोक्ता तस्माद्गोप्यमिदं त्वया॥५६॥

ललिताप्रेरितेनैव मयोक्तं स्तोत्रमुत्तमम्।
रहस्यनामसाहस्रादपि गोप्यमिदं मुने॥५७॥

एवमुक्त्वा हयग्रीवः कुम्भजं तापसोत्तमम्।
स्तोत्रेणनेन ललितां स्तुत्वा त्रिपुरसुन्दरीम्॥५८॥

आनन्दलहरीमग्नमानसः समवर्तत॥५९॥

इति श्रीललितात्रिशतीस्तोत्रं संपूर्णम्।

॥ श्रीललिता-त्रिशती-नामावलिः ॥

क ए ई ल ह्रीं॥

ह स क ह ल ह्रीं॥

स क ल ह्रीं॥

॥ क ॥

ॐ ककार-रूपायै नमः॥

ॐ कल्याण्यै नमः॥

ॐ कल्याण-गुण-शालिन्यै नमः॥

ॐ कल्याण-शैल-निलयायै नमः॥

ॐ कमनीयायै नमः॥

ॐ कलावत्यै नमः॥

ॐ कमलाक्ष्यै नमः॥

ॐ कल्मषघ्न्यै नमः॥

ॐ करुणामृतसागरायै नमः॥

ॐ कदम्ब-काननावासायै नमः॥१०॥

ॐ कदम्ब-कुसुम-प्रियायै नमः॥

ॐ कन्दर्प-विद्यायै नमः॥

ॐ कन्दर्प-जनकापांग-वीक्षणायै नमः॥

ॐ कर्पूर-वीटी-सौरभ्य-कल्लोलित-ककुप्तटायै नमः॥

ॐ कलि-दोष-हरायै नमः॥

ॐ कंज-लोचनायै नमः॥

ॐ कम्र-विग्रहायै नमः॥

ॐ कर्मादि-साक्षिण्यै नमः॥

ॐ कारयित्र्यै नमः।।

ॐ कर्म-फल-प्रदायै नमः।।२०।।

॥ ए ॥

ॐ एकार-रूपायै नमः।।

ॐ एकाक्षर्यै नमः।।

ॐ एकानेकाक्षराकृत्यै नमः।।

ॐ एतत्तदित्यनिर्देश्यायै नमः।।

ॐ एकानन्द-चिदाकृतये नमः।।

ॐ एवमित्यागमाबोध्यायै नमः।।

ॐ एकभक्तिमदर्चितायै नमः।।

ॐ एकाग्रचित्त-निर्ध्यातायै नमः।।

ॐ एषणा-रहितादृतायै नमः।।

ॐ एला-सुगन्धि-चिकुरायै नमः।।

ॐ एनः कूट-विनाशिन्यै नमः।।

ॐ एकभोगायै नमः।।

ॐ एकरसायै नमः।।

ॐ एकैश्वर्य-प्रदायिन्यै नमः।।

ॐ एकातपत्र-साम्राज्य-प्रदायै नमः।।

ॐ एकान्त-पूजितायै नमः।।

ॐ एधमान-प्रभायै नमः।।

ॐ एजदनेक-जगदीश्वर्यै नमः।।

ॐ एक-वीरादि-संसेव्यायै नमः।।

ॐ एक प्रभव-शालिन्यै नमः।।४०।।

॥ ई ॥

ॐ ईकार-रूपायै नमः।।

ॐ ईशित्र्यै नमः।।

ॐ ईप्सितार्थ-प्रदायिन्यै नमः।।

ॐ ईदृगित्यविनिर्देश्यायै नमः।।
ॐ ईश्वरत्व-विधायिन्यै नमः।।
ॐ ईशानादि-ब्रह्ममय्यै नमः।।
ॐ ईशित्वाद्यष्टसिद्धिदायै नमः।।
ॐ ईक्षित्र्यै नमः।।
ॐ ईक्षण-सृष्टाण्ड-कोट्यै नमः।।
ॐ ईश्वर-वल्लभायै नमः।।४०।।
ॐ ईडितायै नमः।।
ॐ ईश्वरार्धांग-शरीरायै नमः।।
ॐ ईशाधिदेवतायै नमः।।
ॐ ईश्वर-प्रेरण-कर्यै नमः।।
ॐ ईश-ताण्डव-साक्षिण्यै नमः।।
ॐ ईश्वरोत्संग-निलयायै नमः।।
ॐ ईति-बाधा-विनाशिन्यै नमः।।
ॐ ईहा-विरहितायै नमः।।
ॐ ईश-शक्त्यै नमः।।
ॐ ईषत्-स्मिताननायै नमः।।६०।।

।। ल ।।

ॐ ल-काररूपायै नमः।।
ॐ ललितायै नमः।।
ॐ लक्ष्मी-वाणी-निषेवितायै नमः।।
ॐ लाकिन्यै नमः।।
ॐ ललना-रूपायै नमः।।
ॐ लसद्दाडिम-पाटलायै नमः।।
ॐ ललन्तिका-लसत्-फालायै नमः।।
ॐ ललाट-नयनार्चितायै नमः।।
ॐ लक्षणोज्ज्वल-दिव्यांग्यै नमः।।

ॐ लक्ष-कोट्यण्ड-नायिकायै नमः॥७०॥

ॐ लक्ष्यार्थायै नमः॥

ॐ लक्षणा-गम्यायै नमः॥

ॐ लब्ध-कामायै नमः॥

ॐ लता-तनवे नमः॥

ॐ ललाम-राज-दलिकायै नमः॥

ॐ लंबि-मुक्ता-लतांचितायै नमः॥

ॐ लम्बोदर-प्रसुवे नमः॥

ॐ लभ्यायै नमः॥

ॐ लज्जाढ्यायै नमः॥

ॐ लय-वर्जितायै नमः॥८०॥

॥ ह्रीं ॥

ॐ ह्रींकार-रूपायै नमः॥

ॐ ह्रींकार-निलयायै नमः॥

ॐ ह्रीं-पद-प्रियायै नमः॥

ॐ ह्रींकार--बीजायै नमः॥

ॐ ह्रींकार-मन्त्रायै नमः॥

ॐ ह्रींकार-लक्षणायै नमः॥

ॐ ह्रींकार-जप-सुप्रीतायै नमः॥

ॐ ह्रींमत्यै नमः॥

ॐ ह्रीं-विभूषणायै नमः॥

ॐ ह्रीं-शीलायै नमः॥९०॥

ॐ ह्रीं-पदाराध्यायै नमः॥

ॐ ह्रीं-गर्भायै नमः॥

ॐ ह्रीं-पदाभिधायै नमः॥

ॐ ह्रींकार-वाच्यायै नमः॥

ॐ ह्रींकार-पूज्यायै नमः॥

ॐ ह्रींकार-पीठिकायै नमः।।

ॐ ह्रींकार-वेद्यायै नमः।।

ॐ ह्रींकार-चिन्त्यायै नमः।।

ॐ ह्रीं नमः।।

ॐ ह्रींशरीरिण्यै नमः।।१००।।

॥ ह ॥

ॐ हकार-रूपायै नमः।।

ॐ हलभृत्पूजितायै नमः।।

ॐ हरिणेक्षणायै नमः।।

ॐ हरप्रियायै नमः।।

ॐ हराराध्यायै नमः।।

ॐ हरि-ब्रह्मेन्द्र-वन्दितायै नमः।।

ॐ हयारूढा-सेवितांघ्र्यै नमः।।

ॐ हयमेध-समर्चितायै नमः।।

ॐ हर्यक्ष-वाहनायै नमः।।

ॐ हंस-वाहनायै नमः।।११०।।

ॐ हत-दानवायै नमः।।

ॐ हत्यादि-पाप-शमन्यै नमः।।

ॐ हरिदश्वादि-सेवितायै नमः।।

ॐ हस्तिकुम्भोत्तुंग-कुचायै नमः।।

ॐ हस्ति-कृत्ति-प्रियांगनायै नमः।।

ॐ हरिद्रा-कुंकुम-दिग्धायै नमः।।

ॐ हर्यश्वाद्यमरार्चितायै नमः।।

ॐ हरिकेश-सख्यै नमः।।

ॐ हादिविद्यायै नमः।।

ॐ हाला-मदोल्लसायै नमः।।१२०।।

॥ स ॥

ॐ सकार-रूपायै नमः।।

ॐ सर्वज्ञायै नमः।।

ॐ सर्वेश्यै नमः।।

ॐ सर्वमंगलायै नमः।।

ॐ सर्वकर्त्र्यै नमः।।

ॐ सर्वभर्त्र्यै नमः।।

ॐ सर्वहन्त्र्यै नमः।।

ॐ सनातनायै नमः।।

ॐ सर्वानवद्यायै नमः।।

ॐ सर्वानवद्यायै नमः।।

ॐ सर्वांग-सुन्दर्यै नमः।।१३०।।

ॐ सर्वसाक्षिण्यै नमः।।

ॐ सर्वात्मिकायै नमः।।

ॐ सर्व-सौख्य-दात्र्यै नमः।।

ॐ सर्व-विमोहिन्यै नमः।।

ॐ सर्वाधारायै नमः।।

ॐ सर्व-गतायै नमः।।

ॐ सर्वावगुण-वर्जितायै नमः।।

ॐ सर्वारुणायै नमः।।

ॐ सर्व-मात्रे नमः।।

ॐ सर्व-भूषण-भूषितायै नमः।।१४०।।

।। क ।।

ॐ ककारार्थायै नमः।।

ॐ कालहन्त्र्यै नमः।।

ॐ कामेश्यै नमः।।

ॐ कामितार्थ-दायै नमः।।

ॐ काम-संजीविन्यै नमः।।

ॐ कल्यायै नमः।।

ॐ कठिन-स्तन-मण्डलायै नमः।।

ॐ करभोर्व्यै नमः।।

ॐ कठिन-स्तन-मण्डलायै नमः।।

ॐ करभोर्व्यै नमः।।

ॐ कलानाथ-मुख्यै नमः।।

ॐ कच-जिताम्बुदायै नमः।।

ॐ कटाक्ष-स्यन्दि-करुणायै नमः।।

ॐ कपालि-प्राण-नायिकायै नमः।।

ॐ कारुण्य-विग्रहायै नमः।।

ॐ कान्तायै नमः।।

ॐ कान्ति-धूत-जपावल्यै नमः।।

ॐ कलालापायै नमः।।

ॐ कम्बु कण्ठ्यै नमः।।

ॐ कर-निर्जित-पल्लवायै नमः।।

ॐ कल्पवल्लीसमभुजायै नमः।।

ॐ कस्तूरी-तिलकांचितायै नमः।।१६०।।

॥ ह ॥

ॐ हकारार्थायै नमः।।

ॐ हंसगत्यै नमः।।

ॐ हाटकाभरणोज्ज्वलायै नमः।।

ॐ हार-हारि-कुचाभोगायै नमः।।

ॐ हाकिन्यै नमः।।

ॐ हल्य-वर्जितायै नमः।।

ॐ हरित्पति-समाराध्यायै नमः।।

ॐ हठात्कार-हतासुरायै नमः।।

ॐ हर्षप्रदायै नमः।।

ॐ हविर्भोक्त्रै नमः।।१७०।।

ॐ हार्द-सन्तमसापहायै नमः।।

ॐ हल्लीस-लास्य-सन्तुष्टायै नमः।।

ॐ हंस-मन्त्रार्थ-रूपिण्यै नमः।।

ॐ हानोपादान-निर्मुक्तायै नमः।।

ॐ हर्षिण्यै नमः।।

ॐ हरि-सोदर्यै नमः।।

ॐ हाहा-हूहू-मुख-स्तुत्यायै नमः।।

ॐ हानि-वृद्धि-विवर्जितायै नमः।।

ॐ हय्यंगवीन-हृदयायै नमः।।

ॐ हरि-गोपारुणांशुकायै नमः।।१८०।।

॥ ल ॥

ॐ लकाराख्यायै नमः।।

ॐ लता-पूज्यायै नमः।।

ॐ लय-स्थित्युद्भवेश्वर्यै नमः।।

ॐ लास्य-दर्शन-सन्तुष्टायै नमः।।

ॐ लाभालाभ-विवर्जितायै नमः।।

ॐ लंघ्येतराज्ञायै नमः।।

ॐ लावण्य-शालिन्यै नमः।।

ॐ लघु-सिद्धिदायै नमः।।

ॐ लाक्षा-रस-सवर्णाभायै नमः।।

ॐ लक्ष्मणाग्रज-पूजितायै नमः।।१९०।।

ॐ लभ्येतरायै नमः।।

ॐ लब्ध-भक्ति-सुलभायै नमः।।

ॐ लांगलायुधायै नमः।।

ॐ लग्न-चामर-हस्त-श्रीशारदा-परिवीजितायै नमः।।

ॐ लज्जा-पद-समाराध्यायै नमः।।

ॐ लम्पटायै नमः।।

ॐ लकुलेश्वर्यै नमः॥
ॐ लब्धमानायै नमः॥
ॐ लब्ध-रसायै नमः॥
ॐ लब्ध-सम्पत्-समुन्नत्यै नमः॥ २००॥

॥ ह्रीं ॥

ॐ ह्रींकारिण्यै नमः॥
ॐ ह्रींकाराद्यायै नमः॥
ॐ ह्रीं-मध्यायै नमः॥
ॐ ह्रीं-शिखामण्यै नमः॥
ॐ ह्रींकार-कुण्डाग्नि-शिखायै नमः॥
ॐ ह्रींकार-शशि-चन्द्रिकायै नमः॥
ॐ ह्रींकार-भास्कर-रुच्यै नमः॥
ॐ ह्रींकारांभोद-चंचलायै नमः॥
ॐ ह्रींकार-कन्दांकुरिकायै नमः॥
ॐ ह्रींकारैक-परायणायै नमः॥२१०॥
ॐ ह्रींकार-दीर्घिका-हंस्यै नमः॥
ॐ ह्रींकारोद्यान-केकिन्यै नमः॥
ॐ ह्रींकारारण्य-हरिण्यै नमः॥
ॐ ह्रींकारालवाल-वल्लयै नमः॥
ॐ ह्रींकार-पंजर-शुक्यै नमः॥
ॐ ह्रींकारांगण-दीपिकायै नमः॥
ॐ ह्रींकार-कन्दरा-सिंह्यै नमः॥
ॐ ह्रींकाराम्भोज-भृंगिकायै नमः॥
ॐ ह्रींकार-सुमनो-माध्व्यै नमः॥
ॐ ह्रींकार-तरु-मंजर्यै नमः॥२२०॥

॥ स ॥

ॐ सकाराख्यायै नमः॥

ॐ समरसायै नमः॥

ॐ सकलागम-संस्तुतायै नमः॥

ॐ सर्व-वेदान्त-तात्पर्य-भूम्यै नमः॥

ॐ सदसदाश्रयायै नमः॥

ॐ सकलायै नमः॥

ॐ सच्चिदानन्दायै नमः॥

ॐ साध्यायै नमः॥

ॐ सद्गति-दायिन्यै नमः॥

ॐ सनकादि-मुनिध्येयायै नमः॥२३०॥

ॐ सदाशिव-कुटुम्बिन्यै नमः॥

ॐ सकलाधिष्ठान-रूपायै नमः॥

ॐ सत्य-रूपायै नमः॥

ॐ समाकृत्यै नमः॥

ॐ सर्व-प्रपंच-निर्मात्र्यै नमः॥

ॐ समानाधिक-वर्जितायै नमः॥

ॐ सर्वोत्तुंगायै नमः॥

ॐ संग-हीनायै नमः॥

ॐ सद्गुणायै नमः॥

ॐ सकलेष्टदायै नमः॥२४०॥

॥ क ॥

ॐ ककारिण्यै नमः॥

ॐ काव्य-लोलायै नमः॥

ॐ कामेश्वर-मनोहरायै नमः॥

ॐ कामेश्वर-प्राणनाड्यै नमः॥

ॐ कामेशोत्संग-वासिन्यै नमः॥

ॐ कामेश्वरालिंगितांग्यै नमः॥

ॐ कामेश्वर-सुख-प्रदायै नमः॥

ॐ कामेश्वर--प्रणयिन्यै नमः।।

ॐ कामेश्वर-विलासिन्यै नमः।।

ॐ कामेश्वर-तपः सिध्द्यै नमः।। २५० ।।

ॐ कामेश्वर-मनः प्रियायै नमः।।

ॐ कामेश्वर-प्राणनाथायै नमः।।

ॐ कामेश्वर-विमोहिन्यै नमः।।

ॐ कामेश्वर-ब्रह्मविद्यायै नमः।।

ॐ कामेश्वर-गृहेश्वर्यै नमः।।

ॐ कामेश्वराह्लाद-कर्यै नमः।।

ॐ कामेश्वर-महेश्वर्यै नमः।।

ॐ कामेश्वर्यै नमः।।

ॐ कामकोटि-निलयायै नमः।।

ॐ कांक्षितार्थ-दायै नमः।।२६०।।

॥ ल ॥

ॐ लकारिण्यै नमः।।

ॐ लब्धरूपायै नमः।।

ॐ लब्ध-धिये नमः।।

ॐ लब्ध-वांछितायै नमः।।

ॐ लब्धाहंकार-दुर्गमायै नमः।।

ॐ लब्ध-पाप-मनो-दूरायै नमः।।

ॐ लब्ध-शक्त्यै नमः।।

ॐ लब्ध-देहायै नमः।।

ॐ लब्धैश्वर्य-समुन्नत्यै नमः।।

ॐ लब्ध-वृध्द्यै नमः।।

ॐ लब्ध-लीलायै नमः।।

ॐ लब्ध-यौवन-शालिन्यै नमः।।

ॐ लब्धातिशय-सर्वांग-सौन्दर्यायै नमः।।

ॐ लब्ध-विभ्रमायै नमः।।

ॐ लब्ध-रागायै नमः।।

ॐ लब्ध-पत्यै नमः।।

ॐ लब्ध-नानागम-स्थित्यै नमः।।

ॐ लब्ध-भोगायै नमः।।

ॐ लब्ध-सुखायै नमः।।

ॐ लब्ध-हर्षाभिपूरितायै नमः।।२८०।।

॥ ह्रीं ॥

ॐ ह्रींकार-मूर्त्यै नमः।।

ॐ ह्रींकार-सौध-शृंग-कपोतिकायै नमः।।

ॐ ह्रींकार-दुग्धाब्धि-सुधायै नमः।।

ॐ ह्रींकार-कमलेन्दिरायै नमः।।

ॐ ह्रींकार-मणि-दीपार्चिषे नमः।।

ॐ ह्रींकार-तरु:शारिकायै नमः।।

ॐ ह्रींकार-पेटक-मण्यै नमः।।

ॐ ह्रींकारादर्श-बिम्बितायै नमः।।

ॐ ह्रींकार-कोशासि-लतायै नमः।।

ॐ ह्रींकारास्थान-नर्तक्यै नमः।।१९०।।

ॐ ह्रींकार-शुक्तिका-मुक्तामण्यै नमः।।

ॐ ह्रींकार-बोधितायै नमः।।

ॐ ह्रींकार-मय-सौवर्ण-स्तम्भ-विभ्रम-पुत्रिकायै नमः।।

ॐ ह्रींकार-वेदोपनिषदे नमः।।

ॐ ह्रींकाराध्वर-दक्षिणायै नमः।।

ॐ ह्रींकार-नन्दनाराम-नव-कल्पक-वल्लयै नमः।।

ॐ ह्रींकार-हिमवद्-गंगायै नमः।।

ॐ ह्रींकारार्णव-कौस्तुभायै नमः।।

ॐ ह्रींकार-मन्त्र-सर्वस्वायै नमः।।

ॐ ह्रींकार-पर-सौख्यदायै नमः।।

।। इति श्रीललिता-त्रिशती-नामावलिः सम्पूर्णा ।।

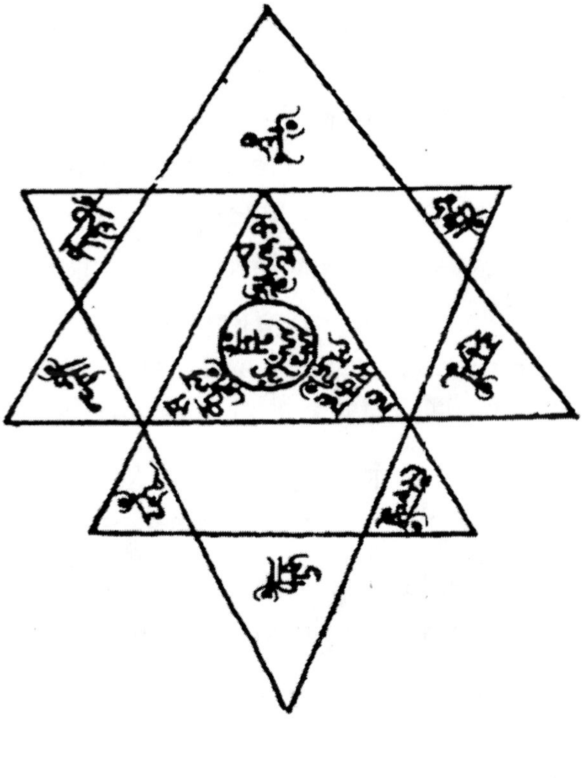

LALITOPĀKYHĀNA

(from Brahmāṇḍa-purāṇa)

॥ श्रीललितोपाख्यानं ॥

चतुर्भुज चंद्रकलावतंसे कुचोन्नते कुङ्कुमरागशोणे।
पुंड्रेक्षुपाशाङ्कुशपुष्पबाणहस्ते नमस्ते जगदेकमातः॥१॥

अस्तु नः श्रेयसे नित्यं वस्तु वामाङ्गसुन्दरम्॥
यतस्तृतीयो विदुषां तृतीयस्तु परं महः॥२॥

INTRODUCTION

(Agastya meets Hayagrīva and discussess with him the method of eradicating the sorrow of human beings).

अगस्त्यो नाम देवर्षिर्वेदवेदाङ्गपारगः॥
सर्वसिद्धान्तसारज्ञो ब्रह्मानन्दरसात्मकः॥३॥

चचाराद्भुतहैतूनि तीर्थान्यायतनानि च॥
शैलारण्यापगामुख्या सर्वाञ्च जनपदानपि॥४॥

तेषु तेष्वखिलाञ्जंतूनज्ञानतिमिरावृतान्॥
शिश्नोदरपरान्दृष्ट्वा चिन्तयामास तान्प्रति॥५॥

तस्य चिन्तयमानस्य चरतो वसुधामिमाम्॥
प्राप्तमासीन्महापुण्यं कांचीनगरमुत्तमम्॥६॥

तत्र वारणशैलेन्द्रमेकाम्रनिलयं शिवम्॥
कामाक्षीं कलिदोषघ्नीमपूजयदथात्मवान्॥७॥

लोकहेतोर्दयार्द्रस्य धीमतश्चिन्तनो मुहुः।।
चिरकालेन तपसा तोषितोऽभूज्जनार्दनः।।८।।

हयग्रीवां तनुं कृत्वा साक्षाच्चिन्मात्रविग्रहाम्।
शङ्खचक्राक्षवलयपुस्तकोज्ज्वलबाहुकाम्।।९।।

पूरयित्रीं जगत्कृत्स्नं प्रभया देहजातया।।
प्रादुर्बभूव पुरतो मुनेरमिततेजसा।।१०।।

तं दृष्ट्वावनन्दभरितः प्रणम्य च मुहुर्मुहुः।।
विनयावनतो भूत्वा सन्तुष्टाव जगत्पतिम्।।११।।

अथो वाच जगन्नाथस्तुष्टोऽस्मि तपसा तव।।
वरं वरय भद्रं ते भविता भूसूरोत्तमः।।१२।।

इति पृष्टो भगवता प्रोंवाच मुनिसत्तमः।।
यदि तुष्टोऽसि भगवन्निमे पामरजन्तवः।।१३।।

केनोपायेन मुक्ताः स्युरेतन्मे वक्तुमर्हसि।।
इति पृष्टो द्विजेनाथ देवदेवो जनार्दनः।।१४।।

The worship of Para-Sakti is the means of securing welfare here and salvation hereafter.

एष एव पुरा प्रश्नः शिवेन चरितो मम।।
अयमेव कृतः प्रश्नो ब्रह्मणा तु ततः परम्।।१५।।

कृतो दुर्वाससा पश्चाद्भवता तु ततः परम्।।१६।।

भवद्भिः सर्वभूतानां गुरुभूतैर्महात्मभिः।।
ममोपदेशो लोकेषु प्रथितोऽस्तु वरो मम।।१७।।

अहमादिर्हि भूतानामादिकर्ता स्वयं प्रभुः।।
सृष्टिस्थितिलयानां तु सर्वेषामपि कारकः।।१८।।

त्रिमूर्तिस्त्रिगुणातीतो गुणहीनो गुणाश्रयः।।१९।।

इच्छाविहारो भूतात्मा प्रधानपुरुषात्मकः।।
एवं भूतस्य मे ब्रह्मंस्त्रिजगद्रुपधारिणः।।१०।।

द्विधाकृतमभूद्रूपं प्रधानपुरुषात्मकम्।।
मम प्रधानं यद्रूपं सर्वलोकगुणात्मकम्।।२१।।

अपरं यद्गुणातीतं परात्परतरं महत्।।
एवमेव तयोर्ज्ञात्वा मुच्यते ते उभे किमु।।२२।।

तपोभिश्चिरकालोत्थैर्यमैश्च नियमैरपि।।
त्यागैर्दुष्कर्मनाशांते मुक्तिराश्वेव लभ्यते।।२३।।

यद्रूपं यद्गुणयुतं तद्रूप्यैक्येन लभ्यते।।
अन्यत्सर्वजगद्रूपं कर्मभोगपराक्रमम्।।२४।।

कर्मभिर्लभ्यते तच्च तत्यागेनापि लभ्यते।।
दुस्तरस्तु तयोस्त्यागः सकलैरपि तापस।।२५।।

अनपायं च सुगमं सदसत्कर्मगोचरम्।।२६।।

आत्मस्थेन गुणेनैव सता चाप्यसतापि वा।।
आत्मैक्येनैव यज्ज्ञानं सर्वसिद्धिप्रदायकम्।।२७।।

वर्णत्रयविहीनानां पापिष्ठानां नृणामपि।।
यद्रूपध्यानमात्रेण दुष्कृतं सुकृतायते।।२८।।

येऽर्चयंति परां शक्तिं विधिनाऽविधिनापि वा।।
न ते संसारिणो नूनं मुक्ता एव न संशयः।।२९।।

शिवो वा यां समाराध्य ध्यानयोगबलेन च।।
ईश्वरः सर्वसिद्धानामर्द्धनारीश्वरोऽभवत्।।३०।।

अन्येऽब्जप्रमुखा देवाः सिद्धास्तद्ध्यानवैभवात्।।
तस्मादशेषलोकानां त्रिपुराराधनं विना।।३१।।

न स्तो भोगापवर्गौ तु यौगपेन कुत्रचित्।।
तन्मनास्तद्गतप्राणस्ताजी तद्गतेहकः।।३२।।

तादात्म्येनैव कर्माणि कुर्वन्मुक्तिमवाप्स्यसि।।
एतद्रहस्यमाख्यातं सर्वेषां हितकाम्यया।।३३।।

सन्तुष्टेनैव तपसा भवतो मुनिसत्तम।।
देवाश्च मुनयः सिद्धा मानुषाश्च तथापरे।।
त्वन्मुखांभोजतोऽवाप्यसिद्धिं यांतु परात्पराम्।।३४।।

इति तस्य वचः श्रुत्वा हयग्रीवस्य शार्ङ्गिणः।।
प्रणिपत्य पुनर्वाक्यमुवाच मधुसूदनम्।।३५।।

भगवन्कीदृशं रूपं भवता यत्पुरोदितम्।।
किंविहारं किंप्रभावमेतन्मे वक्तुमर्हसि।।३६।।

हयग्रीव उवाच।।

एषोंऽशभूतो देवर्षे हयग्रीवो ममापरः।।
श्रोतुमिच्छसि यद्यत्वं तत्सर्वं वक्तुमर्हति।।३७।।

इत्यादिश्य जगन्नाथो हयग्रीवं तपोधनम्।।
पुरतः कुम्भजातस्य पुनरंतरधाद्धरिः।।३८।।

ततस्तु विस्मयाविष्टो हृष्टरोमा तपोधनः।।
हयग्रीर्वेण मुनिना स्वाश्रमं प्रत्यपद्यत।।३९।।

DESCRIPTION OF CHINTAMAṆI GṚHA THE RESIDENCE OF PARĀ-SAKTI

(deities of Śrī-chakra in the enclosure)

हयग्रीव उवाच।।

चिन्तामणिगृहस्याग्निदिग्भागे कुन्दमानकम्।।
योजनायामविस्तारं योजनोच्छासचातकम्।।१।।

तत्र ज्वलति चिद्वह्निः सुधाधाराशतार्चितः।।
परमैश्वर्यजनकः पावनो ललिताज्ञया।।२।।

अनिन्धनो महाज्वालः सुधया तर्पिताकृतिः।।
कंकोलीपल्लवच्छायस्तत्र ज्वलति चिच्छिखी।।३।।

तत्र होत्री महादेवी होता कामेश्वरः परः।।
उभौ तौ नित्यहोतारौ रक्षतः सकलं जगत्।।४।।

अनुत्तरपराधीना ललिता संप्रवर्तितां।
ललिताचोदितः कामः शंकरेण प्रवर्तितः।।५।।

चिन्तामणिगृहेन्द्रस्य रक्षोभागेम्बुजाटवौ।।६।।

चक्रराजरथश्रेष्ठस्तिष्ठत्युन्नतविग्रहः।।
नवभिः पर्वभिर्युक्तः सर्वरत्नमयाकृतिः।।७।।

चतुर्योजनविस्तारो दशयोजनमुन्नतः।।
यथोत्तरं ह्रासयुक्तः स्थूलतः कूबरोज्ज्वलः।।८।।

चतुर्वेदमहाचक्रः पुरुषार्थमहाहयः।।
तत्वैरुपचरद्भिश्च चामरैरभिमंडितः।।९।।

पूर्वेक्तलक्षणैर्युक्ता मुक्ताच्छत्रेण शोभितः।।
भंडासुरमहायुद्धे कृतसाहसिकक्रियः।।१०।।

वर्तते रथमूर्धन्यः श्रीदेव्यासनपाटितः।।
चिन्तामणिगृहेन्द्रस्य वायुभागेम्बुजाटवौ।।११।।

गेयचक्ररथेन्द्रस्तु मन्त्रिण्याः प्रान्त तिष्ठति।।
चिंतामणिगृहेन्द्रस्य रुद्रभागेम्बुजाटवौ।।१२।।

वल्लभो दण्डनाथायाः किरिचक्रे महारथः।।
एतद्रथत्रयं सर्वक्षेत्रश्रीपुरपंक्तिषु।।
समानमेव विज्ञेयमङ्गस्था देवता यथा।।१३।।

आनलं कुंडमाग्नेये यस्तिष्ठति सदा ज्वलत्।।
तप्तमेतत्तु गायत्री तप्तं स्यादभयङ्करम्।।१४।।

घृणिसूर्यस्तु तत्पश्चादोंकारस्य च मन्दिरम्।।
देवी तुरीयगायत्री चक्षुष्मत्यपि तापस।।१५।।

अथ गन्धर्वराजश्च परिषद्रुद्र एव च।।
तारांबिका भगवती तत्पश्चाद्भागतः स्थिताः।।१६।।

चिंतामणिगृहेन्द्रस्य रक्षोभागं समाश्रितः।।
नामत्रय महामन्त्रवाच्योऽस्ति भगवान्हरिः।।१७।।

महागणपतिस्तस्योत्तरसंश्रितकेतनः।।
पञ्चाक्षरीमन्त्रवाच्यस्तस्य चाप्युत्तरे शिवः।।१८।।

अथ मृत्युञ्जयेशश्च वाच्यस्त्र्यक्षरमात्रतः।।
सरस्वती धारणाख्या ह्यस्य चोत्तरवासिनी।।१९।।

अकारादिक्षकारान्तवर्णमूर्तेस्तु मंदिरम्।।
मातृकाया उत्तरतस्तस्यां विन्ध्यनिषूदन।।२०।।

उत्तरे सम्पदेशी वै कालसंकर्षणी तथा।।
श्रीमहाशम्भुनाथा च देव्याविर्भावकारणम्।।२१।।

श्रीः परांबा च विशदज्योत्स्ना निर्मलबिग्रहा।।
उत्तरोत्तरमेतास्तु देवाताः कृतमंदिराः।।२२।।

बाला चैवान्नपूर्णा च हयारूढा तथैव च।।
श्रीपादुकाचतस्रस्तदूत्तरोत्तरमंदिराः।।२३।।

चिन्तामणिगृहेन्द्रस्य वायव्यवसुधादितः।।
महापद्माटवपौ त्वन्या देवताः कृतमंदिराः।।२४।।

उन्मत्तभैरवी चैव स्वप्नवाराहिका परा।।
तिरस्करणिकांबा च तथान्या पञ्चमी परा।।२५।।

यथापूर्वे कृतगृहा एता देव्यो महोदया:।।
श्रीपूर्तिश्च महादेवी श्रीमहापादुकापि च।।२६।।

यथापूर्वे कृतगृहे द्वे एते देवतोत्तमे।।
शंकरेण षडाम्नायस।गरे प्रतिपादिता:।।
या विद्यास्ता: समस्ताश्च महापद्माटवीस्थले।।२७।।

इत्थं श्रीरश्मिमालायामणिक्लृप्ता ग्रहागृहा:।।
उच्चध्वजा उच्चशालास्ससोपानास्तपोधन।।२८।।

चिन्तामणिगृहेन्द्रस्य पूर्वद्वारे समुद्रप।।
दक्षिणे पार्श्वभागे तु मंत्रिनाथागृहं महत्।।२९।।

वामभागे दण्डनाथाभवनं रत्ननिर्मितम्।।
ब्रह्मविष्णुमहेशानामास्थानस्य पूर्वत:।।३०।।

भवनं दीपिताशेषदिक्चक्रं रत्नरश्मिभि:।।
समस्ता देवता एता ललिताभक्तिनिर्भरा:।।
ललितामन्त्रजाप्याश्च श्रीदेवीं समुपासते।।३१।।

पूर्वोक्तर्मस्थानं च पूर्वोक्तं र्चाकल्पनम्।।
याम्यद्वारप्रभृतिषु सर्वेष्वपि समं स्मृतम्।।३२।।

अथ चिन्तामणिगृहं वक्ष्ये श्रृणु महामुने।।
तच्छ्रीपट्टनमध्यस्थं योजनद्वयविस्तृतम्।।३३।।

तस्य चिन्तामणिमयी भित्तिः कोशगुविस्तृता।।
चिन्तामणिशिलाभिश्च च्छादिनीभिस्तथोपरि।।३४।।

संवृता कूटरूपेण तत्रतत्र समुन्नता।।
गृहभित्तिस्तथोन्नम्रा चतुर्योजनमानत:।।३५।।

विंशतिर्योजनं तस्याश्चोन्नम्रा भूमिरुच्यते।।
ततोर्ध्वं ह्राससंयुक्तं स्थौल्यत्रिमुकुटोज्ज्वला।।३६।।

तानि चेच्छाक्रियाज्ञानरूपाणि मुकुटान्यपि।।
सदा देदीप्यमानानि चिन्तामणिमयान्यपि।।३७।।

चिन्तामणिगृहे सर्वं चिन्तामणिमयं स्मृतम्।।
यस्य द्वाराणि चत्वारि क्रोशार्धायामभाञ्जि च।।३८।।

क्रोशार्द्धार्द्धं च विस्तारो द्वाराणां कथितो मुने।।
द्वारेषु सर्वेषु पुनश्चिन्तामणिगृहान्तरे।।३९।।

पिहिता ललिता देव्या मूर्तिर्लोहितसिन्धुवत्।।
तरुणार्कसहस्राभा चन्द्रवच्छीतला ह्यपि।।
द्वारेषु सर्वेषु पुनश्चिन्त्रामणिगृहान्तरे।।
मुहुः प्रवाहरूपेण प्रसरन्तील महामुने।।४०।।

पूर्वाम्नायमयं चैव पूर्वद्वारं प्रकीर्तितम्।।
दक्षिणद्वारदेशस्तु दक्षिणाम्नायलक्षण:।।४१।।

पश्चिमद्वारदेशस्तु पश्चिमाम्नायलक्षण:।।
उत्तरद्वारदेश: स्यादुत्तराम्नायलक्षण:।।४२।।

गृहराजस्यान्तराले भित्तौ खचितदण्डका:।।
रत्नप्रदीपा भास्वंत: कोट्यर्कसदृशत्विष:।।
परितस्तत्र वर्तंते भासयंतो गृहांतरम्।।४३।।

चिंतामणिगृहस्यास्य मध्यस्थाने महीयसि।।
अत्युच्चैर्वेदिकाभागे बिन्दुचक्रं महत्तरम्।।४४।।

चिन्तारत्नगृहोत्तुंगभित्रेर्बिंदोश्चमध्यभू:।।
भित्ति: कोशं परित्यज्य कोशत्रयमुदाहृतम्।।४५।।

तत्र क्रोशत्रयस्थाने ह्यणिमाद्यात्मरोचिषा।।
क्रोशत्रयं समस्तं तद्धस्तसंख्याप्रकारत:।।
चतुर्विंशतिसाहस्रहस्तै: संमितमुच्यते।।४६।।

बिन्दुपीठेशपर्यन्तं चतुर्दशविभेदतः॥
अन्तरे भेदिते जाते हस्तसंख्या मयोच्यते॥४७॥

पद्माटवीस्थलाच्चिन्तामणिवेशमान्तरं मुने॥
हस्तविंशतिरुन्नमं तत्र स्युरणिमादयः॥४८॥

अणिमान्तरविस्तारश्चतुर्नल्वसमन्वितः॥
किष्कुश्चतुःशती नल्वकिष्कुर्हस्त उदीर्यते॥४९॥

तत्रांतरेऽणिमाद्यास्तु पूर्वादिकृतमंदिराः॥
अणिमा महिमा चैव लघिमा गरिमा तथा॥५०॥

ईशित्वं च वशित्वं च प्राकाम्यं मुक्तिरेव च॥
इच्छा प्राप्तिः सर्वकामेत्येताः सिद्धय उत्तमाः॥५१॥

रससिद्धिर्मोक्षसिद्धिर्बलसिद्धिस्तथैव च॥
खड्गसिद्धिः पादुकाया सिद्धिरञ्जनसिद्धिकः॥५२॥

वाक्सिद्धिर्लोकसिद्धिश्च देहसिद्धिरनन्तरम्॥
एता अष्टौ सिद्धयस्तु बह्व्योऽन्य योगिसंमताः॥५३॥

तत्रांतरे तु परितः सेवते परमेश्वरीम्॥
कोटिशः सिद्धयस्तस्मिन्नणिमाद्यन्तरे मुने॥५४॥

नवलावण्यसंपूर्णाः स्मयमानमुखांबुजाः॥
ज्वलच्चिन्तामणिकराः सदा षोडशवार्षिकाः॥
अत्युदारप्रकृतयः खेलंति मदविह्वलाः॥५५॥

तस्याणिमाद्यन्तरस्योपरिष्टात्सुमनोहरम्॥
हस्तविंशतीरुन्नमं चतुर्नल्वप्रविस्तरम्॥५६॥

चतुर्दिक्षु च सोपानपंक्तिभिः सुमनोहरम्॥
ब्रह्माद्यंबरधिष्ण्यं स्यात्तत्रदेवीः स्थिताः श्रृणु॥५७॥

ब्राह्मी माहेश्वरी चैव कौमारी वैष्णवी तथा।।
वाराही चैव माहेन्द्री चामुण्डाप्यथ सप्तमी।।
महालक्ष्मीरष्टमी तु तत्रैताः कृतमंदिराः।।५८।।

नानाविधायुधाढ्याश्च नानाशक्तिपरिच्छदाः।।
पूर्वादिदिशमारभ्य प्रादक्षिण्यकृतालयाः।।५९।।

अथ बाह्यंतरा तस्योपरिष्टात्कुम्भसंभव।।
हस्तविंशतिरुन्नम्रं चतुर्नल्वप्रविस्तरम्।।
मुद्रान्तरमिति त्रैधं तत्र मुद्राः कृतालयाः।।६०।।

सक्षोभद्रावणाकर्षवशेन्मादमहाङ्कुशाः।।
खेचरी बीबजयोन्याख्य त्रिखण्डा दशमी पुनः।।६१।।

पूर्वादिशिमारभ्य मद्रा एताः प्रतिष्ठिताः।।
अत्यन्तपसुन्दराकारा नवयौवनविह्वलाः।।६२।।

कांतिभिः कमनीयाभिः पूरयंत्यो गृहांतरम्।।
सेवंते मुनिशार्दूल ललितापरमेश्वरीम्।।६३।।

अन्तरं त्रयमेतत्तु चक्रं त्रैलोकयमोहनम्।।
एतस्मिञ्छक्तयो यासु ता उक्ताः प्रकटाभिधाः।।६४।।

एतासां समधिष्ठात्री त्रिपुरा चक्रनायिका।।
तच्चक्रपालनकरी मुद्रासंक्षोभणात्मिका।।६५।।

अथ मुद्रांतरस्योर्ध्व प्रोक्ता नित्याकलांतरम्।।
हस्तविंशतिरुन्नम्रं चतुर्नल्वप्रविस्तरम्।।
पर्वतश्चैव सोपानमुत्तरोत्तरमिष्यते।।६६।।

नित्याकलांतरे तस्मिन्कामाकर्षणिका मुखाः।।
परितः कृतसंस्थानाः षोडशेंदुकलात्मिकाः।।६७।।

तर्पयंत्यो दिशां चक्रं सुधास्यंदौ सुशीतलैः।।
तासां नामानि मत्तस्त्वमवधारय कुम्भज।।६८।।

कामाकर्षिणिका नित्या बुद्ध्याकर्षणिकापरा।।
रसाकर्षणिका नित्या गन्धाकर्षणिका कला।।६९।।

चित्ताकर्षणिका नित्या धैर्याकर्षणिका कला।।
स्मृत्याकर्षणिका नित्या नामाकर्षणिका कला।।७०।।

बीजाकर्षणिका नित्या चार्थाकर्षणिका कला।।
अमृताकर्षणी चान्या शरीराकर्षणी कला।।७१।।

एतास्तु गुप्तयोगिन्यस्त्रिपुरेशी तु चक्रिणी।।
सर्वाशापूरिकाभिख्या चक्राधिष्ठानदेवता।।७२।।

एतच्चक्रे पालिका तु मुद्रा द्राविणिकाभिधा।।
नित्या कलांतरादूर्ध्वं धिष्ण्यमत्यंतसुन्दरम्।।७३।।

हस्तविंशतिरुन्नम्रं चतुर्नल्वप्रविस्तरम्।।
प्राग्वत्सोपानसंयुक्तं सर्वसंक्षोभणाभिधम्।।७४।।

तत्राष्टौ शक्तयस्तीव्रा मदारुणविलोचनाः।।
नवतारुण्यमत्ताश्च सेवंते परमेश्वरीम्।।७५।।

कुसुमा मेखला चैव मदना मदनातुरा।।
रेखा वेगिन्यंकुशा च मालिन्यष्टौ च शक्तयः।।७६।।

कोटिशस्तत्परीवारः शक्तयोऽनंगपूर्विकाः।।
सर्वसंक्षोभमिदं चक्रं तदधिदेवता।।७७।।

सुंदरी नाम विज्ञेया नाम्ना गुप्ततरापि सा।।
तच्चक्रपालनकरी मुद्राकर्षणिका स्मृता।।७८।।

अनंगशक्त्यंतरस्योपरिष्टात्कुंभसंभव।।
हस्तविंशतिरुन्नम्रं चतुर्नल्वप्रविस्तरम्।।
संक्षोभिण्याद्यंतरं स्यात्सर्वसौभाग्यदायकम्।।७९।।

सर्वसंक्षोभिणीमुख्यास्तत्र शक्तय उद्धता:।।
चतुर्दश वसंत्येव तासां नामानि मच्छृणु।।८०।।

सर्वसंक्षोभिणी शक्ति: सर्वविद्राविणी तथा।।
सर्वाकर्षणिका शक्ति: सर्वाह्लादनिका तथा।।८१।।

सर्वसंमोहिनी शक्ति: सर्वस्तंभनशक्तिका।।
सर्वजृंभिणिका शक्तिस्तथा सर्ववशंकरी।।८२।।

सर्वरंजनशक्तिश्च सर्वोन्मादनिशक्तिका।।
सर्वार्थसाधिका शक्ति: सर्वसंपत्तिपूरिणी।।८३।।

सर्वमंत्रमयी शक्ति: सर्वद्वंद्वक्षयंकरी।।
एताश्च संप्रदायाख्याश्चक्रिणीपुरवसिनी:।।८४।।

मुद्राश्च सर्ववश्याख्यास्तच्चक्रे रक्षिका मता:।।
कोटिश: शक्तयस्तत्र तासां किंकर्य्य उद्धृता:।।८५।।

संक्षोभिण्याद्यंतरस्योपरिष्टात्कुंभसंभव।।
हस्तविंशतिरुत्रम्रं चतुर्नल्वप्रविस्तरम्।।
सर्वसिद्धिादिकानां तु मंदिरं विष्ट्यमुच्यते।।८६।।

सर्वसिद्धिप्रदा चैव सर्वसंपत्प्रदा तथा।।
सर्वप्रियंकरी देवी सर्वमङ्गलकारिणी।।८७।।

सर्वकामप्रदा देवी सर्वदु:खविमोचनी।।
सर्वमृत्युप्रशमनी सर्वाविघ्ननिवारिणी।।८८।।

सर्वांगसुन्दरी देवी सर्वसौभाग्यदायिनी।।
एता देव्य: कलोत्कीर्णा योगिन्यो नामत: स्मृता:।।८९।।

चक्रिणी श्रीश्च विज्ञेया चक्रं सर्वार्थसाधकम्।।
सर्वोन्मादनमुद्राश्च चक्रस्य परिपालिका:।।९०।।

सर्वासिद्ध्यान्तरस्योपरिष्टात्कुम्भसम्भव।।
हस्तविंशतिरुन्नम्रं चतुर्नल्वप्रविस्तरम्।।९१।।

सर्वज्ञाद्यंतरं नाम्ना सर्वरक्षाकर स्मृतम्।।
चक्रं महत्तरं दिव्यं सर्वज्ञाद्याः प्रकीर्तिताः।।९२।।

सर्वज्ञा सर्वशक्तिश्च सर्वैश्वर्यप्रदायिनी।।
सर्वज्ञानमयी देवी सर्वव्याधिविनाशिनी।।९३।।

सर्वाधारस्वपरूपा च सर्वपापहरी तथा।।
सर्वानन्दमयी देवी सर्वरक्षास्वरूपिणी।।९४।।

सर्वेप्सितप्रदा चैता निर्गर्वा योगिनीश्वराः।।१४।।

मलिनी चक्रिणी प्रोक्ता मुद्रा सर्वमहांकुशा।
इति चिन्तामणिगृहे सर्वज्ञाद्यन्तरावधि।।
चक्राणि कानिचित्प्रोक्तान्यन्यान्यपि मुने श्रुणु।।९६।।

(DESCRIPTION OF INNER APARTMENT OF THE GODDESS)

हयग्रीव उवाच।।

सर्वज्ञाद्यंतरालस्योपरिष्टात्कलशोद्भव।।
हस्तविंशतिरुन्नम्रं चतुर्नल्वप्रविस्तरम्।।१।।

वशिन्याद्यन्तरं प्राग्वत्सोपानमंदिरम्।।
सर्वरोग हरं नाम्नां तच्चक्रमिति विश्रुतम्।।२।।

वशिन्यास्तत्र देव्यः पूर्वादिदिगनुक्रमात्।।
स्वरैस्तु रहितास्तत्र प्रथमा वशिनीश्वरी।।३।।

कवर्गसहिता पश्चात्कामेश्वर्याख्यवाङ्मयी।।
चवर्गजुष्टा वागीशी मोदिनी स्यात्तृतीयका।।४।।

टवर्गमंडिताकारा विमलाख्य सरस्वती।।
तवर्गेण तथोपेता पञ्चमी वाक्प्रधारण।।५।।

पवर्गेण परिस्फीता षष्ठी तु जयिनी मता।।
यादिवर्णचतुष्कोणे सर्वैश्वर्यादिवाङ्मयी।।६।।

साधिकाक्षरषट्केन कौलिनी त्वष्टमी मता।।
एता देव्यो जपरता मुक्ताभरणमंडिता:।।७।।

सदा स्फुरद्गद्यपद्यलहरीललिता मता:।।
काव्यैश्च नाटकैश्चैव मधुरै: कर्णहारिभि:।।
विनोदयन्त्य: श्रीदेवीं वर्तंते कुम्भसम्भव।।८।।

एता रहस्यनाम्नैव ख्याता वातापितापन।।
नयिका स्वस्य चक्रस्य सिद्धानाम्ना प्रकीर्तिता।।९।।

अस्य चक्रस्य संरक्षाकारिणी खेचरी मता।।
वशिन्याद्यंतरालस्योपरिष्टाद्विंध्यमर्दन।।१०।।

हस्तविंशतिरुन्नम्रं चतुर्नल्वप्रविस्तरम्।।
अस्त्रं चक्रमितिज्ञेयं तत्र बाणादिदेवता:।।११।।

पञ्च बाणेश्वरीदेव्य: पञ्च कामेश्वराशुगा:।।
अंकुशद्वितयं, दीप्तमादिस्त्रीपुंसयोर्द्वयो:।।१२।।

धनुर्द्वयं च विंध्यारे नव पुंड्रेषु कल्पितम्।।
पाशद्वयं च दीप्ताभं चत्वार्यस्त्राणि कुम्भज।।१३।।

कामेश्वर्यास्तु चत्वारि चत्वारि श्रीमहेशितु:।।
आहत्याष्टायुधानीति प्रज्वलन्ति विभांति च।।१४।।

भण्डासुरमहायुद्धे दुष्टदानवशोणितै:।।
पीतैरतीव तृप्तानि दिव्यास्त्राण्यतिजाग्रति।।९५।।

एतेषामायुधानां तु परिवारायुधान्यलम्।।
वर्तंतेऽस्त्रांतरे तत्र तेषां संख्या तु कोटिश:।।१६।।

वज्रशक्ति: शतघ्नी च भुशुण्डी मुसलं तथा।।
कृपाण: पट्टिशं चैव मुद्गरंभिन्दिपालकम्।।१७।।

एवमादीनि शस्त्राणि सहस्त्राणां सहस्त्रश:।।
अष्टायुधमहाशक्ती: सेवंते मदविह्वला:।।९८।।

अथ शस्त्रांतरालस्योपरि वातापितापन।।
हस्तविंशतिरुन्नमं चतुनल्वप्रविस्तरम्।।
धिष्ण्यं तु समयेशीनां स्थानं च तिसृणां मतम्।।१९।।

कामेशाद्यास्तत्र देव्यस्तिस्त्रोऽन्या तु चतुर्थिका।।
सैव नि:शेषविश्वानां सवित्री ललितेश्वरी।।२०।।

तिसृणां श्रुणु नामानि कामेशी प्रथमा मता।।
वज्रेशी भगमाला च ता: सेवन्ते सहस्त्रश:।।२१।।

सर्वेषां दर्शनानां च या देव्यो विविधा: स्मृता:।।
ता: सर्वास्तत्र कामेशादिमहोदया:।।२२।।

एतासां च प्रसंगेषु नित्यानां च प्रसञ्जने।।
चक्रिणीनां योगिनीनां श्रीदेवी पूरणात्मिका।।२३।।

या कामेश्वरदेवांकशायिनी ललितांबिका।।
कामेश्यादिचतुर्थी सा नित्यानां पोडशी मता।।२४।।

योगिनी चक्रदेवीनां नवमी परिकीर्तिता।।
समयेश्यन्तरालस्योपरिष्टादिल्वलांतक।।२५।।

नाथांतरमिति प्रोक्तं हस्तविंशतिरुन्नतम्।।
चतुर्नल्वप्रविस्तारं प्राग्वत्सोपानमण्डितम्।।२६।।

तत्र नाथामहादेव्या योगशास्त्रप्रवर्त्तका:।।
सर्वेषां मन्त्रगुरव: सर्वविद्यामहार्णवा:।।२७।।

चत्वारो योगनाथाश्च लोकानामिहगुप्तये।।
सृष्टा: कार्मेशदेवेन तेषां नामानि मे श्रृणु।।२८।।

मित्री च शोडिशश्चैव चर्याख्य: कुम्भसम्भव।।
तै: सृष्टा बहवो लोका रक्षार्थं पादुकात्मका:।।२९।।

दिव्यविद्या मानवौघसिद्धौघा: सुरतापसा:।।
प्राप्तसालोक्यसारूप्यसायुज्यादिकसिद्धय:।।३०।।

महान्तो गुरवस्तांस्तु सेवन्ते प्रचुरां गुरून्।।
अथा नाथांतरालस्योपरिष्टाद्धिष्ण्यमुत्तमम्।।३१।।

हस्तविंशतिरुन्नम्रं चतुर्नल्वप्रविस्तरम्।।
नित्यान्तरमिति प्रोक्तं नित्या: पंचदशात्र वै।।३२।।

अथ कामेश्वरी नित्या नित्या च भगमालिनी।।
नित्यक्लिन्ना अपि तथा भेरुण्डा वह्निवासिनी।।३३।।

महावज्रेश्वरी दूती त्वरिता कुलसुन्दरी।।
नित्या नीलपताका च विजया सर्वमङ्गला।।३४।।

ज्वालामालिनिका चित्रेत्येता: पंचदशोदिता:।।
एता देवीस्वरूपा: स्युर्महाबलपराक्रमा:।।३५।।

प्रथमा मुख्यतिथितां प्राप्ता व्याप्य जगत्त्रया:।।
कालत्रितयरूपाश्च कालग्रासविचक्षणा:।।३६।।

ब्रह्मादीनामशेषाणां चिरकालमुपेयुषाम्।।
तत्तत्काल शतायुष्यरूपा देव्याज्ञया स्थिता:।।३७।।

नित्योद्यता निरातंका: श्रीपराङ्गसमुद्भवा:।।
सेवन्ते जगतामृद्ध्यै ललिता चित्स्वरूपिणीम्।।३८।।

तासां भवनतां प्राप्ता दीप्त: पंचदशेश्वरा:।।
विसृष्टिबिन्दुचक्रे तु षोडश्या भवनं मतम्।।३९।।

अथ नित्यांतरालस्योपरिष्टात्कुम्भसम्भव।।
अङ्गदेव्यंतरं प्रोक्तं हस्तविंशतिरुन्नतम्।।४०।।

चतुर्नल्वप्रविस्तारं प्राग्वत्सोपानमंदिरम्।।
तस्मिन्हृदयदेव्याद्या: शक्तय: संति वै मुने।।४१।।

हृद्देवी च शिरोदेवी शिखादेवी तथैव च।।
वर्मदवी दृष्टिदेवी शस्त्रदेवी षडीरिता:।।४२।।

अत्यंतसन्निकृष्टास्ता: श्रीकामेश्वरसुभ्रुव:।।
नवलावण्यपूर्णाग्य: सावधाना धृतायुधा:।।४३।।

परितो बिन्दुपीठे चभ्राम्यनतो दृप्तमूर्तय:।।
ललिताज्ञाप्रवर्तिन्यो वशीनां पीठवर्तिका:।।४४।।

अथांगदेव्यन्तरस्योपरिष्टान्मण्डलाकृति।।
बिन्दुनाद महापीठं दशहस्तसमुन्नतम्।।४५।।

नल्वाष्टकप्रविस्तारमुद्यदादित्यसंनिभम्।।
बिन्दुपीठमिदं ज्ञेयं श्रीपीठमपि चेष्यते।।४६।।

महापीठमिति ज्ञेयं विद्यापीठमपीष्यते।।
आनन्दपीठमपि च पंचाशत्पीठरूपधृक्।।४७।।

तत्र श्रीललितादेव्या: पंचब्रह्ममये महत्।।
जागर्ति मञ्चरत्नं तु प्रपंचत्रयमूलकम्।।४८।।

तस्य मञ्चस्य पादास्तु चत्वार:परिकीर्तिता:।।
दशहस्तसमुन्नम्रा हस्तत्रितयविष्टिता:।।४९।।

ब्रह्मविष्णुमहेशानेश्वररूपत्वमागता:।।
शक्तिभावमनुप्राप्ता: सदा श्रीध्यानयोगभ:।।५०।।

एकस्तु पंचपादः स्याज्जपाकुसुमन्निभः।।
ब्रह्मात्मकः स विज्ञेयो वह्निदिग्भागमाश्रितः।।५१।।

चतुर्थो मंचपादस्तु कर्णिकारकसाररुक्।।
ईश्वरात्मा स विज्ञेय ईशदिग्भागमाश्रितः।।५२।।

एते सर्वे सायुधाश्च सर्वालंकारभूषिताः।।
उपर्यधः स्तंभरूपा मध्ये पुरुषरूपिणः।।५३।।

श्रीध्यानमीलिताक्षाश्च श्रीध्यानान्निश्चलांगकाः।।
तेषामुपरि मंचस्य फलकन्तु सदशिवः।।५४।।

विकासिदाडिमच्छायश्चतुर्नल्वप्रविस्तरः।।
नल्वषट्कायामवांश्च सदा भास्वरमूर्तिमान्।।५५।।

अंगदेव्यंतरारंभान्मंचस्य फलकावधि।।
चिंतामणिमयांगानि तत्वरूपाणि तापस।।५६।।

सोपानानि विभासंते षट्त्रिंशद्वै निवेशनैः।।
आरोहस्य क्रमेणैव सोपानान्यभिदध्महे।।५७।।

भूमिरापोऽनलो वायुराकाशो गन्ध एव च।।
रसो रूपं स्पर्शशब्दोपस्थपायुपदानि च।।५८।।

पाणिवाग्घ्राणजिह्वाश्चत्वक् चक्षुः श्रोत्रमेव च।।
अहंकारश्च बुद्धिश्च मनः प्रकृतिपूरुषौ।।५९।।

नियतिः कालरागौ च कला विद्ये? च मायया।।
शुद्धविद्येश्वरसदाशिवशक्तिः शिवा इति।।६०।।

एताः षट्त्रिंशदाख्यातास्तत्वसोपानपंक्तयः।।
पूषा सोपानपंक्तिश्च मञ्चपूर्वदिशं श्रिताः।।६१।।

अथ मञ्चस्योपरिष्टाद्धंसतूलिकतल्पकः।।
हस्तमात्रं समुन्नम्रं चतुर्नल्वप्रविस्तरम्।।६२।।

पादोपधानमूर्धोपधानद्वंद्वविराजितम्।।
गड्डुकानां चतु:षष्टिशोभितं पाटलत्विषा।।६३।।

तस्योपरिष्टात्कौसुंभत्सनेनोत्तरच्छद:।।
शुचिना मृदुना क्लृप्तपद्मरागमणित्विषा।।६४।।

तस्योपरि वसन्पूर्वदिङ्भुखो दययान्वित:।।
श्रंगारवेषरुचिरस्सदा षोडशवर्षिक:।।६५।।

उद्यद्भास्करबिंबाभश्चतुर्हस्तस्त्रिलोचन:।।
हारकेयूरमुकुटकटकाद्यैरलंकृत:।।६६।।

क्रमनीयस्मितज्योत्स्नापरिपूर्णकपोलभू:।।
जागर्ति भगवानादिदेव: कामेश्वर: शिव:।।६७।।

तस्योत्संगे समासीना तरुणादित्यपाटला।।
सदा षड्शोडशवर्षा च नवयौवनदर्पिता।।६८।।

अमृष्टपद्मरागाभा चन्दाब्जनखच्छटा।।
यावकश्रीर्निर्व्यपेक्षा पादलौहित्यवाहिनी।।६९।।

कलनिस्वानमञ्जीरपतत्कंकणमोहना।।
अनङ्गवरतूणीरदर्पोन्मथनजंघिगका।।७०।।

करिशुण्डदो:कदलिकाकांतितुल्योरुशोभिनी।।
अरुणेन दुकूलेन सुस्पर्शेन तनीयसा।।
अलंकृतनितंबाढ्याा जघनाभोगभासुरा।।७१।।

अर्धोरुकग्रंथिमती रत्नकांचीविराजिता।।
नतनाभिमहावर्तत्रिवल्यूर्मिप्रभासरित्।।७२।।

स्तनकुड्भलहिंदोलमुक्तादामशतावृता।।
अतिपीवरवक्षोजभारभंगुरमध्यभू:।।७३।।

शिरीषदाममृदुलच्छदाभांश्चतुरो भुजान्।।७४।।

केयूरकंकणश्रेणीमंडितान्सोर्मिकाङ्गुलीन्।।
वहंती पतिसंसृष्टशंखसुन्दरकंधरा।।७५।।

मुखदर्पणवृत्ताभचिबुका पाटलाधरा।।
शुचिभिः पंक्तिशुद्धैश्च विद्यारूपैर्विभास्वरैः।।
कुन्दकुड्भललक्ष्मीकैर्दंतैर्दर्शितचन्द्रिका।।७६।।

स्थूलमौक्तिकसनद्धनानाभरणभासुरा।।
केतकांतर्दलश्रोणी दीर्घदीर्घविलोचना।।७७।।

अर्धेन्दुललिते भाले सम्यक्लृप्तालकच्छटा।।
पालीवतं समाणिक्यकुण्डलामंडितश्रुतिः।।७८।।

नवकर्पूरकस्तूरीसदामोदितवीटिका।।
शरच्चञ्चन्निशानाथमण्डलीमधुरानना।।७९।।

चिन्तामणीनां सारेण क्लृचारुकिरीटिका।।
स्फुरत्तिलकरत्नाभभालनेत्रविराजिता।।८०।।

गाढांधकारनिबिडक्षामकुन्तलसंहतिः।।
सीमन्तरेखाविन्यस्तसिंदूरश्रेणिभासुरा।।८१।।

स्फुरच्चंद्रकलोत्तंसमदलोलविलोचना।।
सर्वश्रृङ्गारवेषाढ्या सर्वाभरणभूषिता।।८२।।

समस्तलोकमाता च सदानन्दविवर्धिनी।।
ब्रह्मविष्णुगिरीशेशसदाशिवनिदानभूः।।८३।।

अपांगरिंखत्करुणान्र्झिरीतर्पिता खिला।।
भासते सा भगवती पापघ्नी ललितांबिका।।८४।।

अन्यदैवतपूजानां यस्याः पूजाफलं विदुः।।
यस्यः पूजाफलं प्राहु र्यस्या एव हि पूजनम्।।८५।।

तस्याश्च ललितादेव्या वर्णयामि कथं पुनः।।
वर्षकोटिसहस्रेणाप्येकांशो वर्ण्यते न हि।।८६।।

वर्ण्यमाना ह्यवग्रूपा वाचस्तस्यां कुतो गतिः।।
यतो वाचो निवर्तंते अप्राप्य मनसा सह।।८७।।

बहुना किमिहोक्तेन तत्वभूतमिदं श्रुणु।।
न पक्षपातान्न स्नेहान्न मोहाद्वा मयोच्यते।।८८।।

संतु कल्पतरोः शाखा लेखिन्यस्तपसां निधे।।
मषीपात्राणि सर्वेऽपि सप्त संतु महार्णवाः।।८९।।

पञ्चाशत्कोटिविस्तीर्णा भूमिः पत्रत्वमृच्छतु।।
तस्य लेखनकालोऽस्तु पराध्यधिकवत्सैरः।।९०।।

लिखंतु सर्वे लोकाश्च प्रत्येकं कोटिबाहवः।।
सर्वे बृहस्पतिसमा वक्तरो यदि कुंभज।।९१।।

अथापि तस्याः श्रीदेव्याः पादाब्जैकाङ्गुलिद्युतेः।।
सहस्रांशेष्वेकैकांशवर्णना न हि जायते।।
अथ वा वृत्तिरखिला निष्फला तद्गुणस्तुतौ।।९२।।

बिन्दुपीठस्य परितश्चतुरस्रवया स्थिता।।
महामायाजवनिका लंबते मेचकप्रभा।।९३।।

देव्या उपरि हस्तानां विंश तिद्वितयोर्ध्वतः।।
इंद्रगोपवितानं तु बद्धं त्रैलोक्यदुर्लभम्।।९४।।

तत्रालंकारजालं तु वर्तमानं सुदुर्लभम्।
मद्वाणी वर्णयिष्यंती कंठ एव ह्रिया हता।।९५।।

सैव जानाति तत्सर्वं तत्रत्यमखिलं गुणम्।।
मनसोऽपि हि दूरे तत् सौभाग्यं केन वर्ण्यते।।१६।।

इत्थं भंडमहादैत्यवधाय ललितांबिका।।
प्रादुर्भूता चिदनलाद्दग्धनिःशेषदानवा।।९७।।

दिव्यशिल्पिजनैः क्लृप्तं षोडशक्षेत्रवेशनम्।।
अधिष्ठाय श्रीनगरं सदा रक्षति विष्टपम्।।९८।।

इत्थमेव प्रकारेण श्रीपुराण्यन्यकान्यपि।।
न भेदकोऽपि विन्यासो नाममात्रं पुरां भिदा।।९९।।

नानावृक्षमहोद्यानमारभ्येतिक्रमेण ये।।
वदंति श्रीपुरकथां ते यांति परमां गतिम्।।१००।।

आकर्णयंति पृच्छंति विचिन्वंति च ये नराः।।
ये पुस्तके धारयंति ते यांति परमां गतिम्।।१०१।।

ये श्रीपुरप्रकारेण तत्तत्स्थानविभेदतः।।
कृत्वा शिल्पिजनैः सर्वे श्रीदेव्यायतनं महत्।।
संपादयंति ये भक्तास्ते यांति परमां गतिम्।।१०२।।

(PARVATI'S PENANCE AND EXPIATION OF SIVA'S SIN)

अगस्त्य उवाच।।

श्रीकामकोष्टपीठस्था महात्रिपुरसुन्दरी।।
कं कं विलासमकरोत्कामाक्षीत्यभिविश्रुता।।१।।

श्रीकामाक्षीति सा देवी महात्रिपुरसुंन्दरी।।
भूमण्डलस्थिता देवी किं करोति महेश्वरी।।
एतस्याश्चरितं दिव्यं वद मे वदतां वर।।२।।

हयग्रीव उवाच।।

अत्र स्थितापि सर्वेषां हृदयस्था घटोद्भव।।
तत्तत्कर्मानुरूपं सा प्रदत्ते देहिनां फलम्।।३।।

यत्किञ्चिद्वर्तते लोके सर्वमस्या विचेष्टितम्।।
किञ्चिञ्चिन्तयते कश्चित्स्वच्छंदं विदधात्यसौ।।४।।

तस्या एवावतारास्तु त्रिपुराद्याश्च शक्तय:।।
इयमेव महालक्ष्मी: ससर्जांडत्रयं पुरा।।५।।

पुरत्रयाणामावासं शक्तीनां तिसृणामपि।।
एकस्मादंडतो जातावंबिकापुरुषोत्तमौ।।६।।

श्रीविरिञ्चौ ततोऽन्यस्मादन्यस्माच्च गिराशिवौ।।
इंदिरा योजयामास मुकुंदने महेश्वरी।।
पार्वत्या परमेशानं सरस्वत्या पितामहम्।।७।।

ब्रह्माणं सर्वलोकानां सृष्टिकार्ये न्ययुंक्त सा।।
वासुदेवं परित्राणे संहारे च त्रिलोचनम्।।८।।

ते सर्वेऽपि महालक्ष्मीं ध्यायंत: शर्मदां सदा।।
ब्रह्मलोके च बैकुंठे कैलासे च वसंत्यमी।।९।।

कदाचित्पार्वती देवी कैलासशिखरे शुभे।।
विहरंती महेशस्य पिधानं नेत्रयो र्व्यधात्।।१०।।

चंद्रसूर्यौ यतस्तस्य नेत्रात्तस्माज्जगत्त्रयम्।।
अंधकारावतमभूदतेजस्कं समंतत:।।११।।

ततश्च सकला लोकास्त्यक्तदेवपितृयिा:।।
इतिकर्त्तव्यतामूढा न प्रजानन्त किञ्चन।।१२।।

तद्दृष्ट्वा भगवान्रुद्र: पार्वतीमिदमब्रवीत्।।
त्वया पापं कृतं देवि मम नेत्रपिधानत:।।१३।।

ऋषयस्त्यक्ततपसो हतसन्ध्याश्च वैदिका:।।
सर्वं च वैदिकं कर्म त्वया नाशितमबिकें।।१४।।

तस्मात्पापस्य शांत्यर्थ तपः कुरु सुदुष्करम्।।
गत्वा काशीं व्रतं तत्र किञ्चित्कालं समाचर।।१५।।

पश्चात्कांचि पुरं गत्वा कामाक्षीं तत्र द्रक्ष्यसि।।
आराधयैतां नित्यां त्वं सर्वपापहरीं शिवाम्।।१६।।

तुलसीमग्रतः कृत्वा कम्पाकूले तपः कुरु।।
इत्यादिश्य महादेवस्तत्रैवान्तरधीयता।।१७।।

तथा कृतवतीशानी भर्तुराज्ञानुवर्तिनी।।
चिरेण तपसा क्लिष्टामनन्यहृदयां शिवाम्।।१८।।

अग्रतः कृतसांनिध्या कामाक्षी वाक्यमब्रवीत्।।
वत्से तपोभिरत्युग्रैरलं प्रीतास्मि सुव्रते।।१९।।

उन्मील्यनयने पश्चात्पार्वती स्वपुरः स्थिताम्।।
बालार्कायुतसंकाशां सर्वाभरणभूषिताम्।।२०।।

किरीटहारकेयूरकटकाद्यैरलंकृताम्।।
पाशांकुशेक्षुकोदंडपञ्चबाणलसत्कराम्।।२१।।

किरीटमुकुटोल्लासिचंद्ररेखाविभूषणाम्।।
विधातृहरिरुद्रेशसदाशिवपदप्रदाम्।।२२।।

सगुणं ब्रह्मतामाउहुरनुत्तरपदाभिधाम्।।
प्रपञ्चद्वयनिर्माणकारिणीं तां परांबिकाम्।।२३।।

तां दृष्ट्वाथ महाराज्ञीं महानंदपरिप्लुता।।
पुलकांचितसर्वांगी हर्षेणोत्फुल्ललोचना।।२४।।

चंडिकामंगलाद्यैश्च सहसा स्वसखीजनैः।।
प्रणिपत्य च साष्टाङ्गं कृत्वा चैव प्रदक्षिणाम्।।२५।।

बद्धांजलिपुटा भूयः प्रणता स्वैक्यरूपिणी।।
तामाह कृपया वीक्ष्य महात्रिपुरसुंदरी।।२६।।

बाहुभ्यां संपरिष्वज्य सस्नेहमिदमब्रवीत्।।
वत्से लभस्व भर्तारं रुद्रं स्वमनसेप्सितम्।।२७।।

लोके त्वमपि रक्षार्थे ममाज्ञामनुवर्तय।।
अहं त्वमिति को भेदस्त्वमेवाहं न संशय:।।२८।।

किं पापं तव कल्याणि त्वं हि पापनिकृंतनी।।
आमनंति हि योगींद्रास्त्वामेव ब्रह्मरूपिणीम्।।२९।।

लीलामात्रमिदं वत्से परलोकविडंबनम्।।
इत्यूचिषीं महाराज्ञीमंबिकां सर्वमंगला।।
भक्त्या प्रणम्य पश्यंती परां प्रीतिमुपाययौ।।३०।।

स्तुवत्यामेव पार्वत्यां तदानीमेव सापरा।।
प्रविष्टा हृदयं तस्या: प्रहृष्टाया महामुने।।३१।।

अथ विस्मयमापन्ना चिंतयंती मुहुर्मुहु:।।
स्वप्न: किमेष दृष्टो वा मया किमथ वा भ्रम:।।३२।।

इत्थं विमृश्य परित: प्रेरयामास लोचने।।
जयां च विजयां पश्चात्सख्यावालोक्य सस्मिते।।
प्रसन्नवदना सा तु प्रणते वदति स्म सा।।३३।।

एतावंतमलं कालं कुत्र याते युवां प्रिये।।
मया दृष्टां तु कामाक्षीं युवां चेत्किमपश्यतम्।।३४।।

सख्यौ तु तद्वच: श्रुत्वा प्रहर्षोत्फुल्ललोचने।।
पुष्पाणि पूजनार्हाणि निधायाग्रे समूचतु:।।३५।।

सत्यमेवाधुना दृष्टा ह्यावाभ्यामपि सा परा।।
न स्वप्नो न भ्रमो वापि साक्षात्ते हृदयं गता।।
इत्युक्त्वा पार्श्वयोस्तस्या निषण्णे विनयानते।।३६।।

एकाम्रमूले भगवान्भवानीविरहार्तिमान्।।
गौरीसंप्राप्तये दध्यौ कामाक्षीं नियतेंद्रियः।।३७।।

तत्रापि कृतसांनिध्या श्रीविद्यादेवता परा।।
आचष्ट कृपया तुष्टा ध्यायंतं निश्चलं शिवम्।।३८।।

अलं ध्यानेन कंदर्पदर्पघ्न त्वं ममाज्ञया।।
अंगीकुरुष्व कंदर्पं भूयो मच्छासने स्थितम्।।३९।।

एकाम्रसंज्ञे मत्पीठे त्विहैव निवसन्सदा।।
त्वमेवागत्य मत्प्रीत्यै संनिधौ मम सुव्रत।।
गौरीमनुगृहाण त्वं कपतीरनिवासिनीम्।।४०।।

तापद्वयं जहीह्याशु योगजं तद्वियोगजम्।।
इत्युक्त्वांतर्दधे तस्य हृदये परमा रमा।।४१।।

शिवो व्युत्थाय सहसा धीरः संहृष्टमानसः।।
तस्य अनुग्रहं लब्ध्वा सर्वदेवनिषेवितः।।४२।।

हृदि ध्यायंश्च तामेव महात्रिपुरसुन्दरीम्।।
यद्विलासात्समुत्पन्नं लयं याति च यत्र वै।।४३।।

जगच्चराचरं चैतत्प्रपंचद्वितयात्मकम्।।
भूषयन्तीं शिवां कम्पामनुकंपार्द्रमानसाम्।।४४।।

अङ्गीकृत्य तदा गौरी वैवाहिकविधानतः।।
आदाय वृषमारुह्य कैलास शिखरं ययौ।।४५।।

पुनरन्यं महप्राज्ञ समाकर्णय कुम्भज।।
आदिलक्ष्म्याः प्रभावं तु कथयामि तवानघ।।४६।।

सभायां ब्रह्मणो गत्वा समासेदुस्त्रिमूर्त्रयः।।
दिक्पालाश्च सुराः सर्वे सनकाद्याश्च योगिनः।।४७।।

देवर्षयो नारदाद्या वशिष्ठाद्याश्च तापसा:।।
ते सर्वे सहितास्तत्र ब्रह्मणश्च कपर्दिन:।।
द्वयो: पंचमुखत्वेन भेदं न विविदुस्तदा।।४८।।

अन्योन्यं पृष्टवंतस्ते ब्रह्मा क: कश्च शङ्कर:।।
तेषां संवदतां मध्ये क्षिप्रमंतर्हित: शिव:।।४९।।

तदा पंचमुखो ब्रह्म सितो नारायणस्तयो:।।
उभयोरपि संवादस्त्वहं ब्रह्मेत्यजायत।।५०।।

अज्ञ मन्नाभिकमलाज्जातस्त्वं यन्ममात्मज:।।
सृष्टिकर्ता त्वहं ब्रह्मा नामसाधर्म्यतस्तथा।।
त्वं च रुद्रश्च मे पुत्रौ सृष्टिकर्तुरुभौ युवाम्।।५१।।

इति मायामोहितयोरुभयोरंतरे तदा।।
तयोश्च स्वस्य माहात्म्यमहं ब्रह्मेति दर्शयन्।।
प्रादुरासीन्महाज्योतिस्तंभरूपो महेश्वर:।।५२।।

ज्ञात्वैवैनं महेशानं विष्णुस्तूष्णीं तत: स्थित:।।
पंचवक्त्रस्ततो ब्रह्मा ह्यवमत्यैवमास्थित:।।
ब्रह्मण: शिरसामूर्ध्वं ज्योतिश्चक्रमभूत्पुर:।।५३।।

तन्मध्ये संस्थितो देव: प्रादुरासोमया सह।।
ऊर्ध्वमैक्षथ भूयस्तमवमत्य वचोऽब्रवीत्।।५४।।

तन्निशम्य भृशं क्रोधमवाप त्रिपुरान्तक:।।
विष्णुमेवं तदालोक्य क्रोधेनैव विकारत:।।५५।।

तयोरेव समुत्पन्नो भैरव: क्रोधसंयुत:।।
मूर्धानमेकं चिच्छेद नखेनैव तदा विधे:।।
हाहेति तत्र सर्वेऽपि क्रन्दंतश्च पलायिता:।।५६।।

अथ ब्रह्मकपालं तु नखलग्नं स भैरवः।।
भूयोभूयो धुनोति स्म तथापि न मुमोच तम्।।५७।।

तद्ब्रह्महत्यामुक्त्यर्थे चचार धरणीतले।।
पुण्यक्षेत्राणि सर्वाणि गंगाद्याश्च महानदीः।।५८।।

न च ताभिर्विमुक्तोऽभूत्कपाली ब्रह्महत्यया।।
विषण्णवदनो दीनो निःश्रीक इव लक्षितः।।
चिरेण प्राप्तवान्कांचीं ब्रह्मणा पूर्वमोषिताम्।।५९।।

तत्र भिक्षामटन्नित्यं सेवमानः परां श्रियम्।।
पंचतीर्थे प्रतिदिनं स्नात्वा भूलक्षणांकिते।।६०।।

कञ्चित्कालमुवासाथ प्रभ्रान्त इव बिल्वलः।।
कांचीक्षेत्रनिवासेन क्रमेण प्रयताशयः।।६१।।

निर्धूतनिखिलातंकः श्रीदेवीं मनसा वहन्।।
उत्तरे सेवितुं लक्ष्म्या वासुदेवेन दक्षिणे।।६२।।

श्रीकामकोष्टमागत्य पुरस्तात्तस्य संस्थितः।।
आदिलक्ष्मीपदध्यानमाततान् यतात्मवान्।।६३।।

यथा दीपो निवातस्थो निस्तरंगो यथांबुधिः।।
तथांतर्वायुरोधेन च चचालाचलेश्वरः।।६४।।

तैलधारावदच्छिन्नामनवच्छिन्नभैरवः।।
वितेने शैलतनयानाथश्रीध्यानसन्ततिम्।।
न ब्रह्मा नैव विष्णुर्वा न सिद्धः कपिलोऽपि वा।।
नान्ये च सनकाद्या ये मुनयो वा शुकादयः।।
तया समाधिनिष्ठायां न समर्थाः कथंचन।।६६।।

अथ श्रीभावयोगेन श्रीभावं प्राप्तवाञ्शिवः।।
ततः प्रसन्ना श्रीदेवी प्रभामण्डलवर्तिनी।।
अर्धरात्रे पुरः स्थित्वा वाचं प्रोवाच वाङ्मयी।।६७।।

श्रीकण्ठ सर्वपापघ्न किं पापं तव विद्यते।।
मद्रूपस्त्वं कथं देहः सेयं लोकविडम्बना।।६८।।

श्वोभूते ब्रह्महत्यायाः क्षणान्मुक्तो भविष्यसि।।
इत्युक्त्वान्तर्दधे तत्र महासिंहासनेश्वरी।।६९।।

भैरवोऽपि प्रहृष्टात्मा कृतार्थः श्रीविलोकनात्।।
विनीय तं निशाशेषं श्रीध्यानैकपरायणः।।७०।।

प्रातः पञ्चमहृतीर्थे स्नात्वा सन्ध्यामुपास्य च।।
पुनः पुनर्धूनुते स्म परलग्नं कपालकम्।।७१।।

तथापि तत्तु नास्रंसत्स निर्वेदं परं गतः।।
स्वप्नः किमेष माया वा मानसभ्रांतिरेव वा।।७२।।

मुहुरेवं विचिंत्येशः शोकव्याकुलमानसः।।
स्वयमेव निगृह्याथ शोकं धीरग्रणीः शिवः।।७३।।

तुलसीमण्डलं गत्वा पूजयित्वा पुरः स्थितः।।
निगृहीतेंद्रियग्रामः समाधिस्थोऽभवत्पुनः।।६४।।

याममात्रे गते देवी पुनः सांनिध्यमागता।।
अलं समाधिना शम्भो निमज्जात्र सरोवरे।।७५।।

इत्या दिश्य तिरोऽधत्त सोऽपि चिंतामुपागमत्।।
इयं च माया स्वप्नो वा किं कर्त्तव्यं मयाथ वा।।७६।।

श्वोभूते ब्रह्महत्यायाः क्षणान्मुक्तो भविष्यसि।।
इत्युक्तं श्रीपरादेव्या यामातीतमिदं दिनम्।।७७।।

एवं सर्वं च मिथ्यैवेत्यधिकं चिन्तयावृतः।।
भगवान्व्योमवाण्या तु निमज्जाप्स्विवति गर्जितम्।।७८।।

श्रुत्वा शङ्कां समुत्सृज्य तत्त्वं निश्चित्य शङ्करः।।
निममज्ज सरस्यां तु गङ्गायां पुनरुत्थितः।।७९।।

तत्र काशीं समालोक्य किमेतदिति चिन्तयन्।।
स मुहुर्तं स्थितस्तूष्णीं नखलीनकपालकः।।८०।।

ललाटंतपमुद्वीक्ष्य तरणिं तरुणेंदुभृत्।।
भिक्षार्थं नगरीमेनां प्रविवेश वशी शिवः।।८१।।

गृहाणि कानिचिद्रत्वा प्रतोल्यां पर्यटन्भवः।।
सोऽपश्यदग्रतः कांचित्कांचीं श्रीदवताकृतिम्।।७२।।

भिक्षां ज्योतिर्मयीं तस्मै दत्वा क्षिप्रं तिरोदधे।।
क्षणाद्ब्रह्मकपालं तत्प्रच्युतं तत्रवाग्रतः।।८३।।

तदृष्ट्वाद्भुतमीशानः कामाक्षीशीलमुत्तमम्।।
प्रसन्नवदनांभोजो बहुमेने मुहुः परम्।।८४।।

पुरी कांची पुरी पुण्या नदी कंपा नदी परा।।
देवता सैव कामाक्षीत्यासीत्संभावना पुरः।।८५।।

इत्थं देवीप्रभावेण विमुक्तः संकटाद्धरः।।
स्वस्थः स्वस्थानमगच्छलाघमानः परां श्रियम्।।८६।।

(DASARATHA'S VISIT TO KANCHI AND PRAYER TO THE THE GOODESS)

पुरनरन्यत्प्रवक्ष्यामि विलासं श्रुणु कुम्भजः।।
प्रभावं श्रीमहादेव्याः कामदं श्रृण्वतां सदा।।८७।।

अयोध्याधिपतिः श्रीमान्नाम्ना दशरथो नृपः।।
सन्तानरहितोऽतिष्टद्बहुालं शुचाकुलः।।८८।।

रहस्याहुय मतिमान्वशिष्टं स्वपुरोहितम्।।
उवाचाचारसंशुद्धः सर्वशास्त्रार्थवेदिनम्।।८९।।

श्रीनाथ बहवोऽतीताः काला नाधिगतः सुतः।।
संततेर्मम संतापः संततं वर्धतेतराम्।।
किं कुर्वे यदि संतानसंपत्स्यात्तन्निवेदय।।९०।।

वशिष्ठ उवाचा।।

मम वंशे महाराज रहस्यं कथयामि ते।।
अयोध्या मथुरा माया काशी कांची ह्यवंतिका।।
एता पुण्यतमाः प्रोक्ताः पुरीणामुत्तमोत्तमाः।।९१।।

अस्याः सांनिध्यमात्रेण महात्रिपुरसुन्दरीम्।।
अर्चयंति ह्ययोध्यायां मनुष्या अधिदेवताम्।।९२।।

नैतस्याः सदृशी काचिद्देवता विद्यते परा।।
एनामेवार्चयंत्यन्ये सर्वे श्रीदेवतां नृपा।।९३।।

ब्रह्मविष्णुमहेशाद्याः सस्त्रीकाः सर्वदा सदा।।
नारिकेलफलालीभिः पनसैः कदलीफलैः।।९४।।

मध्वाज्यशर्कराप्राज्यैर्महापायसाराशिभिः।।
सिद्धद्रव्यविशेषैश्च पूजयेत्त्रिपुरांबिकाम्।।
अभीष्टमचिरेणैव संप्रदास्यति सैव नः।।९५।।

इत्युक्तवन्तमभ्यर्च्य गुरुमिष्टैरुपायनैः।।
स्वाङ्गजप्राप्तये भूयो विससर्ज विशांपतिः।।९६।।

ततोगुरूक्तरीत्यैव ललिता परमेश्वरीम्।।
अर्चयामास राजेंद्रो भक्त्या परमया युतः।।९७।।

एवं प्रतिदिनं पूजां विधाय प्रीतमानसः।।
अयोध्यादेवताधामामशिषत्तत्र सङ्गतः।।९८।।

अर्धरात्रे व्यतीते तु निभृतोल्लासदीपिके।।
किञ्चिन्निदालसस्यास्य पुरतस्त्रिपुरांबिका।।९९।।

पाशांकुशधनुर्बाणपरिष्कृतचतुर्भुजा।।
सर्वश्रृङ्गारवेषाढ्या सर्वाभरणभूषिता।।
स्थित्वा वाचमुवाचेमां मन्दमिन्दुमतीसुतम्।।१००।।

अस्ति पंक्तिरथ श्रीमन्पुत्रभाग्यं तवानघ।।
विश्वासघातकर्माणि संति पूर्वकृतानि ते।।१०१।।

तादृशां कर्मणां शांत्यै गत्वा काञ्चीपुरं वरम्।।
स्नात्वा कम्पासरस्यां च तत्र मां पश्य पावनीम्।।१०२।।

मध्ये काञ्चीपुरस्य त्वं कन्दराकाशमध्यगम्।।
कामकोष्टं विपाप्मपि सप्तद्वारबिलान्वितम्।।१०३।।

साम्राज्यसूचकं पुंसां त्रयाणामपि सिद्धिदम्।।
प्राङ्मुखी तत्र वर्तेऽह महासिंहासनेश्वरी।।१०४।।

महालक्ष्मीस्वरूपेण द्विभुजा पद्मधारिणी।।
चक्रेश्वरी महाराज्ञी ह्यदृश्या स्थूलचक्षुषान्।।१०५।।

ममाक्षिजा महागौरी वर्तते मम दक्षिणे।।
सौन्दर्यसारसीमा सा सर्वाभरणभूषिता।।१०६।।

मया च कल्पिताऽऽवासा द्विभुजा पद्मधारिणी।।
महालक्ष्मीस्वरूपेण किं वा कृत्यात्मना स्थिता।।१०७।।

आपीठमौलिपर्यन्तं पश्य तस्तां ममांशजाम्।।
पातकान्याशु नश्यंति किं पुनस्तूपपातकम्।।१०८।।

कुवासना कुबुद्धिश्च कुतर्कनिचयश्च यः।।
कुदेहश्च कुभावश्च नास्तिकत्वं लयं व्रजेत्।।१०९।।

कुरुष्व मे महापूजां सितामध्वाज्यपायसैः।।
विविधैर्भक्ष्यभोज्यैश्च पदार्थैः षड्रसान्वितैः।।११०।।

तत्रैव सुप्रसन्नाहं पूरयिष्यामि ते वरम्।।
उपदिश्येति सम्राज्ञी दिव्यमूर्तिस्तिरोदधे।।१११।।

राजापि सहसोत्थाय किमेतदिति विस्मितः।।
देवीमुद्बोध्य कौसल्यां शुभलक्षणलक्षिताम्।।११२।।

तस्यै तद्रात्रिवृत्तांतं कथयामास सादरम्।।
तत्समाकर्ण्य सा देवी सन्तोषमभजत्तदा।।११३।।

प्राप्तहर्षो नृपः प्रातस्तया दयितया सह।।
अनीकसचिवोपेतः काञ्चीपुरमुपागमत्।।११४।।

स्नात्वा कंपातरंगिण्यां दृष्ठ्वा देवीं च पावनीम्।।
पञ्चतीर्थे ततः स्नात्वा देव्या कौसल्यया नृपः।।११५।।

गोभूवस्त्रहिरण्याद्यैस्तत्तीर्थक्षेत्रवसिनः।।
प्रीणयित्वा सपत्नीकस्तथा तद्भक्तिपूजकान्।।११६।।

अथालयं समाविश्य महाभक्त्या नृपोत्तमः।।
प्रदक्षिणत्रयं कृत्वा विनयेन समन्वितः।।११७।।

ततः संनिधिमागत्य देव्या कौसल्यया सह।।
श्रीकामकोष्टनिलयं महात्रिपुरसुन्दरीम्।।११८।।

त्रिमूर्तिजननीमंबां दृष्ट्वा श्रीचक्ररूपिणीम्।।
प्रणिपत्य तु साष्टांगं भार्यया सह भक्तिमान्।।११९।।

स्वपुरे त्रैपुरे धाम्नि पुरेक्ष्वाकुप्रवर्तिते।।
दुर्वासा सशिष्येण पूजार्थं पूर्वकल्पिते।।१२०।।

दासीदासध्वजारोहगृहोत्सवसमन्विते।।
तत्र स्वगुरुणोक्तं च कृत्वा स्वात्मार्घपूजनम्।।१२१।।

रात्रौ स्वप्ने तु यद्रूपं दृष्टवान्स्वपुरे महः।।
तदेवात्रापि संदध्यौ सन्निधौ राजसत्तमः।।१२२।।

चिरं ध्यात्वा महाराजः सुवासांसि बहूनि च।।
दिव्यान्यायतनान्यस्यै दत्वा स्तोत्रं चकार ह।।१२३।।

दशरथ उवाच-

पादाग्रलंबिपरमाभरणाभिरामे मञ्जीररत्नरुचिमञ्जुलपादद्मे।।
पीतांबरस्फुरितपेशलहेमकाञ्चि
केयूरकङ्कणपरिष्कृतबाहुवल्लि।।१२४।।

पुंड्रेक्षुचापविलसन्मृदुवामपाणे रत्नोर्मिकासुमशारञ्चितदक्षहस्ते।।
वक्षोजमंडलविलासिवलक्षहारि
पाशांकुशांगदलसद्भुजशोभितांगि।।१२५।।

वक्त्रश्रिया विजितशारदचन्द्रबिम्बे ताटंकरत्नकरमण्डितगंडभागे।।
वामे करे सरसिजं सुबिसं दधाने कारुण्यनिर्झरदपाङ्गयुते
महेशि।।१२६।।

माणिक्यसूत्रमणिभासुरकंबुकंठि
भालस्थचन्द्रशकलोज्ज्वलितालकाढ्ये।।
मंदस्मितस्फुरणशालिनि मंजुनासे नेत्रश्रिया
विजितनीलसरोजपत्रे।।१२७।।

सभ्रूलते सुवदने सुललाटचित्रे योगींद्रमानससरोजनिवासहंसि।।
रत्नानुबद्धतपनीयमहाकिरीटे सर्वागसुन्दरी -
समस्तसुरेन्द्रवंद्ये।।१२८।।

कांक्षानुरूपवरदे करुणार्द्रचित्ते साम्रज्यसम्पदभिमानिनि चक्रनाथे।।
इन्द्रादिदेवपरिसेवितपादपद्मे सिहासनेश्वरि परे मयि
संनिदध्याः।।१२९।।

इति स्तुत्वा न भूपालो बहिर्निर्गत्य भक्तितः।।
तस्यास्तु दक्षिणे भागे महागौरीं ददर्श ह।।१३०।।

प्रणम्य दंडवद्भूमौ कृत्वा चास्याः स्तुतिं पुनः।।
दत्वा चास्यै महार्हाणि वासांसि विविधानि च।।१३१।।

अमूल्यानि महार्हाणि भूषणानि महांति च।।
ततः प्रदक्षिणीकृत्य निर्गत्य सह भार्यया।।१३२।।

स्वगुरूक्तविधानेन महापूजां विधाय च।।
तामेव चिन्तयंस्तत्र सप्तरात्रमुवास सः।।१३३।।

अष्टमे दिवसे देवीं नत्वा भक्त्या विलोकयन्।।
अम्बीभीष्टं प्रदेहीति प्रार्थयामास चेतसा।।१३४।।

सुप्रसन्ना च कामाक्षी सांतरिक्षगिरावदत्।।
भविष्यंति मदंशास्ते चत्वारस्तनया नृपा।।१३५।।

इत्युदीरितमाकर्ण्य प्रमोदविकसन्मुखः।।
श्रियं प्रणम्य साष्टांगमनन्यशरणः पराम्।।१३६।।

आमन्त्र्य मनसैवांबां सस्त्रीकः सह मन्त्रिभिः।।
अयोध्यां नगरीं प्रापदिंदुमत्यास्तु नन्दनः।।१३७।।

एवं प्रभावा कामाक्षी सर्वलोकहितैषिणी।।
सर्वेषामपि भक्तानां कांक्षितं पूरयत्यलम्।।१३८।।

एनां लोकेषु बहवः कामाक्षीं परदेवताम्।।
उपास्य विधिवद्भक्त्या प्राप्ताः कामानशेषतः।।१३९।।

अद्यापि प्राप्नुवंत्येव भक्तिमन्तः फलं मुने।।
अनेके च भविष्यंति कामाक्ष्याः करुणादृशा।।१४०।।

माहात्म्यमस्याः श्रीदेव्याः को वा वर्णयितुं क्षमः।।
नाहं न शुम्भुर्न ब्रह्मा न विष्णुः किमुतापरे।।१४१।।

इति ते कथितं किञ्चित्कामाक्ष्याः शीलमुज्ज्वलम्।।
श्रृण्वतां पठतां चापि सर्वपापहरं स्मृतम्।।१४२।।

(WORSHIP OF GODDESS AND MAGICAL BENEFITS)

अगस्त्य उवाच॥

कीदृशं यंत्रमेतस्या मंत्रो वा कीदृशो वर:॥
उपदेष्टा च कीदृक्स्याच्छिष्यो वा कीदृश: स्मृत:॥१॥

सर्वज्ञस्त्वं हयग्रीव साक्षात्परमपूरुष:॥
स्वमिन्मयि कृपादृष्ट्या सर्वमेतन्निवेदय॥२॥

हयग्रीव उवाच॥

मंत्र श्रीचक्रमेवास्या: सेयं हि त्रिपुरांबिका॥
सैषैव हि महालक्ष्मी: स्फुरच्चैवात्मन: पुरा॥३॥

पश्यति स्म तदा चक्रं ज्योतिर्मयविजृंभितम्॥
अस्य चक्रस्य माहात्म्यपरिज्ञेयमेव हि॥४॥

साक्षात्सैव महालक्ष्मी: श्रीचक्रमिति तत्वत:॥
यदभ्यर्च्य महाविष्णु: सर्वलोकविमोहनम्॥

कामसंमोहिनीरूपं भेजे राजीवलोचन:॥
अर्चयित्वा तदीशान: सर्वविद्येश्वरोऽभवत्॥

तदाराध्य विशेषेण ब्रह्मा ब्रह्मांडसूरभूत्॥
मुनीनां मोहनश्चासीत्स्मरो यद्वरिवस्यया॥६॥

श्रीदेव्या: पुरतश्चक्रं हेमरौप्यादिनिर्मितम्॥
निधाय गन्धैरभ्यर्च्य षोडशाक्षरविद्याया॥७॥

प्रत्यहं तुलसीपत्रै: पवित्रैर्मंगलाकृति:॥
सहस्त्रैर्मूलमंत्रेण श्रीदेवीध्यानसंयुत:॥८॥

अर्चयित्वा च मध्वाज्यशर्करापायसै: शुभै:॥
अनवद्यैश्चनैवैर्माषापूपैर्मनोहरै:॥९॥

य: प्रीणाति महालक्ष्मीं मतिमान्मण्डलत्रये।।
सहसा तस्य सांनिध्यमाधत्ते परमेश्वरी।।१०।।

मनसा वाञ्छितं यच्च प्रसन्ना तत्प्रपूरयेत्।।
धवलै कुसुमैश्चक्रमुक्तरीत्या तु योऽर्चयेत्।।११।।

तस्यैव रसनाभागे नित्यं नृत्यति भारती।।
पाटलै: कुसुमैश्चकं योऽर्चयेदुक्तमार्गत:।।।।
सार्वमौमं च राजानं दासवद्वशयेदसौ।।१२।।

पीतवर्णै: शुभै: पुष्पै: पूर्ववत्पूजयेच्च य:।।
तस्य वक्षस्थले नित्यं साक्षाच्छ्रीर्वसति ध्रुवम्।।१३।।

दुर्गंधैर्गंधहीनैश्च सुवर्णैरपि नार्चयेत्।।
सुगन्धैरेव कुसमै: पुष्पैश्चाभ्यर्चयेच्छिवाम्।।१४।।

कामाक्ष्यैव महालक्ष्मीश्चक्रं श्रीचक्रमेव हि।।
श्रीविद्यैषा परा विद्या नायिका गुरुनायिका।।१५।।

एतस्या मंत्रराजस्तु श्रीविद्यैव तपोधन।।
कामराजांतमत्रांते श्रीबीजेन समन्वित:।।१६।।

षोडशाक्षरीविद्येयं श्रीविद्यति प्रकीर्तिता।।
इत्थं रहस्यमाख्यातं गोपनीयं प्रयत्नत:।।१७।।

तिसृणामपि मूर्तीनां शक्तिर्विद्येयमीरिता।।
सर्वेषामपि मंत्राणां विद्यैषा प्राणरूपिणी।।१८।।

पारंपर्येण विज्ञाता विद्येयं बन्धमोचनी।।
संस्मृता पापहरणी जरामृत्युविनाशिनी।।१९।।

पूजिता दु:खदौर्भाग्यव्याधिदारिद्र्यनाशिनी।।
स्तुता विघ्नौघशमिनी ध्यांता सर्वार्थसिद्धिदा।।२०।।

मुद्राविशेषतत्वज्ञो दीक्षाक्षपितकल्मषः।।
भजेद्यः परमेशानीमभीष्टफलमाप्नुयात्।।२१।।

धवलांबरसंवीतां धवलावासमध्यगाम्।।
पूजयेद्धवलैः पुष्पैर्ब्रह्मचर्ययुतो नरः।।२२।।

धवलैश्चैव नैवेद्यैर्दधिक्षीरोदनादिभिः।।
संकल्पधवलैर्वापि पूजयेत्परमेश्वरीम्।।२३।।

श्रीर्वालंत्र्यक्षीबीजैः क्रमात्खंडेषु योजितयाम्।।
षोडशाक्षरविद्यां तामर्चयेच्छुद्धमानसः।।२४।।

अनुलोमविलोमेन प्रजपन्मातृकाक्षरैः।।२५।।

भावयन्नेव देवाग्रे श्रीदेवीं दीपरूपिणीम्।।
मनसोपांशुना वापि निगदेनापि तापस।।२६।।

श्रीदेवीन्याससहितः श्रीदेवीकृतविग्रहः।।
एकलक्षजपेनैव महापापैः प्रमुच्यते।।२७।।

लक्षद्वयेन देवर्षे सप्तजन्मकृतान्यपि।।
पापानि नश्यंत्येव साधकस्य परा कला।।२८।।

लक्षीत्रितयजापेन सहस्रजनिपातकैः।।
मुच्यते नात्र संदेहो निर्मलो नितरां मुने।।
क्रमात्षोडशलक्षेण देवीसांनिध्यमाप्नुयात्।।२९।।

पूजा त्रैकालिकी नित्यं जपस्तर्पणमेव च।।
होमो ब्राह्मणभुक्तिश्च पुरश्चरणमुच्यते।।३०।।

होमतर्पणयोः स्वाहा न्यासपूजनयोर्नमः।।
मंत्रांते पूजयेद्देवीं जपकाले यथोचितम्।।३१।।

जपाद्दशांशो होमः स्यात्त द्दशांशं तु तर्पणम्।।
तद्दशांश ब्राह्मणानां भोजनं विन्ध्यमर्दन।।३२।।

देशकालोपघाते तु यद्यदंगं विहीयते।।
तत्संख्याद्विगुणं जप्त्वा पुरश्चर्या समापयेत्।।३३।।

ततः काम्यप्रयोगार्थं पुनर्लक्षत्रयं जपेत्।।
व्रतस्थो निर्विकारश्च त्रिकालं पूजने रतः।।
पश्चाद्वसश्यादिकर्माणि कुर्वन्सिद्धिमवाप्स्यति।।३४।।

अभ्यर्च्य चक्रमध्यस्थो मंत्री चिन्तयते यदा।।
सर्वमात्मानमरुणं साध्यमप्यरुणीकृतम्।।३५।।

ततो भवति विन्ध्यारे सर्वसौभाग्यसुन्दरः।।
वल्लभः सर्वलोकानां वशयेन्नात्र संशयः।।३६।।

रोचनाकुंकुमाभ्यां तु समभागं तु चन्दनम्।।
शतमष्टोत्तरं जप्त्वा तिलकं कारयेद् बुधः।।३७।।

ततो यमीक्षते वक्ति स्पृशते चिन्तयेच्च यम्।।
अर्धेन च शरीरेण स वशं याति दासवत्।।३८।।

तथा पुष्पं फलं गन्धं पानं वस्त्र तपोधन।।
शतमष्टोत्तरं जप्त्वा यस्यै संप्रेष्यते स्त्रियै।।
सद्य आकृष्यते सा तु विमूढहृदया सती।।३९।।

लिखेद्रोचनयैकांते प्रतिमानवनीतले।।
सुरूपां च सश्रृङ्गारवेषाभरणमांडितम्।।४०।।

तद्भालगलहृन्नाभिजानुमंडलयोजितम्।।
जन्मनाम महाविद्यामंकुशांतर्विदर्भितम्।।४१।।

सर्वांगसंधिसंलीनामालिख्य मदनाक्षरैः।।
तदाशाभिमुखो भूत्वा त्रिपुरीकृतविग्रहः।।४२।।

बद्धा तु क्षोभिणी मुद्रां विद्यामष्टशतं जपेत्।।
संयोज्य दहनागारे चन्द्रसूर्यप्रभाकुले।।४३।।

ततो विह्वलितापांगीमनङ्गशरपीडिताम्।।
प्रज्वलन्मदनोन्मेषप्रस्फुरज्जघनस्थलाम्।।४४।।

शक्तिचक्रे लसद्रश्मिवलनाकवलीकृताम्।।
दूरीकृतसुचारित्रां विशालनयनाम्बुजाम्।।४५।।

आकृष्टनयनां नष्टधैर्यसंलीनव्रीडनाम्।।
मन्त्रयन्त्रौषधमहामुद्रानिगडबंधनाम्।।
नवानुरागसंधानवेपमानहृदंबुजाम्।।४६।।

मनोऽधिकमहामंत्रजपमानां हृतांशुकाम्।।
विमुढामिव विक्षुब्धामिव प्लुष्टामिवाद्भुताम्।।४७।।

लिखितामिव निः संज्ञामिवप्रमथितामिव।।
निलीनामिव निश्चेष्टामिवान्यत्वं गतामिव।।४८।।

भ्रमन्मन्त्रानिलोद्धूतवेणुपत्राकृतिं च खे।।
भ्रमन्तीं भावयेन्नारीं योजनानां शतादपि।।४९।।

चक्रमध्यगतां पृथ्वीं सशैलवनकाननाम्।।
चतुःसमुद्रपर्यंतं ज्वलंतीं चिंतयेत्ततः।।५०।।

षण्मासाभ्यासयोगेन जायते मदनोपमः।।
दृष्ट्वा कर्षयते लोकं दृष्ट्वैव कुरुते वशम्।।५१।।

दृष्ट्वा संक्षोभयेन्नारीं दृष्ट्वैव हरते विषम्।।
दृष्ट्वा करीति वागीशं दृष्ट्वा सर्वं विमोहयेत्।।
दृष्ट्वा चातुर्थिकादींश्च ज्वरान्नाशयते क्षणात्।।५२।।

पीतद्रव्येण लिखितं चक्रं गूढं तु धारयेत्।।
वाक्स्तंभं वादिनां क्षिप्रं कुरुते नात्र संशयः।।५३।।

महानीलीरसेनापि शत्रुनामयुतं लिखेत्।।
दक्षिणाभिमुखो वह्नौ दग्ध्वा मारयते रिपून्।।५४।।

महिषाश्वपुरीषाभ्यां गोमूत्रैर्नाम टंकितम्।।
आरनालस्थितं चक्रं विद्वेषं कुरुते द्विषाम्।।५५।।

युक्त्वा रोचनया नाम काकपक्षेण मध्यगम्।।
लंबमानस्तदाकारो उच्चाटनकरं परम्।।५६।।

दुग्धलाक्षा रोचनाभिर्महानीलिरसेन च।।
लिखित्वा धारयंश्चक्रं चातुर्वर्ण्यं वशं नयेत्।।५७।।

अनेनैव विधानेन जलमध्ये यदि क्षिपेत्।।
सौभाग्यमतुलं तस्य स्नानपानान्नसंशयः।।५८।।

चक्रमध्यगतं देशं नगरी वा वरांगनाम्।।
ज्वलंतीं चिंतयोन्नित्यं सप्ताहात्क्षोभयेन्मुने।।५९।।

लिखित्वा पीतवर्णं तु चक्रमेतद्यदाचरेत्।।
पूर्वाशाभिमुखो भूत्वा स्तंभयेत्सर्ववादिनः।।६०।।

सिंदूरवर्णालिखितं पूजयेदुत्तरामुखः।।
यदा तदा स्ववशगो लोको भवति नान्यथा।।६१।।

चक्रं गैरिकयालिख्य पूजयेत्पश्चिमामुखः।।
यः स सर्वाङ्गनाकर्षवश्यक्षोभकरो भवेत्।।६२।।

पूजयेद्विंध्यदपरि रहस्येकचरो गिरौ।।
अजरामरतां मन्त्री लभते नात्र संशयः।।६३।।

रहस्यमेतत्कथितं गोपितव्यं महामुने।।
गोपनात्सर्वसिद्धिः स्याद् भ्रंश एव प्रकाशनात्।।६४।।

अविधाय पुरश्चर्यां यः कर्म कुरुते मुने।।
देवताशापमाप्नोति न च सिद्धिं स विंदति।।६५।।

प्रयोगदोषशांत्यर्थं पुनर्लक्षं जपेद्बुधः।।
कुर्याच्च विधिवत्पूजां पुनर्योग्यो भवेन्नरः।।६६।।

निष्कामो देवतां नित्यं योऽर्चयेद्भक्तिनिर्भरः।।
तामेव चिंतयन्नास्ते यथाशक्ति मनुं जपन्।।६७।।

सैव तस्यैहिकं भारं वहेन्मुक्तिं च साधयेत्।।
सदा संनिहिता तस्य सर्वं च कथयेत सा।।६८।।

वात्सल्यसहिता धेनु र्यथा वत्समनुव्रजेत्।।
तथानुगच्छेत्सा देवी स्वभक्तं शरणागतम्।।६९।।

(MANNER OF WORSHIP AND MEANING OF SUB-MISSION)

अगस्त्य उवाच।।

शरणागतशब्दस्य कोऽर्थो वद हयानन।।
वत्सं गौरि धावन्तमनुधावति।।१।।

हयग्रीव उवाच।।

यः पुमानखिलं भारमैहिकामुष्मिकात्मकम्।।
श्रीदेव्तायां निक्षिप्य सदा तद्गतमानसः।।२।।

सर्वानुकूलः सर्वत्र प्रतिकूलविवर्जितः।।
अनन्यशरणो गौरीं दृढं सम्प्रार्थ्य रक्षणे।।७३।।

रक्षिष्यतीति विश्वासस्तत्सेवैकप्रयोजनः।।
वरिवस्यातत्परः स्यात्सा एव शरणागतिः।।४।।

यदा कदाचित्स्तुतिनिंदनादौ निंदन्तु लोकाः स्तुवतां जनो वा।।
इति स्वरूपं सुधिया समीक्ष्य विषादखेदौ न भजेत्प्रपन्नः।।५।।

अनुकुलस्य संकल्पः प्रतिकूलस्य वर्जनम्।।
रक्षिष्यतीति विश्वासो गोप्तृववरणं तथा।।६।।

आत्मनिक्षेपकार्पण्ये षड्विधा शरणागतिः।।
अङ्गीकृत्यात्मनिक्षेपं पञ्चांगानि समर्पयेत्।।
न ह्यस्य सदृशं किंचिद्भुवत्र्योमुक्तयोस्तु साधनम्।।७।।

अमनित्वमदांभित्वमहिंसा क्षांतिरार्जवम्।।
आचार्योपासनं शौचं स्थैर्यमात्मविनिग्रहः।।८।।

इन्द्रियार्थेषु वैराग्यमनहंकार एव च।।
जन्ममृत्युजराव्याधिदुःखदोषानुदर्शनम्।।
असक्तिरनभिष्वंगः पुत्रदारगृहादिषु।।९।।

नित्यं च समचितचत्त्वमिष्टोपपत्तिषु।।
मयि चानन्यभावेन भक्तिख्यभिचारिणी।।१०।।

विविक्तदेशसेवित्वमरतिर्जनसंसदि।।
अध्यात्मज्ञाननित्यत्वं तत्वज्ञानार्थदर्शनम्।।
एतानि सर्वदा ज्ञानसाधनानि समभ्यसेत्।।११।।

तत्कर्मकृतत्परमस्तद्भक्तः संगवर्जितः।।
निर्वैरः सर्वभूतेषु यः स याति परां श्रियतम्।।१२।।

गुरुस्तु मादृशो धीमान्ख्यातो वातापितापन।।
शिष्योऽपि त्वादृशः प्रोक्तो रहस्याम्नायदेशिकः।।१३।।

(THE MUDRAS IN WORSHIP)

अगस्त्य उवाच।।

मुद्राविरचनारीतिमश्वानन निवेदय।।
याभिर्विरचिताभिस्तु श्रीदेवी संप्रसीदति।।१।।

हयग्रीव उवाच।।

आवाहनी महामुद्रा त्रिखण्डेति प्रकीर्तिता।।
परिवृत्या करौ स्पष्टमङ्गुष्ठौ कारयेत्समौ।।२।।

अनामांतर्गते कृत्वा तर्जन्यौ कुटिलाकृती।।
कनिष्ठिके नियुञ्जीत निजस्थाने तपोधन।।
संक्षोभिण्याख्यमुद्रां तु कथयाम्यधुना श्रृणु।।३।।

मध्यमे मध्यगे कृत्वा कनिष्ठांगुष्ठरोधिते।।
तर्जन्यौ दंडवत्कृत्वा मध्यमोपर्यनमिके।।४।।

एतस्या एव मुद्राया मध्यमे सरले यदि।।
क्रियते विंध्यदर्परि मुद्रा विद्राविणी तथा।।५।।

मध्यमातर्जनीभ्यां तु कनिष्ठानामिके समे।।
अंकुशाकाररुपाभ्यां मध्यगे कलशोद्भव।।
इयमाकर्षिणी मुद्रा त्रैलोक्याकर्षणे क्षमा।।६।।

पुटाकारौ करौ कृत्वा तर्जन्यावंकुशाकृती।।
परिवर्तक्रमेणैव मध्यमे तदधोगते।।७।।

क्रमेणानेन देवर्षे मध्यमामध्यगेऽनुजे।।
अनामिके तु सरले तद्वहिस्तर्जनीद्वयम्।।८।।

दंडाकारौ ततोंऽगुष्ठौ मध्यमावर्तदेशगौ।।
मुद्रैषोन्मादिनी नाम्ना ख्याता वातापितापन।।९।।

अस्यास्त्वनामिकायुग्ममधः कृत्वांकुशाकृति।।
तर्जन्यावपि तेनैव क्रमेण विनियोजयेत्।।१०।।

इयं महांकुशा मुद्रा सर्वकार्यार्थसाधिका।।११।।

सव्यं दक्षिणदेशे तु दक्षिणं सव्यदेशतः।।
बाहू कृत्वा तु देवर्षे हस्तौ सम्परिवर्त्य च।।१२।।

कनिष्ठानामिके युक्ते क्रमेणानेन तापस।।
तर्जनीभ्यां समाक्रान्ते सर्वोर्ध्वमपि मध्यमे।।१३।।

लोपामुद्रापतेङ्गुष्ठौ कारयेत्सकलावपि।।
इयं तु खेचरी नाम सर्वोत्तमोत्तमा।।
एतद्विज्ञानमात्रेण योगिनीनां प्रियो भवेत्।।१४।।

परिवर्त्य करौ स्पृष्टावर्धचन्द्रसमाकृती।।
तर्जन्यङ्गुष्ठयुगलं युगपद्योजयेत्ततः।।१५।।

अधः कनिष्ठावष्टब्धमध्यमे विनियोजत्।।
अथैते कुटिले युक्त्वा सर्वाधस्तादनामिके।।
बीजमुद्रेयमचिरात्सर्वसिद्धिप्रवर्तिनी।।१६।।

मध्याग्रे कुटिलाकारे तर्जन्युपरि संस्थिते।।
अनामिकामध्यगते तथैव हि कनिष्टिके।।१७।।

सर्वा एकत्र संयोज्य चाङ्गुष्टपरिपीडिताः।।
एषा तु प्रथमा मुद्रा योनिमुद्रेति संज्ञिता।।१८।।

एता मुद्रास्तु देवर्षे श्रीदेव्याः प्रीतिहेतवः।।
पूजाकाले प्रयोक्तव्या यथानुक्रमयोगतः।।१९।।

INITIATION : ITS VALUE AND KINDS

अगस्त्य उवाच।।

अश्वानन महाप्राज्ञ करुणामृतवारिधे।।
श्रीदेवीदर्शने दीक्षा यादृशी तां निवदेय।।१।।

हयग्रीव उवाच।।

यदि ते देवताभावो यया कल्मषकर्दमाः।।
क्षाल्यन्ते च तथा पुसां दीक्षामाचक्ष्महेऽत्र ताम्।।२।।

हस्ते शिवपुरं ध्यात्वा जपेन्मूलाङ्गमालिनीम्।।
गुरुः स्पृशेच्छिष्यतनुं स्पर्शदीक्षेयमीरिता।।३।।

निमील्य नयने ध्यात्वा श्रीकामाक्षीं प्रसन्नधीः।।
सम्यक्पश्येद्गुरुः शिष्यं दृग्दीक्षा सेयमुच्यते।।४।।

गुरोरालोकमात्रेण भाषणात्स्पर्शनादपि।।
सद्यः सञ्जायते ज्ञानं सा दीक्षा शाम्भवी मता।।५।।

देव्या देहो यथा प्रोक्तो गुरुदेहस्तथैव च।।
तत्प्रसादेन शिष्योऽपि तद्रूपः सम्प्रकाशते।।६।।

चिरं शुश्रूषया सम्यक्तोषितो देशिकेश्वरः।।
तूष्णीं संकल्पयेच्छिष्यं सा दीक्षा मानसी मता।।७।।

दीक्षाणामपि सर्वासामियमेवोत्तमोत्तमा।।
आदौ कुर्यात्क्रियादीक्षां तत्प्रकारः प्रवक्ष्यते।।८।।

शुक्लपक्षे शुभदिने विधाय शुचिमानसम्।।
जिह्वास्यमलशुद्धिं च कृत्वा स्नात्वा यथाविधि।।९।।

संध्याकर्म समाप्याथ गुरुदेहं परं स्मरन्।।
एकान्ते निवसेञ्छ्रीमान्मौनी च नियताशनः।।१०।।

गुरु श्च तादृशो भूत्वा पूजामंदिरमाविशेत्।।
देवीसूक्तेन संयुक्तं विद्यान्यासं समातृकम्।।११।।

कृत्वा पुरुषसूक्तेन षोडशैरुपचारकैः।।
आवाहनासने पाद्यमर्घ्यमाचमनं तथा।।१२।।

स्नानं वस्त्रं च भूषां च गन्धः पुष्पं तथैव च।।
धूपदीपौ च नैवेद्य ताम्बूलं च प्रदक्षिणा।।१३।।

प्रणामश्चेति विख्यातौ प्रीणयेत्त्रिपुरांबिकाम्।।
अथ पुष्पाञ्जलिं दद्यात्सहस्राक्षरविद्याया।।१४।।

ADORATION OF THE DEITIES IN THE NINE EN-CLOSURES OF SRĪ-CHAKRA

ॐ ऐं ह्रीं श्रीं ऐं क्लीं सौः ॐ नमस्त्रिपुरसुन्दरि हृदय देवि शिरोदेवि

शिखादेवि कवचदेवि नेत्रदेवि कामेश्वरि भगमालिनि नित्यक्लिन्नें भैरूंडे वह्निवासिनि महावज्रेश्वरि विद्येश्वरि परशिवदूति त्वरिते कुलसंन्दरि नित्ये नीलपताके विजये सर्वमङ्गले ज्वालामालिनि चित्रे महनित्ये परमेश्वरि मन्त्रेशमयि षष्ठीशमय्युद्यानमयि लोपामुद्रामय्यगस्त्यमयि कालतापनमयि प्रभाकरदेवमयि तेजोदेवमयि मनोजदेवमयि अणिमसिद्धे महिमसिद्धे गरिमसिद्धे लघिमसिद्धे ईशित्वसिद्धे वशित्वसिद्धे प्राकाम्यसिद्धे रससिद्धे सर्वसंक्षोभिणि सर्वाविद्राविणि सर्वाकर्षिणि सर्वस्त्रखंडिनि त्रैलौक्यमोहिनि चक्रस्वामिनि प्रकटयोगिनि बौद्धदर्शनांगि कामार्षिणि बुद्ध्याकर्षिणि अहंकाराकर्षिणि स्पर्शाकर्षिणि रूपाकर्षिणि रसाकर्षिणि गन्धाकर्षिणि चित्ताकर्षिणि स्मृत्याकर्षिणि नामाकर्षिणि बीजाकर्षिणि आत्माकर्षिणि अमृताकर्षिणि शरीराकर्षिणि गुप्तयोगिनी सर्वाशापरिपूरकचक्रस्वामिन अनंगकुसुमे अनंगमेखले अनङ्गमादिनि अनंगमदनातुरेऽनङ्गरेखेऽनंगवेगिन्यनंगांकुशेऽनंगमलिनि गुप्ततरयोगिनि वैदिकदर्शनांगि सर्वसंक्षोभकारक चक्रस्वामिनि पूर्वाम्नायाधिदेवते सृष्टिरूपे सर्वसंक्षोभिणि सर्वविद्राविणि सर्वाकर्षिणि सर्वाह्लदिनि सर्वस्तंभिनि सर्वजृंभिणि सर्ववशङ्करि सर्वरंजिनि सर्वोन्मादिनि सर्वार्थसाधिके सर्वसंपत्प्रपूरिणि सर्वमंत्रमयि सर्वद्वंद्वक्षयकरि सम्प्रदाययोगिनि सौरदर्शनांगि सर्वसौभाग्यदायकचक्रे सर्वसिद्धिप्रदे सर्वसम्पत्प्रदे सर्वाप्रियङ्करि सर्वमङ्गलकारिणि सर्वकामप्रदे सर्वद:खविमोचिनी सर्वमृत्युप्रशमिनि सर्वविघ्ननिवारिणी सर्वांगसुन्दरि सर्वसौभाग्यदयिनि कुलोत्तर्णयोगिनि सर्वार्थसाधकचक्रेशि सर्वज्ञे सर्वशक्ते सर्वैश्वर्यफलप्रदे सर्वज्ञानमयि सर्वव्याधिनिवारिणि सर्वाधारस्वरूपे सर्वपापहरे सर्वानन्दमयि सर्वरक्षारूपिणि सर्वेप्सितफलप्रदे नियोगिनि वैष्णवदर्शनांगि सर्वरक्षाकरचक्रस्थे दक्षिणाम्नायेशि स्थितिरूपे वशिनि कामेशि मोदिनि विमले अरुणे जयिनि सर्वेश्वरि कौलिनि रहस्ययोगिनि रहस्यभोगिनि रहस्यगोपिनि शाक्तदर्शनांगि सर्वरोगहरचक्रेशि पश्चिमाम्नाये धनुर्बाणपाशांकुशदेवते कामेशि वज्रेशि भगमालिनि अतिरहस्ययोगिनि शैवदर्शनांगि सर्वसिद्धिप्रदचक्रगे उत्तराम्नायेशि संहाररूपे शुद्धपरे बिंदुपीठगते महात्रिपुरसुन्दरि परापरातिरहस्ययोगिनि शांभवदर्शनांगि सर्वानन्दमयचक्रेशि त्रिपुरसुंदरि त्रिपुरवासिनि त्रिपुरश्री: त्रिपुरमालिनि त्रिपुरसिद्धे त्रिपुरांब सर्वचक्रस्थे अनुत्तराम्नायाख्यस्वरूपे महात्रिपुरभैरवि चतुर्विधगुणरूपे कुले अकुले कुलाकुले महाकौलिनि सर्वोत्तरे सर्वदर्शनांगि नवासनस्थिते नवाक्षरि नवमिथुनाकृते महेशमाधवविधातृमन्मथस्कन्दनन्दीन्द्र-

मनुचंद्रकुबेरागस्त्यदुर्वासः क्रोध भट्टारकवित्मिके कल्याणतत्वत्रयरूपे शिवशिवात्मिके पूर्णब्रह्मशक्ते महापरमेश्वरि महात्रिपुरसुन्दरि तव श्रीपादुकां पुजयामि नमः।। क एं ईल ह्रीं हस कहल ह्रीं सकल ह्रीं ऐं क्लीं सौः सौः क्लींऐं श्रीं।।

INITIATION PROCEDURE

देव्याः पुष्पांजलिं दद्यात्सस्त्राक्षरविद्यया।।
नोचेत्तत्पूजनं व्यर्थमित्याहुर्वेदवादिनः।।१५।।

ततो गोमयसंलिप्ते भूतले द्रोणशालिभिः।।
तावद्भिस्तण्डुलैः शुद्धैः शस्तार्णैस्तत्र नूतनम्।।१६।।

द्रोणोदपूरितं कुंभं पञ्चरत्नैर्नवैयुतम्।।
न्यग्रोधाश्वत्थमाकंदजंबूदुम्बरशखिनाम्।।१७।।

त्वग्भिश्च पल्लवैश्चैव प्रक्षिप्तैरधिवासिनम्।।
कुम्भाग्रे निक्षिपेत्पक्कं नारिकेलफलं शुभम्।।१८।।

अभ्यर्च्य गंधपुष्पाद्यैर्धूपदीपादि दर्शयेत्।।२०।।

शिष्यमाहूय रहसि वाससा बद्धलोचनम्।।
कारयित्वा प्रणामानां साष्टांगानां त्रयं गुरुः।।२१।।

पुष्पाणि तत्करे दत्वा कारयेत्कुसुमाञ्जलिम्।।
श्रीनाथकरुणाराशे परंज्योतिर्मयेश्वरि।।२२।।

प्रसूनांजलिरेषा ते निक्षिप्ता चरणांबुजे।।
परं धाम परं ब्रह्म मम त्वं परदेवता।।२३।।

अद्यप्रभृति मे पुत्रान्रक्ष मां शरणागतम्।।
इत्युक्त्वा गुरुपादाब्जे शिष्यो मूर्ध्नि विधारयेत्।।२४।।

जन्मान्तरसुकृतत्वं स्यान्न्यस्ते शिरसि पादुके।।
गुरुणा कमलासनमुरशासनपुरशासनसेवया लब्धे।।२५।।

इत्युक्त्वा भक्तिभरितः पुनरुत्थाय शांतिमान्।।
वामपार्श्वे गुरोस्तिष्ठेदमानी विनयान्वितः।।२६।।

ततस्तुंबीजलैः प्रोक्ष्य वामभागे निवेदयेत्।।
विमुच्य नेत्रबंध तु दर्शयेदर्चनक्रमम्।।२७।।

सितामध्वाज्यकदलीफलपायसरूपकम्।।
महात्रिपुरसुन्दर्या नैवेद्यमिति चादिशेत्।।२८।।

षोडशार्णमनुं तस्य वदेद्वामश्रुतौ शनैः।।
ततो बहिर्विनिर्गत्य स्थाप्य दार्वासने शुचिम्।।२९।।

निवेश्य प्राङ्मुखं तत्र पट्टवस्त्रसमास्तृते।।
शिष्यं श्रीकुम्भसलिलैरभिषिंचेत्समंत्रकम्।।३०।।

पुनः शुद्धोदकैः स्नात्वां वासांसि परिगृह्य च।।
अष्टोत्तरशतं मन्त्रं जप्त्वा निद्रामथाविशेत्।।३१।।

शुभे दृष्टे सति स्वप्ने पुण्यं योज्यं तदोत्तमम्।।
दुःस्वप्ने तु जपं कुर्यादष्टोत्तरसहस्त्रकम्।।३२।।

कारयेत्त्रिपुरांबायाः सपर्या मुक्तमार्गतः।।
यदा न दृष्टः स्वप्नोऽपि तदा सिद्धिश्चिराद्भवेत्।।३३।।

स्वीकुर्यात्परया भक्त्या देवी शेषकलाधिकम्।।
सद्य एव स शिष्यः स्यात्पंक्तिपावनपावनः।।३४।।

शरीरमर्थं प्राणं च तस्मै श्रीगुरवे दिशेत्।।
तदधीनश्चरेन्नित्यं तद्वाक्यं नैव लघंयेत्।।३५।।

यः प्रसन्नः क्षणार्धेन मोक्षलक्ष्मीं प्रयच्छति।।
दुर्लभं तं विजानीयाद्गुरुं संसारतारकम्।।३६।।

गुकारस्यांधकारोऽर्थो रुकारस्तन्निरोधकः।।
अंधकारनिरोधित्वाद्गुरुरित्यभिधीयते।।३७।।

बोधरूपं गुरुं प्राप्य न गुर्वंतरमादिशेत्।।
गुरूक्तं परुषं वाक्यमाशिषं परिचिंतयेत्।।३८।।

लौकिकं वैदिकं वापि तथाध्यात्मिकमेव च।।
आददीत ततो ज्ञानं पूर्वं तमभिवादयेत्।।३९।।

CONTEMPLATION

एवं दीक्षात्रयं कृत्वा विधेयं बोधयेत्पुनः।।
गुरुभक्तिस्सदाचारस्तद्द्रोहस्तत्र पातकम्।।४०।।

तत्पदस्मरणं मुक्तिर्यावद्देहमयं क्रमः।।
यत्पापं समवाप्नोति गुर्वग्रेऽनृतभाषणात्।।४१।।

गोब्राह्मणवधं कृत्वा न तत्पापं समाश्रयेत्।।
ब्रह्मादिस्तंबपर्यतं यस्य मे गुरुसंततिः।।४२।।

तस्य मे सर्वपूज्यस्य को न पूज्यो महीतले।।
इति सर्वानुकूलो यः स शिष्यः परिकीर्तितः।।४३।।

शीलादिविमलानेकगुणसंपन्नभावनः।।
गुरशासनवर्तित्वाच्छिष्य इत्यभिधीयते।।४४।।

जपाच्छांतः पुनर्ध्यायेद्ध्यानाच्छांतः पुनर्जपेत्।।
जपध्यानादियुक्तस्य क्षिप्रं मन्त्रः प्रसिध्यति।।४५।।

यथा ध्यानस्य सामर्थ्यात्कीटोऽपि भ्रमरायते।।
तथा समाधिसामर्थ्याद्ब्रह्मीभूतो भवेन्नरः।।४६।।

यथा निलीयते काले प्रपञ्चो नैव दृश्यते।।
तथैव मीलयेन्नेत्रे एतद्ध्यानस्य लक्षणम्।।४७।।

विदिते तु परे तत्वे वर्णातीते ह्यविक्रिये।।
किंकरत्वं च गच्छंति मंत्रा मंत्राधिपैः सह।।४८।।

आत्मैक्यभावनिष्ठस्य या चेष्टा सा तु दर्शनम्॥
योगस्तपः स तन्मंत्रस्तद्धनं यन्निरीक्षणम्॥४९॥

देहाभिमाने गलिते विज्ञाते परमात्मनि॥
यत्र यत्र मनो याति तत्र तत्र समाधयः॥५०॥

यः पश्येत्सर्वगं शांतमानंदात्मानमद्वयम्॥
न तस्य किंचिदाप्तव्यं ज्ञातव्यंवावशिष्यते॥५१॥

पूजाकोटिसमं स्तोत्रं स्तोत्रकोटिसमो जपः॥
जपकोटिसमं ध्यानं ध्यानकोटिसमो लयः॥५२॥

Right conduct

देहो देवालयः प्रोक्तो जीव एव महेश्वरः॥
त्यजेदज्ञानं निर्माल्यं सोहंभावेन योजयेत्॥५३॥

तुषेण बद्धो व्रीहिः स्यात्तुषाभावे तु तंडुलः॥
पाशबद्धः स्मृतो जीवः पाशमुक्तो महेश्वरः॥५४॥

आकाशै पक्षिजातीनां जलेषु जलचारिणाम्॥
यथा गतिर्न दृश्येत महावृत्तं महात्मनाम्॥५५॥

नित्यार्चनं दिवा कुर्यांद्रात्रौ नैमित्तिकार्चनम्॥
उभयोः काम्यकर्मा स्यादिति शास्त्रस्य निश्चयः॥५६॥

कोटिकोटिमहादानात्कोटिमहाव्रतात्॥
कोटिकोटिमहायज्ञात्परा श्रीपादुकास्मृतिः॥५७॥

ज्ञानतोऽज्ञानतो वापि यावद्देहस्य धारणम्॥
तावद्वर्णाश्राचारः कर्तव्यः कर्ममुक्तये॥५८॥

निर्गतं यद्गुरोर्वक्त्रात्सर्वं शास्त्रं तदुच्यते॥
निषिद्धमपि तत्कुर्याद्गुर्वाज्ञां नैव लंघयेत्॥५९॥

जातिविद्याधनाढ्यो वा दूरे दृष्ट्वा नरं मुदा।।
दंडप्रणामं कृत्वैकं त्रि:प्रदक्षिणमाचारेत्।।६०।।

गुरुबुद्ध्या नमेत्सर्वं दैवतं तृणमेव वा।।
प्रणमेद्देवबुद्ध्या तु प्रतिमां लोहमृन्मयीम्।।६१।।

गुरुं हुंकृत्य तुंकृत्य विप्रं वादैर्विजित्य च।।
विकासस्य गुह्यशास्त्राणि भवति ब्रह्मराक्षसा:।।६२।।

अद्वैतं भावयेन्नित्यं नाद्वैतं गुरुणा सह।।
न निंदेदन्यसमयान्वेदशास्त्रगमादिकान्।।६३।।

एकाग्रमास्थित: शिष्यस्त्रिसंध्यं प्रणमेद्गुरुम्।।
क्रोशमात्रस्थितो भक्त्या गुरुं प्रतिदिनं नमेत्।।६४।।

अर्थयोजनग: शिष्य: प्रणमेत्पंचपर्वसु।
एकयोजनमारभ्य योजनद्वादशावधि।।६५।।

तत्तद्योजनसंख्यातमासेषु प्रणमेद्गुरुम्।।
अतिदूरस्थित: शिष्यो यदिच्छा स्यात्तदा व्रजेत्।।६६।।

रिक्तपाणिस्तु नोपेयाद्राजानं देवतां गुरुम्।।
फलपुष्पांबरादीनि यथाशक्ति समर्पयेत्।।६७।।

मनुष्यचर्मणा बद्ध: साक्षात्परशिव: स्वयम्।।
सच्छिष्यानुग्रहार्थाय गूढं पर्यटति क्षितौ।।६८।।

सद्भक्तरक्षणायैव निराकारोऽपि साकृति:।।
शिव: कृपानिधिर्लोके संसारीव हि चेष्टते।।६९।।

अत्रिनेत्र: शिव: साक्षादचतुर्बाहुरच्युत:।।
अचतुर्वदनो ब्रह्मा श्रीगुरु: परिकीर्तित:।।७०।।

श्रीगुरुं परतत्त्वाख्यं तिष्ठंतं चक्षुरग्रत:।।
भाग्यहीना न पश्यंति सूर्यमन्धा इवोदितम्।।७१।।

उत्तमा तत्त्वचिंता स्याज्जपचिंता तु मध्यमा।।
अधमा शास्त्रचिंता स्याल्लोकचिंतास्त्वधमाधमा।।७२।।

नास्ति गुर्वधिकं तत्त्वं नास्ति ज्ञानाधिकं सुखम्।।
नास्ति भक्त्यधिका पूजा न हि मोक्षाधिकं फलम्।।७३।।

सर्ववेदेषु शास्त्रेषु ब्रह्मविष्णुशिवादिषु।।
तत्र तत्रोच्यते शब्दैः श्रीकामाक्षी परात्परा।।७४।।

शचींद्रौ रोहिणीचंद्रौ स्वाहाग्नी च प्रभारवी।।
लक्ष्मीनारायणौ वाणीधातारौ गिरिजाशिवौ।।७५।।

अग्नीषोमौ बिंदुनादौ तथा प्रकृतिपूरुषौ।।
आधाराधेयनामानौ भोगमोक्षौ तथैव च।।७६।।

प्राणपानौ च शब्दार्थौ तथा विधिनिषेधकौ।।
सुखदःखादि यद्द्वंद्वं दृश्यते श्रूयतेऽपि वा।।७७।।

सर्वलोकेषु तत्सर्वं परं ब्रह्म न संशयः।।
उत्तीर्णमपरं ज्योतिः कामाक्षीनामकं विदुः।।७८।।

यदेव नित्यं ध्यायंति ब्रह्मविष्णुशिवादयः।।
इत्थं हि शक्तिमार्गेऽस्मिन्यः पुमानिह वर्तते।।७९।।

प्रसादभूमिः श्रीदेव्या भुक्तिमुक्त्योः स भाजनम्।।
अमन्त्रं वा समंत्रं वा कामाक्षीमर्चयंति ये।।८०।।

स्त्रियो वैश्याश्च शूद्राश्च ते यांति परमां गतिम्।।
किं पुनः क्षत्रिया विप्रा मंत्रपूर्वं यजंति ये।।८१।।

संसारिणोऽपि ते नूनं विमुक्ता नात्र संशयः।।
सितामध्वाज्यकदलीफलपायसरूपकम्।।८२।।

पञ्चपर्वसु नैवेद्यं सर्वदैव निवेदयेत्।।
यो नार्चयति शक्तोऽपि स देवीशापमाप्नुयात्।।७३।।

अशक्तौ भावनाद्रव्यैरर्चयेन्नित्यमंबिकाम्।।
गृहस्थस्तु महादेवीं मंगलाचारसंयुत:।।८४।।

अर्चयेत महालक्ष्मीमनुकूलांगनासख:।।
गुरुस्त्रिवारमाचारं कथयेत्कलशोद्भव।।८५।।

शिष्यो यदि य गृह्णीयाच्छिष्ये पापं गुरोर्न हि।।
लक्ष्मीनारायणौ वाणीधातारौ गिरिजाशिवौ।।८६।।

श्रीगुरुं गुरुपत्नीं च पितरौ चिंतयेद्धिया।।
इति सर्व।: मया प्रोक्तं समासेन घटोद्भव।।८७।।

एतावदवधानेन सर्वज्ञो मतिमान्भवेत्।।८८।।

CONSECRATION : ĀSANA AND NYĀSA

ग्रीव उवाच।।

प्रविश्य तु जपस्थानमानीय निजमासनम्।।
अभ्युक्ष्य विधिवन्मंत्रैर्गुरूक्तक्रमयोगत:।।१।।

स्वात्मानं देवातामूर्तिं ध्यायंस्तत्राविशेषत:।।
प्राङ्भुखो दृढमाबध्य पद्मासनमनन्यधी:।।२।।

त्रिखण्डामनुबध्नीयाद्दुर्वादीनभिवंद्य च।।
द्विरुक्तबालबीजानि मध्याद्यंगुलिषु क्रमात्।।३।।

तलयोरपि विन्यस्य करशुद्धिपुर:सरम्।।
अग्निप्राकारपर्यंतं कुर्यात्स्वास्त्रेण मन्त्रवित्।।४।।

प्रतिलोमेन पादाद्यमनुलोमेन कादिकम्।।
व्यापकन्यासमारोप्य व्यापयन्वाग्भवादिभि:।।५।।

व्यक्तै: कारणसूक्ष्मस्थूलशरीराणि कल्पयेत्।।
नाभौ हृदि भ्रुवोर्मध्ये बालाबीजान्यथ न्यसेत्।।६।।

मातृकां मूलपुटितां न्यसेन्नाभ्यादिषु क्रमात्।।
बालाबीजानि तान्येव द्विरावृत्याथ विन्यसेत्।।७।।

मध्यादिकरशाखासु तलयोरपि नान्यथा।।
नाभ्यादावथ विन्यस्य न्यसेदथ पदद्वये।।८।।

जानूरुस्फिग्गुह्यमूलनाभिहृन्मुर्धसु क्रमात्।।
नवासनानि ब्रह्माणं विष्णुं रुद्रं तथेश्वरम्।।९।।

सदाशिवं च पूषाणं तूलिकां च प्रकाशकम्।।
विद्यासनं च विन्यस्य हृदये दर्शयेत्ततः।।१०।।

पद्मत्रिखण्डयोन्याख्यां मुद्रामोष्ठपुटेन च।।
वायुमापूर्य हुं हुं हुं त्विति प्रबोध्य कुण्डलीम्।।११।।

मन्त्रशक्त्या समुन्नीय द्वादशान्ते शिवकैकताम्।।
भावयित्वा पुनस्तं च स्वस्थाने विनिवेश्य च।।१२।।

वाग्भवादीनि बीजानि मूलहृद्वाहुषु न्यसेत्।।
समस्तमूर्ध्निदोर्मूलमध्याग्रेषु यथाक्रमम्।।१३।।

हस्तौ विन्यस्य चांगेषु ह्यङ्गुष्टादितलावधि।।
हृदयादौ च विन्यस्य कुंकुमं न्यासमाचरेत्।।१४।।

शुद्धा तृतीयबीजेन पुटितां मातृकां पुनः।।
आद्यबीजद्वयं न्यस्य ह्यंत्यबीजं न्यसेदिति।।१५।।

पुनर्भूतलविन्यासमाचरेन्नातिविस्तरम्।।
वर्गाष्टकं न्यसेन्मूले नाभौ हृदयकण्ठयोः।।१६।।

प्रागाधायैषु शषसान्मूलहृन्मूर्द्धसु न्यसेत्।।
कक्षकट्यंसवामांसंकटिहृत्सु च विन्यसेत्।।१७।।

प्रभूताधः षडंगानि दादिवर्गैस्तु विन्यसेत्।।
ऋषिस्तु शब्दब्रह्म स्याच्छंदो भूतलिपिर्मता।।१८।।

श्रीमूलप्रकृतिस्त्वस्य देवता कथिता मनोः।।
अक्षस्त्रक्पुस्तके चोर्ध्वे पुष्पसायककार्मुके।।१९।।

वराभीतिकराब्जैश्च धारयंतीमनूपमाम्।।
रक्षणाक्षमयीं मालां वहन्ती कण्ठदेशतः।।२०।।

हारकेयूरकटकच्छत्रवीरविभूषिणाम्।।
दिव्यांगरागसंभिन्नमणिकुंण्डलमण्डिताम्।।२१।।

लिपिकल्पद्रुमस्याधो रूपिपंकजवासिनीम्।।
साक्षाल्लिपिमयीं ध्यायेद्भैरवीं भक्तवत्सलाम्।।२२।।

अनेककोटिदूतीभिः समंतात्समलंकृताम्।।
एवं ध्यात्वा न्यसेद्भूयो भूतलेप्यक्षरान्क्रमात्।।२३।।

मूलाद्याज्ञावसानेषु वर्गाष्टकमथो न्यसेत्।।
शषसान्मूर्ध्नि संन्यस्य स्वरानेष्वेव विन्यसेत्।।२४।।

हादिरूर्ध्वादिपञ्चास्येष्वग्रे मूले च मध्यमे।।
अङ्गुली मूलमणिबन्धयोर्दोष्णोश्च पादयोः।।२५।।

जठरे पार्श्वयोर्दक्षवामयोर्नाभिपृष्ठयोः।।
शषसान्मूलहृन्मूर्धस्वेतान्वा लादिकान्न्यसेत्।।२६।।

ह्रस्वाः पञ्चाथ सन्ध्यर्णाश्चत्वारो हयरा वलौ।।
अकौ खगेनगश्चादौ क्रमोयं शिष्टवर्गके।।२७।।

शषसा इति विख्याता द्विचत्वारिंशदक्षराः।।
आद्यः पञ्चाक्षरो वर्गा द्वितीयश्चतुरक्षरः।।२८।।

पञ्चाक्षरी तु षङ्वर्गी त्रिवर्णो नवमो मतः।।
ब्रह्मा विष्णुश्च रुद्रश्च धनेशेंद्रयमाः क्रमात्।।२९।।

वरुणश्चैव सोमश्च शक्तित्रयमिमे नव।।
वर्णानामीश्वराः प्रोक्ताः क्रमो भूतलिपरेयम्।।३०।।

एवं सृष्टौ पाठो विपरीतः संहृतावमून्येव।।
स्थानानि योजनीयौ विसर्गबिंदू च वर्णातौ।।३१।।

ध्यानपूर्वं ततः प्राज्ञो रत्यादिन्यासमाचरेत्।।
जपाकुसुमसंकाशाः कुंकुमारुणविग्रहाः।।३२।।

कामवामाधिरूढांका ध्येयाः शरधनुर्धराः।।
रतिप्रीतियुतः कामः कामिन्याः कांत इष्यते।।३३।।

कांतिमान्मोहिनीयुक्तकामांगः कलहप्रियाम्।।
अन्वेति कामचारैस्तु विलासिन्या समन्वितः।।३४।।

कामः कल्पतलायुक्तः कामुकः श्यामवर्णया।।
शुचिस्मितान्वितः कामो बंधको विस्मृतायुतः।।३५।।

रमणो विस्मिताक्ष्या च रामोऽयं लेलिहानया।।
रमण्या रतिनाथेपि दिग्वस्त्रद्यो रतिप्रिया।।३६।।

वामया कुब्जया युक्तो रतिनाथो धरायुतः।।
रमाकांतो रमोपास्यो रममाणो निश्चारः।।३७।।

कल्याणो मोहिनीनाथो नन्दकश्चोत्तमान्वितः।।
नन्दी सुरोत्तमाढ्यो नन्दनो नन्दयिता पुनः।।३८।।

सुलावण्यान्वितः पंचबाणो बालनिधीश्वरः।।
कलहप्रियया युक्तस्तथा रतिसखः पुनः।।३९।।

एकाक्ष्या पुष्पधन्वापि सुमुखेशो महाधनुः।।
नीली जटिल्यो भ्रमणः क्रमशः पालिनीपतिः।।४०।।

भ्रममाणः शिवाकांतो भ्रमो भ्रान्तश्च मुग्धया।।
भ्रामको रमयो प्राप्तो भ्रामितो भृङ्ग इष्यते।।४१।।

भ्रांताचारो लोचनया दीर्घजिह्विकया पुनः।।
भ्रमावहं समन्वेति मोहनस्तु रतिप्रियाम्।।४२।।

मोहकस्तु पलाशाक्ष्य। गृहिण्या मोह इष्यते।।
विकटेशो मोहधरो वर्धनोयं धरायुत:।।४३।।

मदनाथोऽनूपमस्तु मन्मथो मलयान्वित:।।
मादकोह्लादिनीयुक्त: समिच्छन्विश्वतोमुखी।।४४।।

नायको भृंगपूर्वस्तु गायको नंदिनीयुत:।।
गणकोऽनामया ज्ञेय: काल्या नर्तक इष्यते।।४५।।

क्ष्वेल्लक: कालकर्ण्याढ्य: कंदर्पो मत्त इष्यते।।
नर्तक: श्यामलाकांतो विलासी झषयान्वित:।।४६।।

उन्मत्तामुपसंगम्य मोदते कामवर्धन:।।
ध्यानपूर्वं तत: श्रीकण्ठादिविन्यासमाचरेत्।।४७।।

सिंदूरकांचनसमोभयभागमर्धनारीश्वरं गिरिसुताहरभूपचिह्नम्।।
पाशद्वयाक्षवलयेष्टदहस्तमेव स्मृत्वा न्यसेल्लिपिपदषु समीहितार्थम्।।४८।।

SHOḌHĀ-NYĀSA

श्रीकंठानंतसूक्ष्मौ च त्रिमूर्तिरमेश्वर:।।
उर्वीशो भारभूतिश्चातिथीश: स्थाणुको हर:।।४९।।

चण्डीशो भौतिक: सद्योजातश्चानुग्रहेश्वर:।।
अक्रूरश्च महासेन: स्युरेते वरमूर्त्तय:।।५०।।

तत: क्रोधीशचण्डीशौ पञ्चांतशिवोत्तमौ।।
तथैकरुद्रकूमैकनेत्रा: सचतुरातना:।।५१।।

अजेश: सर्वसोमेशौ हरो लांगलिदारुकौ।।
अर्धनारीश्वरश्चोमाकांतश्चापाद्यदंडिनौ।।५२।।

अत्रिर्मीनश्च मेषश्च लोहितश्च शिखी तथा।।
खड्गदंडद्विदंडौ च सुमहकालव्यालिनौ।।५३।।

भुजंगेशः पिनाकी च खड्गेशश्च बकस्तथा।।
श्वेतोह्यमश्च लकुलीशिवः संवर्तकस्तथा।।५४।।

पूर्णोदरी च विरजा तृतीया शाल्मली तथा।।
लोलाक्षी वर्तुलाक्षी च दीर्घघोण तथैव च।।५५।।

सुदीर्घखिगो मुख्यौ नवमी दीर्घजिह्विका।।
कुञ्जरीचोर्ध्वकेशा च द्विमुखी विकृतानना।।५६।।

सत्यलीलाकलाविद्यामुख्याः स्युः स्वरशक्तयः।।
महाकालीसरस्वत्यौ सर्वसिद्धिसमन्विते।।५७।।

गौरी त्रैलोक्यविद्या च तथा मंत्रात्मशक्तिका।।
लंबोदरी भूतमाता द्राविणी नागरी तथा।।५८।।

खेचरी मञ्जरी चैव रूपिणी वारिणी तथा।।
कोटरा पूतना भद्रा काली योगिन्य एव च।।५९।।

शंखिनीगर्जिनीकालरात्रिकूर्दिन्य एव च।।
कपर्दिनी तथा वज्रा जया च सुमुखेश्वरी।।६०।।

रेवती माधवी चैव वारुणी वायवी तथा।।
रक्षावधारिणी चान्या तथा च सहजाह्वया।।६१।।

लक्ष्मीश्च व्यापिनीमाये संख्याता वर्णशक्तयः।।
द्विरुक्तवालाया वर्णै रंगं कृत्वाथ केवलैः।।६२।।

षोढान्यासं प्रकुर्वीत देवतात्मत्वसिद्धये।।
विघ्नेशादीस्तु तत्रादौ विन्यसेद्ध्यानपूर्वकम्।।६३।।

तरुणाऽरुणसंकाशान्गजवक्त्रांस्त्रिलोचनान्।।
पाशांकुशवराभीतिहस्ताञ्छक्तिसमन्वितान्।।६४।।

विघ्नेशो विघ्नराजश्च विनायकशिवोत्तमौ।।
विघ्नकृद्विघ्नहन्ता च विघ्नराड्गणनायकः।।६५।।

एकदन्तो द्विदन्तश्च गजवक्त्रो निरञ्जन:।।
कपर्दवान्दीर्घमुख: शंकुकर्णो वृषध्वज:।।६६।।

गणनाथो गजेन्द्रास्य: शूर्पकर्णास्त्रिलोचन:।।
लम्बोदरो महानादश्चतुर्मूर्ति: सदाशिव:।।६७।।

आमोदो दुर्मदश्चैव सुमुखश्च प्रमोदक:।।
एकपादो द्विपादश्च शूरो वीरश्च षण्मुख:।।६८।।

वरदो नाम देवश्च वक्रतुण्डो द्विदन्तक:।।
सेनानीर्ग्रामणीर्मत्तो मत्तमूषकवाहन:।।६९।।

जटी मुण्डी तथा खड्गी वरेण्यो वृषकेतन:।।
भक्ष्यप्रियो गणेशश्च मेघनादो गणेश्वर:।।७०।।

एते गणेशा वर्णानामेकपञ्चाशत: क्रमात्।।
श्रीश्च ह्रीश्चैव पुष्टिश्च शांतिस्तुष्टि: सरस्वती।।७१।।

रतिर्मेधा तथा कांति कामिनी मोहिनी तथा।।
तीव्रा च ज्वालिनी नंदा सुयशा: कामरूपिणी।।७२।।

उग्रा तेजोवती सत्यविघ्नेशानी स्वरूपिणी।।
कामार्त्ता मदजिह्वा च विकटा घूर्णितानना।।७३।।

भूतिर्भूमिर्द्विरस्या चामारूपा मकरध्वजा।।
विकर्णभ्रुकुटी लज्जा दीर्घघोणा धर्नुर्धरी।।७४।।

तथैव यामिनी रात्रिश्चंद्रकांतां शशिप्रभा।।
लोलाक्षी चपला ऋज्वी दुर्भगा सुभगा शिवा।।७५।।

दुर्गा गुहप्रिया काली कालजिह्वा च शक्तय:।।
ग्रहन्यासं तत: कुर्याद्ध्यानपूर्वं समाहित:।।७६।।

वरदाभयहस्ताढ्याञ्छक्त्यालिंगितविग्रहान्।।
कुंकुमक्षीररुधिरकुंदकांचनकंबुभि:।।७७।।

अम्भोदधूमतिमिरैः सूर्यादीन्सदृशान्स्मरेत्।।
हृदयाधो रविं न्यस्य शीर्ष्णि सोमं दृशोः कुजम्।।७८।।

हृदि शुक्रं च हृन्मध्ये बुधं कण्ठे वृहस्पतिम्।।
नाभौ शनैश्चरं वक्त्रे राहुं केतुं पदद्वये।।७९।।

ज्वलत्कालानलप्रख्यावरदाभयपाणयः।।
तारा न्यसेत्ततो ध्यायन्सर्वाभरणभूषिताः।।८०।।

भाले नयनयोः कर्णद्वये नासापुटद्वये।।
कण्ठे स्कन्धद्वये पश्चात्कूर्पयोर्मणिबन्धयोः।।८१।।

स्तनयोर्नाभिकट्यूरुजानुजङ्धापदद्वये।।
योगिनीन्यासमादध्याद्विशुद्धो हृदये तथा।।८२।।

नामौ स्वाधिष्ठिते मूले भ्रूमध्ये मूर्धनि क्रमात्।।
पद्मेदुकर्णिकामध्ये वर्णशक्तीर्दलेष्वथ।।८३।।

दलाग्रेषु तु पद्मस्य मूर्ध्नि सर्वाश्च विन्यसेत्।।
अमृता नंदिनीन्द्राणी त्वीशानी चात्युमा तथा।।८४।।

ऊर्ध्वकेशी ऋद्विदुषी ऌकारिका तथैव च।।
एकपादात्मिकैश्वर्यकारिणी चौपधात्मिका।।८५।।

ततोंबिकाथो रक्षात्मिकेति षोडश शक्तयः।।
कालिका खेचरी गायत्री घण्टाधारिणी तथा।।८६।।

नादात्मिका च चामुण्डा छत्रिका च जया तथा।।
झङ्कारिणी च संज्ञा च टंकहस्ता ततः परम्।।८७।।

टंकारिणी च विज्ञेयाः शक्तयो द्वादशा क्रमात्।।
डंकारी टंकारिणी चणामिनी तामसी तथा।।८८।।

थंकारिणी दया धात्री नादिनी पार्वती तथा।।
फट्कारिणी च विज्ञेयाः शक्तयो द्वयपत्रगाः।।८९।।

वर्धिनी च तथा भद्रा मज्जा चैव यशस्विनी।।
रमा च लामिनी चेति षडेताः शक्तयः क्रमात्।।९०।।

नारदा श्रीस्तदा षंढाशश्चत्यपि च शक्तयः।।
चतस्रोऽपि तथैव द्वे हाकिनी च क्षमा तथा।।९१।।

ततः पादे च लिंगे च कुक्षौ हृद्दोःशिरस्सु च।।
दक्षादिवामपादान्तं राशीन्मेषादिकान्न्यसेत्।।९२।।

ततः पीठानि पञ्चाशदेकं चक्रं मनो न्यसेत्।।
वाराणसी कामरूपं नेपालं पौण्ड्रवर्धनम्।।९३।।

वरस्थिरं कान्यकुब्जं पूर्णशैलं तथार्बुदम्।।
आम्रातकेश्वरैकाम्रं त्रिस्रोतः कामकोष्ठकम्।।९४।।

कैलासं भृगुनगरं केदारं चन्द्रपुष्करम्।।
श्रीपीठं चैकवीरां च जालन्ध्रं मालवं तथा।।९५।।

कुलात्रं देविकोटं च गोकर्णं मारुतेश्वरम्।।
अट्टहासं च विरजं राजवेश्म महापथम्।।९६।।

कोलापुरकैलापुरकालेश्वरजयन्तिकाः।।
उज्जयिन्यपि चित्रा च क्षीरकं हस्तिनापुरम्।।९७।।

उडीरां च प्रयागं च षष्टिमायापुरं तथा।।
गौरीशं सलयं चैव श्रीशैलं मरुमेव च।।९८।।

पुनर्गिरिवरं पश्चान्महेन्द्रंवामनं गिरिम्।।
स्याद्धिरण्यपुरं पश्चान्महालक्ष्मीपुरं तथा।।९९।।

पुरोद्यानं तथा छायाक्षेत्रमाहुर्ननीषिणः।।
लिपिक्रमसमायुक्ताँल्लिपिस्थानेषु विन्यसेत्।।१००।।

अन्यान्यथोक्तस्थानेषु संयुक्ताँल्लिपिसङ्क्रमात्।।
षोढा न्यासो मयाख्यातः साक्षादीश्वरभाषितः।।१०१।।

एवं विन्यस्तदेहस्तु देवताविग्रहो भवेत्।।
तत: षोढा पुर: कृत्वा श्रीचक्रन्यासमाचरेत्।।१०२।।

अंशाद्यानन्द्यमूर्त्यन्तं मन्त्रैस्तु व्यापकं चरेत्।।
चक्रेश्वरी चक्रसमर्पणमन्त्रान्हृदि न्यसेत्।।१०३।।

अन्यान्यथोक्तस्थानेषु गणपत्यादिकान्न्यसेत्।।
दक्षिणोरुसमं वामं सर्वांश्च क्रमशो न्यसेत्।।१०४।।

गणेशं क्षेत्रपालं च योगिनीं बटुकं तथा।।
आदाविन्द्रादयो न्यस्या: पदाङ्गुष्ठद्वया ग्रके।।१०५।।

जानुपार्श्वासमूर्धास्यपार्श्वजानुषु मूर्धनि।।
मूलाधारेऽणिमादीनां सिद्धीनां दशकं तत:।।१०६।।

न्यस्तव्यंमदसदो: पृष्टवक्षस्तु प्रपदो: स्फिजि।।
दोर्देशपृष्ठयोर्मूर्धपादद्वितययो: क्रमात्।।१०७।।

अणिमा चैव लधिमा तृतीया महिमा तथा।।
ईशित्वं च वशित्वं च प्राकाभ्यं प्राप्तिरेव च।।
इच्छासिद्धी रससिद्धिर्मोक्षसिद्धिरिति स्मृता:।।१०८।।

ततो विप्र न्यसेद्धीमान्मातृणामष्टकं क्रमात्।।
पादाङ्गष्टयुगे दक्षपार्श्वे मूर्द्धनि वामत:।।१०९।।

वामजनौ दक्षजानौ दक्षवामांसयो स्तथा।।११०।।

ब्राह्मी माहेश्वरी चैव कौमारी वैष्णवी तथा।।
वारही च तथेन्द्रणी चामुण्डा चैव सप्तमी।।१११।।

महालक्ष्मीश्च विज्ञेया मातरो वै क्रमाद् बुधै:।।
मुद्रादेवीर्न्यसेदाष्टावेष्टवेव द्वे च ते पुन:।।११२।।

मूर्द्राध्योरपि मुद्रास्तु सर्वसंक्षोभिणी तथा।।
सर्वविद्राविणी पश्चात्सर्वार्थाकर्षणी तथा।।११३।।

सर्वाद्या वशकरिणी सर्वाद्या प्रियकारिणी।।
महाङ्कुशी च सर्वाद्या सर्वाद्याश्चेचरी तथा।।११४।।

त्रिखण्डा सर्वबीजा च मुद्रा सर्वप्रपुरिका।।
योनिमुद्रेति विज्ञेयास्तत्र चक्रेश्वरीं न्यसेत्।।११५।।

त्रैलोक्यमोहन चक्रं समर्प्य व्याप्य वर्ष्मणि।।
ततः कलानां नित्यानां क्रमात्षोडशकं न्यसेत्।।११६।।

कामाकर्षणरूपा च शब्दाकर्षणरूपिणी।।
अहंकाराकर्षिणी च शद्धकर्षणरूपिणी।।
स्पर्शाकर्षणरूपा च रुपाकर्षणरूपिणी।।
रसाकर्षरूपा च गन्धा कर्षणरूपिणी।।१९७।।

चित्ताकर्षणरूपा च धैर्याकर्षरूपिणी
स्मृत्याकर्षणरूपा च हृदाकर्षणरूपिणी।।११९।।

श्रद्धाकर्षणरूपा च ह्यात्माकर्षणरूपिणी।।
अमृताकर्षिणी प्रोक्ता शरीराकर्षिणी तथा।।१२०।।

स्थानानि दक्षिणं श्रोत्रं पृष्ठमंसश्च कूर्परः।।
दक्षहस्ततलस्याथ पृष्टं तत्स्फिक्ंच जानुनी।।१२१।।

तज्जंघाप्रपदे वामप्रपददिविलोमतः।।
चक्रेशीं न्यस्य चक्रं च समर्च्य व्याप्य वर्ष्मणि।।१२२।।

न्यसेदनंगकुसुमदेव्यादीनामथाष्टकम्।।
शंखजत्रुरुजङ्धासु वामे तु प्रतिलोमतः।।१२३।।

अनङ्गकुसमा पश्चाद्द्वितीयानंगमेखला।।
अनंगमदना पश्चादनंगमदनातुरा।।१२४।।

अनंगरेखा तत्पश्चाद्वेगाख्यानंगपूर्विका।।
ततोऽनंगांकुशा पश्चादनंगाधारमालिनी।।१२५।।

चक्रेशीं न्यस्य चक्रं च समर्प्य व्याप्य वर्ष्मणि।।
शक्तिदेवीर्न्यसेत्सर्वसंक्षोभिण्यादिका अथ।।१२६।।

ललाटगण्डयोरंसे पादमूले च जानुनि।।
उपर्यधश्च जंघायां तथा वामे विलोमतः।।१२७।।

सर्वसंक्षोभिणी शक्तिः सर्वविद्राविणी तथा।।
सर्वाद्याकर्षणी शक्तिः सर्वप्रह्लादिनी तथा।।१२८।।

सर्वसंमोहिनी शक्तिः सर्वाद्या स्तंभिनी तथा।।
सर्वाद्या जृंभिणी शक्तिः सर्वाद्यावशकारिणी।।१२९।।

सर्वाद्या रञ्जिनी शक्तिः सर्वाद्योन्मादिनी तथा।।
सर्वार्थसाधिनी शक्तिस्सर्वाशापूरिणी तथा।।१३०।।

सर्वमन्त्रमयी शक्तिः सर्वद्वन्द्वक्षयङ्करा।।
चक्रेशीं न्यस्य चक्रं च समर्प्य व्याप्य वर्ष्मणि।।१३१।।

सर्वसिद्धिप्रदादीनां दशकं चाथ विन्यसेत्।।
दक्षनासापुटे दंतमूले दक्षस्तने तथा।।१३२।।

कूर्परे मणिबन्धे च न्यस्येद्वामे विलोमतः।।
सर्वसिद्धिप्रदा नित्यं सर्वसंपत्प्रदा तथा।।१३३।।

सर्वप्रियंकरा देवी सर्वमङ्गलकारिणी।।
सर्वाघमोचिनी शक्तिः सर्वदुःखविमोचिनी।।१३४।।

सर्वमृत्युप्रशमनी सर्वविघ्नविनाशिनी।।
सर्वांगसुन्दरी चैव सर्वसौभाग्यदायिनी।।१३५।।

चक्रेशीं न्यस्य चक्रं च समर्प्य व्याप्यवर्ष्मणि।।
सर्वज्ञाद्यान्यसेद्वक्षस्यपि दन्तस्थलेष्वथ।।१३६।।

सर्वज्ञा सर्वशक्तिश्च सर्वज्ञानप्रदा तथा।।
सर्वज्ञानमयी देवी सर्वव्याधिविनाशिनी।।१३७।।

सर्वाधारस्वरूपा च सर्वपापहरा तथा।।
सर्वानन्दमयी देवी सर्वरक्षास्वरूपिणी।।
विज्ञेया दशमी चैव सर्वेप्सितफलप्रदा।।१३८।।

चक्रेशीं न्यस्य चक्रं च समर्प्य व्याप्य वर्ष्मणि।।
प्राग्वामाद्याश्च विन्यस्य पक्षिण्याद्यास्ततः सुधीः।।१३९।।

दक्षे तु चिबुके कण्ठे स्तने नाभौ च पार्श्वयोः।।
वामा विनोदिनी विद्या वशिता कामिकी मता।।१४०।।

कामेश्वरी परा ज्ञेया मोहिनी विमला तथा।।
अरुणा जयिनी पश्चात्तथा सर्वेश्वरी मता।।
कौलिनीति समुक्तानि तासां नामानि सूरिभिः।।१४१।।

चक्रेश्वरी न्यसेच्चक्रं समर्प्य व्याप्य वर्ष्मणि।।
हृदि त्रिकोणं संभाव्य दिक्षु प्रागादितः क्रमात्।।१४२।।

तद्वहिर्विन्यसेद्धीमानायुधानां चतुष्टयम्।।
न्यसेदग्न्यादिकोणेषु मध्ये पीठचतुष्टयम्।।१४३।।

मध्यवृत्तंन्यसित्वा च नित्याषोडशकं न्यसेत्।।
कामेश्वरी तथा नित्या च भगमालिनी।।१४४।।

नित्याक्लिन्ना तथा नित्या नित्या भेरुण्डिनी मता।।
बह्निवासिनिका नित्या महावज्रेश्वरी तथा।।१४५।।

नित्या च दूती नित्या च त्वरिता तु ततः परम्।।
कुलसुन्दरिका नित्या कुल्या नित्या ततः परम्।।
नित्या नीलपताका च नित्या तु विजया परा।।
ततस्तु मङ्गला चैव नित्यपूर्वा प्रचक्ष्यते।।१४७।।

प्रभामालिनिका नित्या चित्रा नित्या तथैव च।।
एतास्त्रिकोणान्तरेण पादतो हृदि विन्यसेत्।।
नित्या प्रमोदिनी चैव नित्या त्रिपुरसुन्दरी।।
तन्मध्ये विन्यसेद्देवीमखण्डजगदात्मिकाम्।।१४९।।

चक्रेश्वरी हृदि न्यस्य कृत्वा चक्रं समुद्धतम्।।
प्रदर्श्य योन्याख्यां सर्वानन्दमनुं जपेत्।।
इत्यात्मनस्तु चक्रस्य चक्रदेवी भविष्यति।।१५०।।

॥ श्रीललिताष्टोत्तरशतनामावलिः ॥

ॐ रजताचल-श्रृंगारग्रमध्यस्थायै नमो नमः।

ॐ हिमाचल-महावंश-पावनायै नमो नमः।

ॐ शंकरार्धांग-सौन्दर्य-शरीरायै नमो नमः।

ॐ लसन्-मरकत-स्वच्छ-विग्रहायै नमो नमः।

ॐ यहातिशय-सौन्दर्य-लावण्यायै नमो नमः।

ॐ शशांकशेखर-प्राणवल्लभायै नमो नमः।

ॐ सदा-पंचदशात्मैक्य-स्वरूपायै नमो नमः।

ॐ वज्र-माणिक्य-कटक-किरीटायै नमो नमः।

ॐ कस्तूरी-तिलकोल्लास-निटिलायै नमो नमः।

ॐ भस्म-रेखांकित-लसन्-मस्तकायै नमो नमः॥१०॥

ॐ विकचांभोरुह-दल-लोचनायै नमो नमः।

ॐ शरच्चांपेय-पुष्पाभ-नासिकायै नमो नमः।

ॐ लसत्-कांचन-ताटंक-युगलायै नमो नमः।

ॐ मणि-दर्पण-संकाश-कपोलायै नमो नमः।

ॐ ताबूंल-पूरित-स्मरे-वदनायै नमो नमः।

ॐ सुपक्क-दाडिमी-बीज-रदनायै नमो नमः।

ॐ कंबु-पूग-समच्छाय-कन्धरायै नमो नमः।

ॐ स्थूल-मुक्ताफलोदार-सुहारायै नमो नमः।

ॐ गिरीश-बद्ध-मांगल्य-मंगलायै नमो नमः।

ॐ पद्म-पाशांकुश-लसत्-कराब्जायै नमो नमः॥२०॥

ॐ पद्म-कैरव-मन्दार-सुमालिन्यै नमो नमः।

ॐ सुवर्णकुंभ-युग्माभ-सुकुचायै नमो नमः।

ॐ रमणीय-चतुर्बाहु-संयुक्तायै नमो नमः।

ॐ कनकांगद-केयूर-भूषितायै नमो नमः।

ॐ बृहत्-सौवर्ण-सौन्दर्य-वसनायै नमो नमः।

ॐ बृहन्नितंब-विलसज्जघनायै नमो नमः।

ॐ सौभाग्य-जात-शृंगार-मध्यमायै नमो नमः।

ॐ दिव्य-भूषण-सन्दोह-रंजितायै नमो नमः।

ॐ पारिजात-गुणाधिक्य-पदाब्जायै नमो नमः।

ॐ सुपद्मराग-संकाश-चरणायै नमो नमः।।३०।।

ॐ कामकोटि-महापद्म-पीठस्थायै नमो नमः।

ॐ श्रीकण्ठ-नेत्र-कुमुद-चन्द्रिकायै नमो नमः।

ॐ सुचामर-रमा-वाणी-वीजितायै नमो नमः।

ॐ भक्त-रक्षण-दाक्षिण्य-कटाक्षायै नमो नमः।

ॐ भूतेशालिंगनोद्भूत-पुलकांग्यै नमो नमः।

ॐ अनंग-जनकापांगवीक्षणायै नमो नमः।

ॐ ब्रह्मोपेन्द्र-शिरोरत्न-रंजितायै नमो नमः।

ॐ शची-मुख्यमार-वधू-सेवितायै नमो नमः।

ॐ लीला-कल्पित-ब्रह्माण्ड-मण्डलायै नमो नमः।

ॐ अमृतादि-महाशक्ति-संवृतायै नमो नमः।।४०।।

ॐ एकातपत्र-साम्राज्य-दायिकायै नमो नमः।

ॐ सनकादि-समाराध्य-पादुकायै नमो नमः।

ॐ देवर्षिभिस्तूयमान-वैभवायै नमो नमः।

ॐ कलशोद्भव-दुर्वास-पूजितायै नमो नमः।

ॐ मत्तेभ-वक्त्र-षड्वक्त्र-वत्सलायै नमो नमः।

ॐ चक्रराज-महायंत्र-मध्यवर्तिन्यै नमो नमः।

ॐ चिदग्निकुण्ड-संभूत-सुदेहायै नमो नमः।

ॐ शशांक-खण्ड-संयुक्त-मुकुटायै नमो नमः।

ॐ मत्त-हंस-वधू-मन्दगमनायै नमो नमः।

ॐ वन्दारुजन-सन्दोह-वन्दितायै नमो नमः।।५०।।

ॐ अन्तर्मुख-जनानन्द-फलदायै नमो नमः।

ॐ प्रतिव्रतांगनाभीष्टफलदायै नमो नमः।

ॐ अव्याज-करुणा-पूर-पूरितायै नमो नमः।

ॐ नितान्त-सच्चिदानन्द-संयुक्तायै नमो नमः।

ॐ सहस्र-सूर्य-संयुक्त-प्रकाशायै नमो नमः।

ॐ रत्न-चिन्तामणि-गृहमध्यास्थायै नमो नमः।

ॐ हानि-वृद्धि-गुणधिक्य-रहितायै नमो नमः।

ॐ महापद्माटवी-मध्यनिवासायै नमो नमः।

ॐ जाग्रत्-स्वप्न-सुषुप्तीनां साक्षिभूत्यै नमो नमः।

ॐ महापापौघ-पापानां विनाशिन्यै नमो नमः।।६०।।

ॐ दुष्टभीति-महाभीति-भंजानायै नमो नमः।

ॐ समस्त-देव-दनुज-प्रेरकायै नमो नमः।

ॐ समस्त-हृदयांभोज-निलयायै नमो नमः।

ॐ अनाहत-महापद्म-मन्दिरायै नमो नमः।

ॐ सहस्रार-सरोजात-वासितायै नमो नमः।

ॐ पुनरावृत्तिरहित पुरस्थायै नमो नमः।

ॐ वाणी-गायत्री-सावित्री-सन्नुतायै नमो नमः।

ॐ रमा-भूमिसुताराध्य-पदाब्जायै नमो नमः।

ॐ लोपामुद्रार्चितश्रीमच्चरणायै नमो नमः।

ॐ सहस्र-रति-सौन्दर्य-शरीरायै नमो नमः।।७०।।

ॐ भावना-मात्र-सन्तुष्ट-हृदयायै नमो नमः।

ॐ सत्य-संपूर्ण-विज्ञान-सिद्धिदायै नमो नमः।

ॐ श्रीलोचन-कृतोल्लास-फलदायै नमो नमः।

ॐ श्रीसुधाब्धि-मणिद्वीप-मध्यगायै नमो नमः।

ॐ दक्षाध्वर-विनिर्भेद-साधनायै नमो नमः।

ॐ श्रीनाथ-सोदरीभूत-शोभितायै नमो नमः।

ॐ चन्द्रशेखर-भक्तार्ति-भंजनायै नमो नमः।

ॐ सर्वोपाधि-विनिर्मुक्त-चैतन्यायै नमो नमः।

ॐ नाम-पारायणाभीष्ट-फलदायै नमो नमः।

ॐ सृष्टि-स्थिति-तिरोधान-संकल्पायै नमो नमः।।८०।।

ॐ श्रीषोडशाक्षरीमन्त्रमध्यगायै नमो नमः।

ॐ अनाद्यन्त-स्वयंभूत-दिव्यमूर्त्यै नमो नमः।

ॐ भक्त-हंस-परित्राण-नियोगायै नमो नमः।

ॐ मातृ-मण्डल-संयुक्त-ललितायै नमो नमः।

ॐ भण्डदैत्य-महासत्व-नाशनायै नमो नमः।

ॐ क्रूर-भण्ड-शिरच्छेद-निपुणायै नमो नमः।

ॐ धाताच्युत-सुराधीश-सुखदायै नमो नमः।

ॐ चण्ड-मुण्ड-निशुंभादि-खण्डनायै नमो नमः।

ॐ रक्ताक्ष-रक्तजिह्वादि-शिक्षणायै नमो नमः।

ॐ महिषासुर-दोर्वीर्य-निग्रहायै नमो नमः।।९०।।

ॐ अभ्रकेश-महोत्साह-कारणायै नमो नमः।

ॐ महेश-युक्त-नटन-तत्परायै नमो नमः।

ॐ निजभर्तृ-मुखांभोज-चिन्तनायै नमो नमः।

ॐ वृषभध्वज-विज्ञान-भावनायै नमो नमः।

ॐ जन्म-मृत्यु-जरा-रोग-भंजनायै नमो नमः।

ॐ विधेय-मुक्त-विज्ञान-सिद्धिदायै नमो नमो नमः।

ॐ काम-क्रोधादि-षड्वर्ग-नाशनायै नमो नमः।

ॐ राजराजार्चित-पद-सरोजायै नमो नमः।

ॐ सर्व-वेदान्त-संसिद्ध-सुतत्त्वायै नमो नमः।

ॐ श्री-वीर-भक्त-विज्ञान-निधानायै नमो नमः।।१००।।

ॐ अशेष-दुष्ट-दनुज-सूदनायै नमो नमः।

ॐ साक्षाच्छ्री-दक्षिणामूर्ति-मनोज्ञायै नमो नमः।

ॐ हयमेधाग्र-संपूज्य-महिमायै नमो नमः।

ॐ दक्षप्रजापति-सुरा-वेषाढ्यायै नमो नमः।

ॐ सुम-बाणेक्षु-कोदण्ड-मण्डितायै नमो नमः।

ॐ नित्य-यौवन-पांगल्य-मंगलायै नमो नमः।

ॐ महादेव-समायुक्त-शरीरायै नमो नमः।

ॐ महादेव-रतौत्सुक्य-महादेव्यै नमो नमः।

।। इति श्रीललिताष्टोत्तरशतनामावलिः संपूर्णा।। श्रिये नमः ।।

॥ श्रीललिताष्टोत्तरशतनामावलिः ॥

ॐ भूरूप-सकलाधारयै नमः॥

ॐ बीजौषध्यन्नरूपिण्यै नमः॥

ॐ जरायुजाण्डजोद्भिज्जस्वेदजादिशरीरिण्यै नमः॥

ॐ क्षेत्ररूपायै नमः॥

ॐ तीर्थरूपायै नमः॥

ॐ गिरिकाननरूपिण्यै नमः॥

ॐ जलरूपाखिलाप्यायायै नमः॥

ॐ तेजः पुंजशरीरिण्यै नमः॥

ॐ जगत्प्रकाशिकायै नमः॥

ॐ अज्ञानतमोहृद्भानुरूपिण्यै नमः॥१०॥

ॐ वायुरूपायै नमः॥

ॐ अखिलव्याप्यायै नमः नमः॥

ॐ उत्पत्यादि-विधायिन्यै नमः॥

ॐ नभोरूपायै नमः॥

ॐ इन्दु-सूर्यादि-ज्योतिर्भूतावकाशदायै नमः॥

ॐ घ्राणरूपायै नमः॥

ॐ गन्धरूपायै नमः॥

ॐ गन्धग्रहण-कारिण्यै नमः॥

ॐ रसनायै नमः॥

ॐ रसरूपायै नमः॥२०॥

ॐ रसग्रसण - कारिण्यै नमः॥

ॐ चक्षुरूपायै नमः॥

ॐ रूपरूपायै नमः॥

ॐ रूपग्रहण - कारिण्यै नमः।।

ॐ त्वग्रूपायै नमः।।

ॐ स्पर्शरूपायै नमः।।

ॐ स्पर्शग्रहण-कारिण्यै नमः।।

ॐ श्रोत्ररूपायै नमः।।

ॐ शब्दरूपायै नमः।।

ॐ शब्दग्रहण-कारिण्यै नमः।।३०।।

ॐ वागिन्द्रियस्वरूपायै नमः।।

ॐ वाचावृत्तिप्रदायिन्यै नमः।।

ॐ पाणीन्द्रिय स्वरूपायै नमः।।

ॐ क्रियावृत्तिप्रदायिन्यै नमः।।

ॐ पादेन्द्रियस्वरूपायै नमः।।

ॐ गतिप्रवृत्तिदायिन्यै नमः।।

ॐ पाय्विन्द्रियस्वरूपायै नमः।।

ॐ विसर्गार्थैक कारिण्यै नमः।।

ॐ रहस्येन्द्रिय रूपायै नमः।।

ॐ विषयानन्द दायिन्यै नमः।।४०।।

ॐ मनोरूपायै नमः।।

ॐ संकल्पविकल्पादिस्वरूपिण्यै नमः।।

ॐ सर्वोपलब्धिहेतु रूपायै नमः।।

ॐ बुद्धिनिश्चयरूपिण्यै नमः।।

ॐ अहंकार स्वरूपायै नमः।।

ॐ चित्तचेतनारूपायै नमः।।

ॐ सर्वचैतन्य दायिन्यै नमः।।

ॐ गुणवैषम्य रूपाद्य महत्तत्त्वाभिमानिन्यै नमः।।

ॐ गुणसाम्याव्यक्तमायामूल प्रकृति संज्ञाय नमः।।५०।।

ॐ पंचीकृत महाभूतसूक्ष्मभूतस्वरूपिण्यै नमः।।

ॐ विद्याविद्यात्मिकायै नमः।।

ॐ मायाबन्धमोचन कारिण्यै नमः।।

ॐ ईश्वरेच्छारोगरूपायै नमः।।

ॐ प्रकृतिक्षोभकारिण्यै नमः।।

ॐ कालशक्त्यै नमः।।

ॐ कालरूपायै नमः।।

ॐ नियतात्मनियामिकायै नमः।।

ॐ धूम्रादिपरमव्योमात्मिकायै नमः।।

ॐ यंत्रमंत्रकलात्मिकायै नमः।।६०।।

ॐ ब्रह्मरूपायै नमः।।

ॐ विष्णुरूपायै नमः।।

ॐ रुद्ररूपायै नमः।।

ॐ महेश्वर्यै नमः।।

ॐ सदाशिवस्वरूपायै नमः।।

ॐ शिवायै नमः।।

ॐ वाणीलक्ष्म्युमारूपायै नमः।।

ॐ सदाख्यायै नमः।।

ॐ चित्कलात्मिकायै नमः।।७०।।

ॐ प्राज्ञतैजसविश्वाख्यविराट्सूत्रेश्वरात्मिकायै नमः।।

ॐ स्थूलदेहस्वरूपायै नमः।।

ॐ सूक्ष्मदेहस्वरूपिण्यै नमः।।

ॐ बाच्यवाचकस्वरूपिण्यै नमः।।

ॐ ज्ञानज्ञेयस्वरूपिण्यै नमः।।

ॐ कार्यकारणरूपायै नमः।।

ॐ तत्त्वतत्त्वाधिदेवतायै नमः।।

ॐ दशनादस्वरूपायै नमः।।

ॐ नाडीकुण्डलरूपायै नमः।।

ॐ अकारादिक्षकारान्तवैखरीवाक्स्वरूपिण्यै नमः।।८०।।

ॐ वेदवेदांगरूपायै नमः।।

ॐ सूत्रशास्त्रादिरूपिण्यै नमः।।
ॐ पुराणरूपायै नमः।।
ॐ सद्धर्मशास्त्ररूपायै नमः।।
ॐ परात्परायै नमः।।
ॐ आयुर्वेदस्वरूपायै नमः।।
ॐ धनुर्वेदस्वरूपायै नमः।।
ॐ गांधर्वविद्यारूपायै नमः।।
ॐ अर्थशास्त्रादिरूपिण्यै नमः।।
ॐ चतु:षष्टिकलारूपायै नमः।।
ॐ निगमागमरूपिण्यै नमः।।
ॐ काव्येतिहासरूपायै नमः।।
ॐ गानविद्यादिरूपिण्यै नमः।।
ॐ पदवाक्यस्वरूपायै नमः।।
ॐ सर्वभाषास्वरूपिण्यै नमः।।
ॐ पदवाक्यस्फोट रूपायै नमः।।
ॐ ज्ञानेच्छाक्रियात्मिकायै नमः।।
ॐ सर्वतन्त्रमय्यै नमः।।
ॐ सर्वतन्त्र यन्त्रादिरूपिण्यै नमः।।
ॐ वेदमात्रे नमः।।१००।।
ॐ महाव्याहृतिरूपिण्यै नमः।।
ॐ अव्याकृतपदानाद्याचिन्त्यशक्त्यै नमः।।
ॐ तमोमय्यै: नमः।।
ॐ परस्मै ज्योतिषे नमः।।
ॐ परब्रह्म साक्षात्कारस्वरूपिण्यै नमः।।
ॐ परब्रह्ममय्यै नमः।।
ॐ सत्यासत्यज्ञानसुधात्मिकायै नमः।।
ॐ श्री ललितायै नमः।।१०८।।

APPENDIX

WORSHIP OF LALITĀ

Lalitā is one of the more popular names under which the mother-goddess is worshipped. In the reckoning of the one hundred and eight or fifty-one centres of Śakti-worship in the county the name Lalitā is associated with Prayāga (the present day Allahabad in Uttar pradesh) (*Mastya-purāṇa,* 291, 26) And among the twelve major Śakti-pīṭhas recounted in Tripurā*rahasya,* Māhātmya-Khaṇḍa, chap-48, Lalitā is worshipped in Prayāga ; Kāmakshi in Kāñchīpuram, Bhrāmari in Malaya, Kumārī in Kerala, Aṁbā in the Ānarta country, Viśālākshī in Vārāṇasī, Maṅgalāvati in Gayā, Mahā-lakshmī in Karavīra (Kolhapur), Kālikā in Mālavā and Vindhya-vāsinī in the Vindhyā mountains.

Lalitā is also one of the nine forms of Gaurī, worshipped in different locations within Vārāṇasī : others being Mukha-nirmālikā, Jyeshṭhā, Saubhāgyā, Śriṅgārā, Viśālākshī, Bhavānī, Maṅgalā, and Mahā-lakshmī Gaurīs. *Skānda-purāṇa* (Kāśī-khaṇḍa, 70) gives Lalitā as one of the names of the mother-goddesses along with names like Viśālākshi, Śiva-dūti, Aindrī, Viśva-bhujā, Bhadrakālī, Mahā-lakshmī, Hara-siddhi, Triloka-sundarī and Chāmuṇḍī.

Among the ten great Vidyās, Lalitā is another name for Shoḍaśī. The form of Lalitā is regarded as a variant (bheda) of Tripura-sundarī, and hence known as Lalitā parā-bhaṭṭārikā or Rāja-rājeśvarī. This is also the reason why the worship of Lalitā takes the form of the worship of Śrīchakra in its nine enclosures, and with homa prescribed for the Śrīchakra. The worship of Śrīchakra is usually accompained by the recitation of the thousand names of Lalitā (Sahasra-nāma). More particularly, Lalitā is identified with Bālā-tripura-sundari, and therefore has associations with Bālā-sarasvatī.

At the folk level, Lalitā is worshipped in the form of a 'Vrata', a chosen ritual elaborately and meticulously observed. There are two well-known vratas in the name of Lalitā, and Lalitā is here identified with Durgā ('yā durgā saiva Lalitā', *Padma-purāṇa,* Pātālakhaṇḍa). 'Lalitā-saptami' is performed on the seventh day of the first fortnight of the month Bhādrapada. Śiva and Lalitā are together worshipped in a maṇḍala. This is also known as Kukkuṭī-Vratra, and it is undertaken by those who desire progeny and welfare of the offsprings. Works like Tithyādi-tattva explain the significance of this Vrata on the basis of the legends recounted in *Bhavishyottara-purāṇa* about Nahusha, the king of Ayodhyā and his queen 'Chandramukhi having performed this vrata and having secured not only progeny but the welfare and longevity of the children, and about Devakī (the mother of Krishṇa) having performed this rite on the advice of the sage Lomaśa after her seven children were killed by Kaṁsa. The rite involves the tying of a consecrated thread with eight knots and dipped in milk to the left wrist of the devotee.

The other Vrata is known as Lalitā-pañchamī, performed every year on the fifth day of the Navarātri in the month of Aśvin (Śarannava-rātri). The background story is given in *Adbhuta-rāmāyana.* After Rāma killed the ten-headed Rāvaṇa and returned to Ayodhyā, the hundred- headed Rāvaṇa (śata-mukha-rāvaṇa) oppeared in Laṅkā and at the instance of Vibhīshaṇa, Rāma arrived in Laṅkā to fight with this demon. Rāma, however, was worsted in the fight and on the advice of the sage Nārada, Hanumān was sent to Ayodhyā to request Sītā to help kill the demon. Sītā took the form of the mighty Lalitā and killed the hundred-headed Rāvaṇa. Rāma is said to have worshipped Sītā as Śakti on this occasion. His father Daśaratha is also said to have worshipped Lalitā before Rāma was born.

A variant of this Vrata is Upāṅga-Lalitā-pañchamī, associated with a legend in *Skanda-purāṇa*. The name 'Upāṅga' as prefix to Lalitā is derived from the ruler of the Upāṅga city, who was also named Upāṅga. Gautama of Bhṛgu-Kshetra had a son Gopati by name who began as a wastrel but was tranformed into wise, wealthy and virtuous householder as a result of having performed this Vrata in a temple to Lalitā in Upāṅga. This Vrata is described as a 'kāmya-vrata', a ceremonial meant to secure a material benefit. The Dhyāna-śloka which visualizes the goddess on the occasion emphasizes this purpose.

While worshipping Lalitā in Śrī-Chakra, the usual procedure in Tripura-sundarī-Saparyā is followed. Tripura-sundarī is identified here with Lalitā and is visualized as being accompained by the sixty-four yoginī-śaktis, who are mentioned in the Sahasra-nāma These are secondary forms of the mother-goddess Lalitā herself, and they are separately invoked for granting material benefits ('Chatus-shashṭi-śaktayas siddhi-dayikāh'). Their names are (1) Kuleśī (2) Kulānandā (3) Vāgīśī (4) Bhairavī (5) Umā (5) Śrī (7) Śāntā (8) Chaṇḍā (9) Dhūmrā (10) Kālī (11) Karālinī (12) Mahālakshmī (13) Kaṅkālī (14) Rudra-Kāli, (15) Sarasvatī, (16) Vāg-vādinī, (17) Nakulī, (18) Bhadra-Kālī (19) Śaśi-prabhā (20) Pratyaṅgirā (21) Siddhi-lakshmī (22) Amṛteśi (23) Chaṇḍikā (24) Khecharī (25) Bhūcharī (26) Siddhā (27) Kāmākshī (28) Hiṅgulā (29) Bālā (30)

Jayā (31) Vijayā (32) Ajitā (33) Nityā (34) Aparājitā (35) Vilāsinī (36) Aghorā (37) Chitrā (38) Mugdhā (39) Dhaneśvarī (40) Someśvarī (41) Mahā-chaṇḍā (42) Vidyā (43) Haṁsī (44) Vināyikā (45) Veda-garbhā (46) Bhīmā (47) Ugrā (48) Vaidyā (49) Sad-gatī (50) Ugreśvarī (51) Chaṇḍa-garbha (52) Jyotsnā (53) Satyā (54) Yaśovatī (55) Kulikā (56) Kāminī (57) Kamya (58) Jñāna-vati (59) Ḍākinī (60) Rākinī (61) Lākinī (62) Kākinī (63) Śakinī and (64) Hākinī.

An important sequence in the worship is what is known as 'shoḍhā-nyāsa', placement of the deities of six categories - Ganeśa, graha, nakshatra, yoginī, rāśi and pīṭ ha, on different parts of the devotee's body. This is followed by the sixteen ministrations (upachāra) and worship of the attendant deities in the nine enclosure of Śrī-Chakra. During the worship, the thousand names of Lalitā (sahasra-nāma) or one hundred and eight names of Lalitā (Lalitāshṭottara-śata-nāmāvalī) are recited.